World Enough and Time

Conversations with Canadian Women at Midlife

For all who venture to live life fully,
and especially the women of my family

World Enough and Time

Conversations with Canadian Women at Midlife

Andrea Mudry

Dundurn Press
Toronto • Oxford

Editor: Judith Turnbull
Designer: Andy Tong
Printer: Webcom
[Cover photo from an art video, *Still Point,* courtesey of Charlotte Wilson Hammond and Paula Fairfield.]

Canadian Cataloguing in Publication Data

Main entry under title:

Mudry, Andrea
    World enough and time: conversations with Canadian women at midlife

ISBN 1-55002-268-7

1. Middle aged women — Canada — Interviews.   I. Title

HQ1059.5.C3M87 1996   305.24'4'092271   C96–932104–X

Publication was assisted by the **Canada Council,** the **Book Publishing Industry Development Program** of the **Department** of **Canadian Heritage,** and the **Ontario Arts Council.**

Care has been taken to trace the ownership of copyright material used in this book. The author and the publisher welcome any information regarding references or credit for attribution in subsequent editions.

Printed and bound in Canada

Printed on recycled paper.

Dundurn Press
2181 Queen Street East
Suite 301
Toronto, Ontario, Canada
M4E 1E5

Dundurn Press
73 Lime Walk
Headington, Oxford
England
OX3 7AD

Dundurn Press
250 Sonwil Drive
Buffalo, NY
U.S.A. 14225

CONTENTS

ACKNOWLEDGMENTS

Putting this collection together has – literally and figuratively – been a trip, and many people helped along the way. I apologize if there are omissions in the following.

Kirk Howard, publisher of Dundurn Press, took an immediate interest in my concept and contributed many excellent suggestions throughout the book's evolution, including the idea that the scope should be national. Grants from Ontario Arts Council made the necessary travel financially possible. I regret that I was unable to travel to Newfoundland or the Northwest Territories.

I am indebted to the women in this collection who generously shared their thoughts with me and entrusted our conversations to my editing skills. I have endeavoured to represent them accurately.

Gloria Hazell provided excellent work as a transcriber, which certainly facilitated the editing process. Bernice Lever Farrar and Jackie Buxton read parts of the manuscript and made suggestions that were invariably helpful. Paul Stack frequently assisted in my research in the University of Guelph library. At the early stages of the project, Marianne Quirk McInnis provided much needed encouragement and assistance from the Canadian West. And at Dundurn Press, my editor Judith Turnbull skilfully helped the project through to completion.

The following people suggested names of women for the collection and provided related helpful assistance. I received many excellent suggestions, but unfortunately could not accommodate them all: Di Brandt; Silver Donald Cameron; CBC: Angelica Fox, George Jamieson, Mary Stinson; Leo Cheverie, University of Prince Edward Island library; Hanya Cirka; Carolyn Drake, P.E.I. *Guardian and Patriot*; Marielle Fleury; Susan Foche, Art Gallery of Nova Scotia; Heather Frayne, Buffalo Gal Pictures; Perry Goldsmith, National Speakers Bureau; Louise Halfe; Douglas Hughes, Saint John *Telegraph-Journal*; Betty Ann Jordon, *Canadian Art Magazine*; Angela Lee, Vancouver *Chinatown News*; Suzanne McAdam; Karen MacDonald, Ste-Foy *Quebec Chronicle Telegraph*; Jane McNamee; Penni Mitchell, *Herizons Magazine*; Gwen Parker, Manitoba Women's Institute; Dara Rowland, Doubleday; Dorothy Shannon; Mary Sharpe; Darlene Shea, P.E.I. *Journal Pioneer*; Mary Sparling; Lois Stevenson, Atlantic Canada Opportunities Agency;

University of Guelph: Joanna Boehnert, David Gaskin, David Noakes, Mary Rogers; Mika Walsh, *Border Crossing Magazine*; Nancy Wardle; Women's Television Network: Laura Michalchyshyn, Michelle Van Beusekom.

The following helped in numerous ways by variously generously sharing their time, thoughts and resources: Barbara Barde, Eileen Brett Schwarz, Betty Ann Davis, Lorna May Durstling, Denise Gregoire, Dorothy Hogan, Helena Holub, Gilda Katz, Douglas Killam, Ann Koral Anderson, Ghislaine Lesevre, Ellen Malos, Ursula McMurray, Marianne Microse, Heather Moreau, Sister Marion Norman, Marion Steele, Tim Struthers, Pam Watts, Suzanne Wise.

I am especially indebted to my mother, Mary Mudry Keefe, my daughters, Natalie and Tanya Fawcett, and my brother, Russell Mudry, for their interest and support regarding this project and all of my undertakings through the years. My husband, Peter Brigg, co-habited with my book project as well as me since our marriage last year; both he and his daughter, Emma Brigg, were unfailingly supportive. Peter provided editing expertise that was invaluable in many ways, from vetting the manuscript to making many informed suggestions.

I thank you all.

INTRODUCTION

The women in this collection differ from each other in areas such as lifestyle, attitudes, occupations and accomplishments, but they are united by one characteristic: all believe that at midlife, despite problems, there is world enough and time for them to achieve and enjoy. I believe this is a message women need to hear. At midlife a few may be able to shrug and say, "I don't know what all the fuss is about," but along with positive changes, many encounter varying kinds and degrees of discomfort.

The idea for this book arose from my own experiences and those of women whom I originally talked to in an effort to cope with changes that were confusing and sometimes difficult. I found it so enormously helpful to share experiences and concerns with others that I subsequently collected the conversations that appear in these pages, in order to extend the circle to include as many women as possible.

***

"You can die now." This statement, so simple and factual, was my first indication that life as I had known it was about to change. I heard the voice, which came from the recesses of my own mind, while walking with other mourners to a reception after attending the funeral of an old family friend. It immediately deafened me to the chatter of my companions, and even now I remember that incident with daunting clarity.

What exactly did these words mean? To me, then forty-five years old with two daughters leaving home, they seemed to signal the end of my biological mission, a kind of dismissal from "Mother Nature." After some eighteen years of parenting, the last six of them on my own, I had – as the saying goes – succeeded in working myself out of a job. My daughters could manage on their own. "Thank you very much, you can go now. You are dismissed."

For a long time afterwards, I tried to deny the fact that my life had reached a turning point. However, bit by bit, tangible and intangible proof appeared in the form of white strands of hair too numerous to pluck out, eyes that couldn't see the print for the glare on a page, the onset of uncomfortable hot flashes. Fertility was definitely on the way out, and with it any of my grasping claims to youth.

It was in trying to work through this unwelcome transformation that I started talking with unusual candour to female friends and acquaintances. Whether or not to take hormones, how to keep fit, the difficulty of being promoted over a younger person, these were some of the more constant subjects of our discussions. Through such exchanges I developed a heightened awareness of our society's negative attitudes towards aging, but I also gained strength to deal with such attitudes as well as with my own fears and weaknesses.

It is a truism to say that North American society is youth centred. Instances abound, from skeletal young models, endlessly featured on billboards and television and in magazines, to the burgeoning billion-dollar cosmetic and cosmetic surgery industries. In the workplace, "Freedom 55" now frequently arrives unexpectedly when men and women are unceremoniously handed a pink slip because they're considered "past it." On the streets, the sight of a twenty-something woman on the proud arm of a fifty-something male is commonplace. Meanwhile fifty-something females often say that they've become invisible to men. One woman tells the story of a determined female friend who plans to wear extravagant hats to ensure continued visibility and attention.

After this collection was under way, I came across the following quote in Germaine Greer's book *The Change: Women, Aging and Menopause*. Some may think that she overstates the case, but it is a situation that cannot be ignored: "What if we, the horde of women of fifty, cannot see what business we have in the world? Most of us are no longer sought as lovers, as wives, as mothers, or even as workers ... We are supposed to mind our own business; if we are to do this we need to find a business of our own" (New York: Ballantine, 1991, page 22).

"Whatever it takes!" might well be our war cry. Extravagant hats may be the more frivolous part of the ammunition supply, but in order to have an acceptable place for ourselves, we undoubtedly do have to contend with our world as well as with ourselves. And considering the changes in women's lives, especially in the last thirty years, we may well play a part in altering our society's attitude towards older women.

Women in North America who are now at midlife have helped to create a radical change in the lives and expectations of females since the 1960s. Lest we forget, Toronto therapist Gilda Katz keeps an old Osterizer advertisement from the fifties pinned up on her office door. It shows an aproned woman proudly standing beside a stove graced with a cake, pie and other delicacies, and underneath are admonitions: "Keep the children quiet when he comes home." "Put a ribbon in your hair."

"Talk softly."

Brought up with the expectation that our lives would be completely fulfilled through the roles of wife and mother, white picket fence and all, many of us found ourselves altogether elsewhere: clambering up a professional ladder, raising children as a single parent, running for political office. Consciously and unconsciously, willingly and unwillingly, throughout the whole of adult life most women have been challenging, changing and redefining the status quo.

Statistics underline just how recent and rapid the changes have been. Between 1960 and 1990, the percentage of women over the age of twenty-five in the Canadian work force rose from 23.9 to 52.8 percent. For approximately the same period, the birthrate dropped from 118.3 to 54.8 births per 1,000 women age fifteen to forty-nine, and the divorce rate rose from 5 to 40 percent of marriages performed in a given year.

Statistics also tell a tale that cries out for a redefinition of human potential at midlife and far beyond: life expectancy has surged by an average of almost three years a decade during this century to approximately eighty-one years for females and seventy-six years for males. In 1891 the life expectancy for women was fifty-four and for men forty-nine.

In his book *50: Midlife in Perspective*, Herant Katchadourian notes the dramatic changes in our life patterns during this century, including the facts that women today tend to remain healthier as they get older, have fewer children than their grandmothers and finish giving birth earlier. He concludes: "A fifty year old woman now faces a stretch of approximately thirty years of post parental life" (New York: W.H.Freeman, 1987, page 104).

For me personally, the potential of that thirty-year stretch of time was certainly a factor in my thinking when I made a landmark journal entry a full three years after I heard "the voice":

> Time to face the fact that a period in my life is over, and that I'm in the position of being able to choose and create a new life for myself ... The real problem/question is – what do I want? Where do I want to live? What kind of work do I want to do? What kinds of friends do I want? Do I want a boyfriend, live-in or husband? ... and if I'm going to create a new life, I'd better get moving while I still have the energy. I know now that my resources won't last forever.

It took me quite a while to fully realize that although I'd lost some options, especially the ability to have children, I still had many others, including the choice to create this book.

***

The women in this collection developed an awareness of their needs, desires and abilities, and then – sometimes with great difficulty – dared to follow their own paths. One has embarked on an internal journey, while another has mapped out the next twenty years in a series of five-year plans that will require constant changes in lifestyle and will probably take her halfway around the world. Some of the women have embarked on new careers, and others are flourishing in their chosen or related fields of work, contrary to the prevalent belief that midlife presages decline. Several have blazed entirely new trails, thereby redefining what is possible.

In talking about their lives, a few of the women discuss other societies and Canadian society at an earlier time, and it again becomes apparent that societal norms can and do change. Wilma Stewart reveals just how much and how quickly our society has changed as she describes her mother's and grandmother's lives and discusses the circumstances of Nova Scotia's female settlers some two hundred years ago.

Midlife may have brought struggles to some of these women, but it also brought gifts. Lesia Gregorovitch lyrically expresses her changing sense of self and the world: "My view of the world is slowly becoming more integrated. Sometimes I feel as if I've walked to the top of a mountain, can look down and see all around. I can feel such a strong sense of internal growth, of being more comfortable with myself and with the world."

Some of the women find that such self-acceptance gives them the courage to take on new challenges; others decide that they can relax and "just be me." Often hard won, self-acceptance is briefly but memorably expressed by Beth Kellett as she reflects on her reaction to a mastectomy: "Everything in our lives makes up who we are. This is part of who I am, and I can't change it."

Midlife has been the beginning of a more intense search for truth and meaning for a number of the women – a burgeoning of the inner life. For several this results in adherence to a traditional religion, and for others, a heightened awareness of nature or an eclectic approach to spirituality.

As perceptions change, so do values. Many of the women express a deeper appreciation for the intimates in their lives – their husbands, children, grandchildren and friends. Friends are often mentioned as a major source of support and encouragement.

***

In this collection, menopause and midlife are treated jointly. The two are intertwined. Alterations in the functioning of the ovaries which signal the end of the menses are a result of time and part of the aging process. Throughout their conversations, the women variously allude to both: they discuss the physical changes they are experiencing and also changes in such areas as the psychological, intellectual and spiritual. The women's ages are roughly in the range of forty-five to fifty-five, the period during which menopause usually begins and ends, and which is also frequently referred to as midlife.

Several of the women featured are my friends or acquaintances; others were recommended via friends or organizations. The high-profile women will, I trust, provide insights into the character, attitudes and problems of women who are trailblazers in their fields.

In selecting and talking to the women and presenting them in this volume, I've perceived them as unique, well-developed personalities but have tried to avoid treating them as superwomen or as role models. The superwoman myth of the seventies, which blithely assumed that a woman should be able to cope with a high-powered job, a family and entertaining, then climb Mount Everest in her spare time, is, hopefully, dead. As for role models, people in our generation have struggled to avoid the strangulating confines of society's pre-ordained roles in an effort to find and follow their own paths. It would be incongruous, then, to present these women as alternative models. Rather, I think of them as friends and companions on a journey. And, like good friends, they can help to mitigate our anxieties as they relate their feelings and experiences, state convictions and deliberate over their unresolved problems. Since they have differing viewpoints on various subjects, such as the wisdom of taking hormones, their comments should also provoke some disagreement and further useful deliberation.

The conversation format of this book tends to create a portrait of each of the women against the background of her life as it is being lived at a particular place and time. The women comment on midlife throught their words, but also through their actions and the patterns of their lives. This volume, with its experiential approach, can complement some of the recent books on the subject of women at midlife that use various combinations of analysis, argument, statistics and anecdote. This approach may also encourage personal exchanges on the part of readers by heightening their awareness of the significance of their own life stories and the stories of the women all around them.

In *Understanding Menopause*, Janine O'Leary Cobb observes that there is often a pattern in women's relationships which brings them closer together at midlife: "Now we are rediscovering friendship as we experienced it in our late teens and early twenties. And it is good. We wonder why it ever stopped" (Toronto: Key Porter, 1988, page 194).

Relationships also can extend to other generations for the benefit of all. I certainly agree with Barbara Barde, the first programming executive for the Women's Television Network (WTN), regarding the need to reach out to younger women: "There's a whole new generation of women coming up, and we have to be sure that those coming after us have it better than we did." There's also much to be gained from the experiences of the older generations. In *Fountain of Age*, a pioneering study that embraces these groups, Betty Friedan suggests that development is possible well beyond retirement age for both men and women.

The statement "You can die now" will inevitably become an imperative for us all, but it is becoming clear that the opportunities to grow, achieve and enjoy life are being considerably prolonged.

When I asked film and video maker Marjorie Beaucage why she decides to do particular works, her answer mirrored my own motivation in creating this collection: "Necessity. There are things that have to be said or done." Travelling the country to produce this collection has been an extraordinary venture into my own inner world as well as the worlds that these women have so generously shared with me. Many of their thoughts continue to resonate for me and will, I expect, indefinitely. I hope that this will also be true for the reader..

ANNE COWAN-BUITENHUIS

In line with **Anne Cowan-Buitenhuis**'s belief that midlife is usually a "harvest time" in one's career, her work as a program director in the area of professional development at Simon Fraser University has yielded considerable results. In her forties, Anne co-founded the Canadian Centre for Studies in Publishing. She also began research on healing and the creative arts.

In her personal life, two teenagers at home who financially depend mainly on Anne, five grown stepchildren, and stepgrandchildren create a scenario for her middle years that certainly differs from the expectations Anne had in her twenties. So do the changes in her mirror and mind's eye, expressed in her letter to Adrien Arpel cosmetics.

ANDREA MUDRY: This letter that you wrote to Adrien Arpel cosmetics asking for a make-over because of the physical changes that come with age is wonderfully witty and can be all too true:

> I seem to have disappeared. When I look in the mirror, I see my mother. In my mind's eye, I see my daughter. For the first time in my forty-six years, nothing looks or feels right. Neither my mother's style (a very chic seventy-five year old) nor my daughter's is appropriate ...
>
> It is not simply a matter of weight or weight distribution. Somehow my whole image has blurred. Clothes, hats, and accessories that contributed to a witty and dramatic style now make me look like a bag lady. Makeup that used to accentuate high cheekbones and slightly oriental eyes is too much or too little – I'm not sure which...
>
> I would greatly appreciate having some one look at the whole picture, assess the ravages of middle age, and give me some advice on how to get through this awkward stage. It is worse than adolescence, pregnancy or anything else I've experienced. I have no desire to look younger than my years, nor am I particularly concerned about old age; it's this passage through the middle that has me confused and has left me puzzled and hesitant at the makeup counter and in the dressing room.

Have you discovered any compensations for this transformation?
ANN COWAN-BUITENHUIS: There are many, and in different areas of my life. In the physical realm, learning to be comfortable in my skin is a great benefit. Some friends of mine who are accustomed to being gorgeous, really feel the loss of the hush that used to descend on a room when they walked in. I now have a greater understanding of certain things, even fairy tales. I never really appreciated what Snow White was all about when I was a young girl because I didn't read it from the queen's point of view. She is a middle-aged woman who resents the growing beauty of a girl. So, I think that being comfortable with who you are and not having the burden of beauty are compensations. To some extent, not having to wonder whether someone is talking to you because they are

interested in what you are saying or whether they are just looking for an opportunity to make a pass is a plus.

Generally, I now have less concern about whether or not I'll be perceived as "nice." I probably have more empathy with people's sensitivities and situations and extend myself more than in the past. On the other hand, now I am not going to take a lot of nonsense from some idiot out of a concern for appearing to be too pushy, too bossy. That's part of our generation: women were taught to use the velvet glove and to be more deferential toward men and authority. I feel less inclined to do that now. All that is liberating. I feel I could cope with most situations – with the exception of the death of my children – and that the things in my life that I have worried about have not been the things that have proven difficult, so why worry?

AM: Is part of that because you've had to cope with a lot?

ACB: When I think of the horrible things that have happened to people in the world, no. I have had a relatively easy life. I've had no serious physical problems, my children are healthy, my husband is healthy, my parents are alive, my house has never burnt down. Any of the things that could happen to me have been relatively minor in relation to the terrible things that happen to other people.

AM: I understand that you had some difficulties at menopause.

ACB: Yes. It's different for everybody. For me, it came suddenly several years ago, and the first effects were mental. I had extreme mood swings and thought, "This is what middle age has done. Am I going to be a true manic depressive?" There were rages, where I'd lose my temper, then feel extremely depressed. Coupled with that was really serious memory loss. I couldn't remember a phone number long enough to dial it. Then that was followed by the inability to read a page of text and retain any of it. So then I thought, "Aah, Alzheimer's, I'm really losing my marbles here." And then I got hot flashes, and I thought "Oh, is this what's going on?"

AM: What did you do?

ACB: I went to see my doctor, who gave me some hormone tests and said, "Yes, you're in there, it's not perimenopause, you're really menopausal. And there's a variety of things you can do about it or not do about it." Meanwhile, my friends were giving me Evening Primrose Oil and lots of vitamin advice. I also thought that if the menopause was in fact the problem, it would go away eventually and I would begin to feel normal again. But then, I couldn't do my job, couldn't handle the mood swings. One day, I was so angry that I almost killed my husband by driving over him. As I was bearing down on him with my car, I realized that maybe this wasn't normal behaviour. So I decided not to fiddle around anymore. This had been going on for months, from Christmas time into the spring.

I saw my doctor and started hormone replacement therapy, which made an immediate difference. It was as if somebody had turned the lights back on in the room. Before that everything seemed dim. People who have been depressed say that's the way recovery is: as if someone has washed the windows or turned the lights on. Suddenly, I had tons of energy, I could think again, make sense of things. At work, in a period of three weeks I developed a whole year's worth of programs and wrote many pages of copy. Just suddenly, I could cope again. It took about a year to get the right dose to settle my body down, but the mental and emotional stuff sorted out very quickly.

After it was over, I wondered, "Why is it that I didn't know this could happen and that it would be like this?" If you're a baby-boomer, whatever is happening to you is happening to many people. Because I'm an early baby-boomer, this happened before the appearance of all the books that made menopause a subject for everyday conversation. When I started telling people what had happened to me, I discovered that horrible things had happened to many women. Some of my older colleagues had suffered enormously.

One woman, who is a very distinguished medical historian, told me that it happened to her when she was quite young. She decided to research and write a paper on the subject and discovered all kinds of interesting things about the way menopause was handled in France around the nineteenth century. But she couldn't get the paper published, although she had never had a paper turned down in her whole career. Also, many women whom I met didn't want their male colleagues to know that this was happening to them.

AM: Women didn't want anyone to know this was happening to them.

ACB: I would also lie in bed awake and think about what happened to my mother's generation. Some of them got shipped off to a mental institution in St. Thomas, a little town not far from my Ontario hometown, where they had their brains fried with electro-shock therapy. One of my schoolmates went home and found her mother in the bathtub with her wrists cut. I started thinking about all of these women.

AM: No one talked about it. You're certainly making the point that it's important for women to feel free to talk about menopause to convey knowledge and overcome that sense of isolation.

ACB: Well, the other thing is the differences in our lives. If I had been able to go to bed for a couple of years, I think I probably would have been fine. But I didn't have that opportunity. I think about our mothers' generation. When they were fifty years old, they were at the stage where the children had gone away; they may or may not have had anything they had to do tomorrow, because they might not have been working. They didn't usually have the demands that we have – careers and everything else. I can remember my mother saying of a friend, "Oh well, Marilyn isn't herself these days, so we won't ask her to bring sandwiches to the tea." There was an accommodation, I think, among women of other women who were not quite themselves, and it was recognized that they were going through "the change," as they referred to it. They kind of took care of each other.

Hormone replacement therapy, like natural childbirth, is very political. There are women who consider that their greatest failure in life was to deliver their child by caesarian rather than by natural childbirth, and the same philosophy informs menopause. If you can't do it somehow or other without any interventions, you feel inadequate, or you could feel inadequate. It's very political.

AM: Do you feel that way at all?

ACB: No, I don't. Somebody said to me: "You do what you have to do with a certain amount of dignity, and that's that." I don't question people's choices about these things. It's so different for everyone, as is having a baby. Some people have babies with great ease and others don't. So how anybody could know what's the right decision for another person, I just can't see.

I asked my doctor what kind of longitudinal studies have been done on women who take hormones for a long time. It's interesting to now look at the backlash against birth control pills. We all took the pill. It was the greatest thing that could have happened. There are a lot of women now who are not willing to use that method of birth control because of side effects.

One of the things that will probably happen in twenty years is that there will be more information about the longitudinal effects of hormone replacement therapy. My doctor, who is a very good gynaecologist/obstetrician, told me there really wasn't very much literature on what happens to a woman after twenty years of hormone replacement therapy. And they've been doing it for quite a long time. So I think that we will have better information, and people will make whatever decision they make with more confidence.

Maybe in future, all of the other environmental factors in our lives will have changed our bodies to some extent. I don't know. I don't know why the breast cancer rate is going up. Maybe we will all be infertile in fifty years. I'm exaggerating, but the effects of the environment, our diet and everything else on our bodies seem to be fairly dramatic. It's difficult to project forward. However, the habit of everybody talking openly about whatever is going on with them is not going to go away. So whatever people do, they'll do it with better information and a bit more confidence.

AM: How have all these changes affected you sexually?

ACB: Really, I think the biggest blow to my sex life was motherhood. I remember being sleep-deprived and energy-deprived during those years of childbearing and child-raising, and trying to keep it together at work. My sexuality was at a fairly low ebb at that point. I didn't feel that my body was my own; I felt sucked on and very much a part of some kind of physical mass that included my children and my household and my job. After my second child, I had my tubes zapped, so there has not been the fear of pregnancy. Right now, I feel more comfortable in my body and certainly enjoy my sexual relationship with my husband, probably more now than ever before. We've always had a very happy and very powerful relationship, but the years of early motherhood certainly didn't enhance my sexuality. Now I feel that coming back.

My husband is twenty-two years older than I am. When we met, he already had five children and serious financial commitments to them. So if I wanted to have children of my own, I had to realize that I would be financially responsible for raising and educating them. That was certainly not something that I was raised to believe would happen. Previously, I had been married to a man who did not want children.

In my youth, I had no expectations of doing anything other than marrying somebody that I loved, having children and working part-time. I never thought in terms of a career. If I had done, I think I would have chosen a profession, probably law, rather than doing two degrees in literature.

AM: How was it, coping with babies and a demanding job?

ACB: It was difficult. I had a daughter and a son who were born eighteen months apart in 1980 and 1981. Because there was a recession in the early eighties in Vancouver, I was concerned about losing my job and took very little time off work. We had a nanny, and we also had my husband's other children with us in the summers, which was great. The stepchildren have always made things easier rather than harder, because they've been helpful and encouraging. Also, I could look at them and say, "Right, these kids have turned out fine, so mine will, too." And my husband was an experienced parent, so I was spared a lot of the anxieties that my friends had about motherhood.

AM: Interesting. Some of the stepchildren couldn't have been much younger than you.

ACB: My oldest stepchild is ten years younger than I am, and there are grandchildren now. I aged in some ways because if you're thirty years old and you are confronted with a stepchild who is twenty-two, it becomes very clear that you are no longer in your early twenties. Without such a comparison, you can have illusions about your age for years.

I've also had the chance to go through adolescent rebellion with three sets of children. The latest is my own daughter. I had more perspective with the stepchildren because I wasn't so emotional. Much as I loved them, I could forgive them more than I could forgive my own daughter. They were not required to be perfect, because they didn't have a perfect mother. I, on the other hand, expected my own daughter would be much different.

AM: Many younger men find it difficult to deal with the changes in women's lives and attitudes over the last few decades. How is your husband in this regard?

ACB: Peter certainly is not like any other seventy-year-old man I know. They're not taking their kids to baseball, doing the shopping and cooking and all that kind of stuff. Generally, he treats women in the same way as we treat each other. There's none of this, "Okay now, I'm going to speak, women, and I am the man, so listen!" I've seen men do that to women. He probably seems younger because he has younger children. Peter is also someone who is very much in the moment and doesn't sit around reminiscing about the past. He was an English professor before he retired. Physically, I don't see that Peter does less: he skis, runs, sails and just doesn't seem much different from when we married. We have tons of energy, stamina and ability to enjoy life.

I am feeling some pressure of time, however, because of Peter's age and the fact that the children have a limited number of years at home. I would like to have more time for us to do things together than I have right now. I'm still very interested in my work, and it gives me a great deal of pleasure, but I'm less inclined to sacrifice family time to it.

AM: Tell me about your work and the kind of pleasure you derive from it.

ACB: In my job at Simon Fraser University, I'm a program director, which entails determining and meeting community needs in the area of professional development. When I was in France recently, I met an incredibly interesting woman from Los Angeles who is a dowser and works with divining rods. She did this thing with divining rods, where she would walk around the floor and ask a series of questions about me, empty her mind, and then the rods would part. Sounds like witchcraft and, in a way, it is.

She described me as an artisan. There are six or seven categories of people: healer, scholar, priest, artisan, and so on. An artisan is essentially somebody who has a sense of making or connecting things, a sense of wanting to help change the world. I think that fairly accurately describes what gives me pleasure intellectually and defines my purpose. I'm not necessarily an artist, but basically someone who draws together disparate elements and crafts something.

The largest long-term projects that I've been involved in concern writing and publishing. In the late 1980s I was a co-founder of the Canadian Centre for Studies in Publishing. This fall, we're taking our first group of master's students. We annually run a program that has about 130 short-term courses a year in areas of writing and publishing. More recently, I've also become interested in the subject of healing.

That's essentially what I do. Program development in the non-credit area is like a small business. It's a matter of trying to figure out what people want, getting the right ingredients together, presenting it in an attractive way, and hoping they'll buy it.

AM: What does the publishing centre entail?

ACB: It's a combination of things: research, teaching, education and information. We developed an undergraduate minor in communications that relates to publishing, a graduate master's program in publishing, and non-credit courses. At the same time, research is carried out. I did a study funded by the Bronfman Foundation that looked at the economics of publishing by museums and galleries. I also had a five-year grant with a research partner from the Social Sciences and Humanities Research Council to find and describe the existing primary documentation of the publishing industry. I don't have a faculty position, but I and my colleagues have often been involved in academic projects and teaching.

AM: What about the healing you mentioned?

ACB: I was the associate dean for a while, and when I finished my term, my dean asked me to explore the liberal arts area. I took a practical approach to liberal arts by asking what it is about the liberal arts that is important to people. It became very clear to me that the integrating, connecting nature of the arts has great value. Much of what ails people is a sense of dislocation, disconnection. In fact, art and medicine were at one time part and parcel of the same enterprise and were divorced unnaturally. One of our instructors, who is a writer, suggested doing a conference on healing and the creative arts, looking at the relationship between alternative therapies, traditional healing and an integrated approach to health care that would be inclusive. The conference was very successful and led to further work in this area.

This was very appealing to me. I believe the saying that you teach what you have to learn. I was at a point in my life where I was trying to make sense of the world and trying to understand life, death – the big questions: where did I come from, where am I going? I was not too surprised to learn that there were a lot of other people going along the same exploratory path. So that's what I've been really focusing on in the past year, and it's changed the way that I look at the world. It's been very helpful.

AM: You're fortunate to have such involvement in your work.

ACB: Yes. I've looked at a whole new area of literature. I've also looked at social organization. This comes at a time when the institutions that we designed at the end of the Second World War aren't working very well, according to some people.

Essentially, social institutions – the universities, hospitals, the health care system and so on – are reorganizing themselves. And people are having to realize that we must be more responsible as individuals and as a society for each other, and that the relationship between government and the individual is shifting. I'm not suggesting that this now means that everyone is on their own. I think it means that individuals are going to look after each other, whereas before there was a third party that individuals could expect to take over that responsibility. There is, I believe, a much stronger feeling now that communities are going to have to become self-sufficient. Whether that community is defined as a neighbourhood or a union or a university, there's going to be more consideration of the context in which people function, not just for the nine-to-five day. Institutions are part of a system, not isolated from each other, and they can no longer be "islands unto themselves."

The "ecosystem" model suggests more individual responsibility and, at the same time, more responsibility for the consequences of our actions. I think that has major implications for how we regard health – our own, our family's and our community's. When we look at healing, when we look at medicine, we don't have a group of specialists who are solely responsible for these functions in our society any more. We are all responsible, individually and collectively, and in a sense we all become healers.

AM: Instead of simply telling a patient what to do, some doctors now give information and their opinion, then allow the patient to make a decision. Is this indicative of the change?

ACB: Oh, sure. It's a less paternalistic model. Also, families will have to be more involved in health care. The point has been made that this could fall on the unpaid backs of women. If you have an elderly parent or a seriously ill child, there may not be anybody else to look after that person. Clearly, we need to ensure that the supports are there for this broader definition of the healing community. As government becomes "leaner and meaner," it's not enough to say that the community must take over.

Some of these questions fit in with what I am thinking about my own life. When you reach fifty and some friends have died around you and your parents are aging, you face your own mortality. You begin to question your values and also appreciate life. Before, I don't think I valued and cherished my life as much as I do now; I took it for granted.

One of the things that interested me about becoming a mother was that the wings of death are very close to you at the moment of birth. It's a transforming experience. Maybe it happens to other people in other ways. But for me, my first real brush with the power of death came when I became a mother and realized that if anything ever happened to my child, I'd want to evaporate, pulverize. Being a mother has made me fear death for my children. And the fear of my own death has to do with their well-being.

AM: Then there's the sense of uselessness that can come when children get old enough to manage without you.

ACB: I just read a review of Anne Tyler's new book. Apparently, it is about a woman who is at the beach with her kids, then just goes away from them, partly because she's become, in a sense, inessential to them. And so she has to say, "So if I am inessential to them, am I essential to myself?" I think that's a very common transition, too. Before this recent trip to France I thought, "I can go away; I don't have to always do things with my family; I can just go by myself."

AM: Where else have you been looking for some of the answers to your questions?

ACB: Well, literature, of course, because that's my background and my training. I've also become a practising Anglican. My family were churchgoing people. We went to the Presbyterian church, and I was active in church as a teenager, which was not all that unusual for my generation. When I was twenty, I married a Jew, and through my twenties, I was interested in religion, but I wasn't a practising member of any congregation. Then the children were christened, and we occasionally went to church. Just in the last two or three years, I have probably become more involved in taking time to contemplate some kind of spiritual life. But it could be anything, it could be practising t'ai chi or Zen. It's not Christianity that grabs me, but some kind of fairly regular spiritual practice. It just happens that Christianity is very available and part of my tradition.

AM: Has middle age affected you professionally as well as spiritually?

ACB: Yes. I am certainly aware of a younger generation of people with wonderful ideas, very good skills and a new perspective. They remind me of me. I remember when I was young and thought everybody who was old and established was probably not going to come up with any great ideas. So I really am thrilled that we have young people coming into our organization, and I have a strong sense of the need to move over, but not because I feel that I am washed up. I hope to work at the university for many years, because I still have lots of good ideas and am beginning to get a perspective on what I can do, the value of my experience, and how to use that experience to the benefit of other people who are following me. There are some things that I can do very well that I couldn't have done twenty years ago. I've got a lot of connections, political smarts, and wisdom about what might work and what might not work.

So, I certainly have become very aware of being a senior member of my profession, and also I have thought quite a lot about what you do in an organization to make sure that everyone is used most effectively.

In one's work, I believe that middle age is usually a time of harvesting the seeds that you planted or of expanding things that you have started. It's not necessarily a time for people to start new things. It's more difficult to start new things at middle age, unless you make a complete departure, I believe. It would be interesting to look at projects or work people did earlier in life and things they began in middle age to see if there's any qualitative difference. Generally, I suspect that the work that requires a keen sense of synthesis and wisdom would come more out of middle age.

AM: Yes, that would be interesting.

ACB: Middle age has also made me think again about the relationship between mothers and daughters. When I became a mother myself, I felt that I had entered into a whole new relationship with the women of my mother's and grandmother's generations. That experience seemed to complete a chain. But as I became middle-aged and went through menopause, I remembered things my mother said that I just didn't understand. I hear her words a lot.

AM: What sorts of things?

ACB: I remember my mother saying how unhappy she was when my grandparents died. She said, "Well, now we are the older generation." I thought, "Sure, look at you, you are old." But I didn't understand the feeling of vulnerability when you are the oldest generation.

In middle age, you start recognizing yourself in your parents or your parents in yourself. I also see a poignant desire in my friends and in myself to quickly get all the information we can from parents. All the stories they told that I found boring and ignored are becoming very interesting. A lot of my friends are gathering together photographs and trying to create some sort of family history. They are engaged in various projects, using video, old photograph albums, computers and scanners, and all the technology. It's interesting. I think it's part of a middle-aged desire to collect information to pass on, because you recognize how little attention you paid, and you want to ensure that your children will have the information when their time comes.

CAROLYN COLE

As head of New Brunswick's Aitken Bicentennial Exhibition Centre (ABEC), **Carolyn Cole** takes particular pleasure in a fundraising "moveable feast" that brings together a variety of people and organizations. Now that she has finally gained a position appropriate to her talents, Carolyn's own life has become a kind of movable feast because she is able to use her daily experiences, contacts and ideas to imaginatively create new programming for ABEC.

At midlife, forced to reassess many aspects of her life and make changes after a divorce, Carolyn has succeeded in overcoming numerous obstacles, although she would still like to be "slimmer," "richer" and "healthier."

CAROLYN COLE: I remember getting Betty Friedan's *Feminine Mystique* when my daughter was just a baby. After I started reading it, I thought, "This is too disturbing, I can't do it," and put it down. Little did I know that I was going to have great need for it later on. I thought I would always be secure because I was a good wife, worked hard, loved my children and loved being a mother. Looking back now, I realize that Friedan struck a chord, but I was really terrified. It meant questioning everything, what my whole life was about.

So, in a way, it was thrust upon me when my husband left some years later. He walked out. He had another woman and had a baby with her. I was supposed to cope, and I was really scared. My identity was as his wife and as a mother. My former husband is very talented and came from a wealthy family, and I was Mrs. So-and-so; wasn't that nice. My two sons and daughter, who were eight, fourteen and sixteen when we separated, are also very accomplished. So I was a mother too. That was all.

ANDREA MUDRY: What schooling did you have?

CC: I was married when I was twenty and had finished high school and business college; I'd also studied a lot of music. So I had married and settled down. I know I was a good mother. That part was fine. I loved being pregnant and being a mother, but when I looked around the house and I realized I wasn't a good housekeeper, and when that's all you do ...

AM: That was an important criterion for housewives then.

CC: That's right. I looked at the women on television who had these shiny floors; I didn't know how to do that. And I didn't like it either. My satisfaction came from having dinner parties. When I was really fed up and down on myself, I would have a dinner party. They were always great successes.

I wanted to go to work. More than anything, I wanted to get out of the house. The most challenging thing I did was teach bridge at the Y. Well, that was fun, but I should have been doing a lot more. Somehow I knew I should be making some kind of contribution apart from organizing concerts for the PTA, but I didn't really know what.

One of the times I remember so vividly is when I got a part-time job working for a psychiatrist back in the 1960s. I had made all the necessary arrangements to have the children looked after and picked up. I even arranged to work at home sometimes if necessary. When I told my husband, he said, "No wife of mine is going to work." Of course, wh￼ he later walked out he expected me to immediately be able to mar￼

So, in the early eighties, after my divorce had gone through, I found myself stuck in the steno ghetto, unqualified for anything and very frustrated. In fact, I had what could be classified as a kind of breakdown; it was diagnosed as a reactive depression. My doctor said it wasn't a chronic condition, it was a reaction to circumstances.

Then there were years of drudgery in jobs that were hellish, just hellish, where I was sexually harassed and treated like nothing by some people who would say, "Get me this," "Do that." It was so demoralizing. A couple of men in particular were really awful creatures. Knowing what I do now, I would report them to the human rights commission. I especially remember one job with the federal government where they effectively said that as long as I showed up, it didn't matter what I did. So there I was, just middle-aged and squeaking by financially. I had a lovely home, but had to sell it because I couldn't afford a six-thousand-dollar roof on a secretary's salary. There just didn't seem to be any future.

AM: Sounds grim.

CC: A major reason for my lack of job mobility was the fact that I didn't speak French. Although I had a lot of friends and contacts in Fredericton, where I was living, everyone said, "Oh, if only you were bilingual." I heard that so many times.

My former mother-in-law, to her eternal credit, and my former sister-in-law both really encouraged me to go back to school. "You can do it," they said, and kept gently pushing. So, finally, that's what I started doing, by taking a spring course in sociology just to see if my brain still worked. I had no faith in myself. On my first exam, I got a C+ and was devastated. But I ended up doing very well because, after checking with the professor, I realized I had forgotten how to write an exam.

From there, I went to a French immersion program at Université Sainte-Anne in Nova Scotia. That was the most amazing summer of my life! I left my son and my dog with my parents. There I was for six weeks, and all I had to do was make my bed – if I felt like it – and go to the cafeteria for meals. It was heavenly; I started playing the piano again, acting and writing. I hadn't done any of these things for ages, and I did everything in French.

The unbelievable was happening. I remember leaving residence with my music books in my arms, tears running down my face: life could be fun and interesting and challenging! That really was the beginning of a major change in my life.

AM: What do you think happened?

CC: It was the carefree life – not having to do anything but what I love, which is music, theatre and classes. As it turned out, once I got going, languages were my thing, and I studied French, Spanish, Latin and Greek. If you're musical, languages are probably a natural adjunct. This is especially true of French, because it is not phonetic; you have to have a good ear. So, although I started out to learn French in order to get a good job, I ended up being incredibly turned on.

After that experience, I started as a student at the University of New Brunswick in the fall, and was in school full-time for five years. When I was beginning my first year, I was so enthusiastic that I wanted to take everything. My sociology professor, who had taught me in the spring, said, "The best plan for somebody like you is to pick excellent professors; don't worry about the subject." So I did that. I went out and talked to the profs and to their former students, and chose accordingly. My sociology prof was so right: a poor professor can make any subject boring, and a good one can make any subject fascinating.

After my first semester, I gained a full scholarship. At the end of my second year, I won a gold medal.

AM: Those are motivating rewards.

CC: The positive feedback was a great stimulant. I couldn't wait to get my essays back. It seemed like everything was so straightforward. You worked hard, and then somebody said, "Congratulations. Here's an A+. That was wonderful." Whereas in the real world, things didn't seem to work that way at all.

AM: How did you react to the fact that a lot of the students were younger than you?

CC: Since I was forty-four when I started, I expected age to be a problem, but I soon met a group of mature students, all exceedingly motivated because it was costing a fortune to be there. Also, I'm a social animal and don't have difficulty meeting people of any age.

I was enjoying myself so much at university, I felt that even if the experience didn't translate into work, it really didn't matter. It was amazing.

But as time went on, I was also forced to realize that I had become reliant upon substances to help me cope, and had done so for years. But now they were starting to cause me real problems. One semester I didn't do well at all. I knew that I had to stop taking anything that altered my moods because it was getting difficult to study at night.

AM: Was it alcohol?

CC: It was also drugs, mainly prescribed by doctors for sleeplessness and depression, and in some cases overprescribed. I have a strange chemical make-up and suffered from side effects. I didn't do anything dramatic on drugs. They just slowed me down a lot, and I needed to have my wits about me all the time in order to do well.

AM: Did you have depressions earlier?

CC: I had a serious post-partum depression after my last baby was born. Now I realize what it was, but at the time the tendency was to victimize the victim. People, including family, would say, "What do you mean you're depressed? What right have you got to be depressed? You've got everything. You've got a lovely home, three beautiful children, a good husband." But I was truly depressed, and I felt guilty. Now this is widely recognized as a serious condition.

In any case, life's turning points are amazing. The summer after I began to recognize my problem, I was at Laval University for a French immersion program. The thing about French immersion is that it is a very intimate experience, because your language capabilities are limited and you're on a first-name-only basis with everybody. In one class, we were asked to introduce ourselves. One man said he was Dale from Cleveland, Ohio, and he was an alcoholism and drug counselor. Well, here I am in Quebec City, where nobody knows me. I went up to him and said, "Dale, I want to see you in my room. I desperately need to talk to you in English."

When we talked, I was very honest with him about my past. I told him about getting into school, how it was a slippery slope, and that at times I was out of control. "I don't want to do it," I said. "Why am I doing this? I have this wonderful opportunity now, but unless I can be more stable, I'll lose it. I've lost everything else, and I don't want to lose my last chance." He listened, then said to me point-blank, "You're an alcoholic. What you've got to do is get yourself to Alcoholics Anonymous fast." I listened to him, but I didn't do it, I slipped and slid, coasted ...

AM: But it was a beginning.

CC: It was a big beginning. When I got back to Fredericton, I called a friend up one night after I had been drinking. When I did it again another night, she said, "Carolyn, you've got a problem." Then she told me that she had talked to a friend of hers, a professional artist. "She goes to an AA group in Fredericton," my friend said, "and has given me permission to tell you that she has the same problem, and she wants you to go to a meeting." So I went to the meeting, walked in and – I'll never forget this – the woman who was chairing was a brilliant writer from Fredericton.

AM: I have a friend who goes to AA in Ottawa, and tells me how full it is of senior government officials.

CC: That's right, exactly. It's such an eye-opener. The next time that I walked into a meeting, there was one of my professors. He came up to me and said, "You don't know what goes on behind closed doors."

In time, I developed other means of emotional support as well. I went on retreats and hooked into what was almost an underground network of women who were extremely bright and left wing. Most of them were radical feminists and very supportive. It made me feel good about myself because I respected these women so much. Some had food problems. Some had marriage problems – perfect on the surface but awful in fact – and had walked out. But, for me, the main support and motivation for change were my studies at the university.

So I went on to graduate with distinction and got an assistantship to do graduate work in Latin and Greek. I took ill during that year with a yeast syndrome. It was the sort of thing you die with, rather than of, but I had to quit. Then later I started to work.

Now the only drug I take is Anacin for migraines. It has caffeine and that seems to be the only thing that, if I take it in time, will do something with the migraine, but I don't take anything else.

AM: Even though you do have some medical conditions?

CC: That's right. I take vitamins now, and I'm using natural treatments. Last fall, I travelled to Toronto to see a naturopath, and I go to dietitians and chiropractors – that kind of thing. I simply can't handle chemicals; I don't process them like other people.

AM: I hope you allow yourself to take great pride in overcoming these problems.

CC: People always say that to me. I feel very grateful. From time to time I've spoken to women's groups; it's satisfying and I feel that I'm "paying back." There are so many women with difficulties and addictions to food or whatever it is that helps them to temporarily kill the pain. It can be a painful world for women, especially if they have no security.

I also feel almost blessed that, for some reason, I wanted to stop, and the motivating factor was school, no question. After all those years in terrible jobs, it was wonderful to be able to go into a situation where I was allowed to be as creative as I wanted to be – writing and playing music. And now, in my present position, I'm limited only by my imagination. It's fabulous and so exciting. But, if I hadn't gone back to school, I don't think I would have got the self-confidence to tackle some of the things the way I have.

AM: What does your job as executive director of ABEC entail?

CC: The Aiken Bicentennial Exhibition Centre – ABEC for short – is an arts and science centre. We have a permanent hands-on children's science gallery, plus five other galleries that are constantly changing to exhibit fine art, photography, crafts, science. We're thinking of doing a "Listen'n Lunch" series throughout the year. And we're doing set-up shows for a series of plays.

The ABEC itself is an attractive building that was formerly a Carnegie library; it has a beautiful stained-glass ceiling in the foyer. Recently, we launched a Scott Joplin compact disc. It was a really magical summer evening with the doors open and Scott Joplin wafting out into the street. I think of us as a community cultural centre with great variety. One week we host one of the world's foremost experts on Shakespeare, and the next week we might feature Saint John fiddlers.

I always hope we'll lure in people who might not have been able to have these experiences elsewhere. Then, after their experiences at the ABEC, they may say, "Hey, wow … I really like Shakespeare, or Handel, or Joplin." There are people who say, "Oh, those things are for people who have a lot more education than I do." They're dead wrong, and I want to show them that they are and that it's fun. My staff enjoy the centre; they often come to our events after hours.

AM: How do you choose the programming?

CC: I play my hunches; I listen to people; I go out a lot and meet people at the supermarket, flea market, auctions, theatre, and at dinner parties who make suggestions. We try to feature regional talent and bring shows in from outside as well.

Some collaborative efforts that we do with other organizations, such as a fundraising moveable feast in the spring, have been especially successful. Last year, the dinner started with strawberry soup and jazz at the ABEC and then, for different courses and entertainments, moved on to the library, then to the museum and out to the French Centre. Such an event gets a lot of us working together.

I'm president of Hospitality Saint John, the city's tourism organization, which is time-consuming. And, as a result of my mother's fairly lengthy illness, I'm on the board of a hospice as a volunteer. However, most of my activities are arts and culture related. That's what I really love, and sometimes it's hard for me to draw the line between my work and my play.

AM: That's perfect. There's a saying that when work becomes play, the gods have called you.

CC: When I wake up in the morning, it's usually great. I wonder what's on the agenda and who I'm going to meet that day. Because I married young and had my children young, now I've got another life. My children are still a great joy to me, each one of them, and we're constantly in touch. But now I have this other life where I'm free to study and learn, and they have their lives. They're all involved in the arts: Allen is a composer and artistic director of a theatre company in B.C., Holly is a jazz singer, and Ted is an actor.

I love Saint John and I love being an uptowner. You know, I'm the suburban housewife from hell who has never lived in a house with windowsills before. This house is probably 150 years old. I've never lived in a neighbourhood like this before, where you walk to the corner store. I've always driven to the supermarket. And I love the neighbourhood. It's so erratic: one house is a slum and the next is renovated.

I hate clichés in some ways, but clichés exist for a reason: because they're true. And it's true: "no pain, no gain." I have had a lot of pain and I still have significant worries ...

AM: What are you thinking of?

CC: Well, you know, I'm very lucky. I love my job and I love my home, but there's no security. I have no pension. I didn't really start working until I was almost fifty in a real job. So what do I have to look forward to? I have a friend in Fredericton who says to me, "I hope I don't live to be old. I'm going to be destitute."

I'm really afraid of the future. I had something like a mantra, really an affirmative statement, that I used to write over and over: "I'm no longer the victim of my past, nor do I fear my future." Somebody told me, if I did that for days and days on end, that it would come true. Well it hasn't come true. I do fear my future.

I've had a stressful life and have some health problems, such as fibromyalgia. It's a muscular problem that can cause excruciating pain, then disappear. And my mother recently died of cancer. My dad was there for her, but now Dad is a widower and his health isn't great. If I ever took ill, I'd really be on my own.

One idea that I've really talked a lot about is a women's commune in a really nice apartment building. So many single women are struggling to keep a house going. If we just banded together, we could afford a lovely place – a co-op or a condo. Each person would have her own flat, but when the roof or furnace goes, the cost of it would be divided five ways. And when you're sick, there's somebody to make chicken soup for you.

AM: Have you encountered any examples of that?

CC: I thought up the idea, and then somebody sent me an article about a group of women out on the West Coast who had established a commune. Right now I'm busy, but eventually living alone may be a problem. It is only since my mother took ill that I began to give some serious thought to the fact that I'm not getting any younger and that I'm alone.

I've been engaged three times since my marriage breakup, but I've never quite been able to do it. Twice, I was the one who broke it up. I think I'm often attracted to inappropriate men. Some had addiction problems. I love the company of men, and I do seem to have a lot of gay men friends. They're wonderful friends; maybe that satisfies my need for male companionship, and it's safe. There's not going to be a physical relationship obviously, so I can't get burned.

My mother and my father had a close, loving relationship. But for me, I'm beginning to think that I was really meant to be alone. Maybe I'm happier this way. I don't know. We're programmed to think we should have a partner. But I've had a number of suitors and relationships, none of which has worked out. And I know intellectually that the "Father Knows Best" family doesn't exist. It just isn't there – the white house and the picket fence.

Actually, life for me right now is very exciting. I'm having a good time. So, on balance, I have been fortunate. But this business of the unfair treatment of the women of our generation has to be dealt with. There's a whole army of middle-aged women who have done their jobs as wives and mothers well but are going to be destitute because they've been abandoned. Society rewards men for walking out. It's a fact of life that when men leave their families, their income jumps by a huge amount, and the income of the women and children decreases by a huge amount. When the man goes, the pension goes with him, everything goes.

AM: I like to think that more young women are now learning to look after their own careers and finances as a matter of course.

CC: I hope so. I wish women had more faith in themselves and believed in themselves more. The big con is that we need men because they're so much smarter and stronger. That is not the case at all. Women are much stronger physically, not in terms of lifting things, but in terms of tolerating pain. We're stronger when it comes to looking after ourselves. That con has kept us – metaphorically and in reality – pregnant and barefoot. It's kept us dependent. It's made us think that we really need men to look after us. In fact it's the other way around.

I have a friend whose partner died a few years ago. She was just bereft, saying, "Well, what am I going to do? Who am I going to look after?" When she originally met this man, she was alone with four small children. They got together, and he was going to look after her. Somewhere along the way it shifted. She looked after him, and when he was gone, she was lost because she had put so much time and energy into looking after him. He was a high-powered executive, yet was incapable of making some decisions. Once, she went away on vacation for two weeks and told him: "Stop at the Hilton Hotel on your way home and have chicken dinner." When she returned two weeks later, he said, "I'm so glad you're back; I'm so tired of that chicken dinner."

AM: Are you serious?

CC: Isn't that funny? He was a millionaire. It's a true story.

MARJORIE BEAUCAGE

In her forties, Marjorie Beaucage left the life of a community worker to become a video and film artist. Her main aim remains unchanged: to assist people, especially members of the. Aboriginal community, to change, to heal and to celebrate. "Storytellers create and re-create the cosmos, giving form and meaning to the moment, connecting us to the sacred power that is in all things," she says. For her latest project, a film on menopause, she wants to gather the wisdom of Aboriginal and other ancient cultures to assist women in the present and future.

A Métis, Marjorie views her mixed ancestry as a gift that enables her to act as a bridge between various worlds. She currently lives in Saskatoon, Saskatchewan.

ANDREA MUDRY: What prompted you to start working on "Women's Power," your film about menopause?

MARJORIE BEAUCAGE: Menopause is an "in" subject in magazines and books. From what I've picked up and seen, the discussions are around its biological and emotional aspects in Western society. People seem to refer to it as the end of something, not the beginning of something: the end of childbearing years, of attractiveness, of desirability as a woman. A woman's place is determined a lot by that biological function, so when it is no longer there, she has no place. Because of my life and where it's brought me, in this film I want to explore the spiritual and ritual aspects, and the things that affirm "woman" rather than express loss.

In the Aboriginal culture, when you've finished your moon time, you become a grandmother, and that is your place of power as a woman in the community. The moon is the grandmother, not your physical grandmother. Your moon time is tied to grandmother moon because she governs the waters of life and of the earth, whether it's your blood or the water you drink or the tides; it's all connected. Your moon time is your connection to the grandmother, and your responsibility is also to the waters of life as a woman. That's a very strong power and a big responsibility. So, your woman time and your monthly times teach you different things about that power; that's why we have those moods every month, as a teaching.

AM: What sort of teaching?

MB: Just like the moon has different phases, if you pay attention to your own phases and your own moon times, you will learn different things about your life and what life is about. For example, when I started to pay attention to what was happening to me, I recognized that sometimes I had angry moods and other times I had really soft and gentle moods, and I was learning different things or responding from different places. Over a number of years, I saw that every spring or every winter I would be in a different phase in my own life. I recognized that I had strong rhythms, weak rhythms and restorative rhythms. During new moons, I was very creative, and there were times when I wasn't.

So I started to plan my calendar and my activities around my moons. Then, when I went into meetings, and everybody would pull out their day books and say, "Well, let's have our next meeting on such and such a day." If I had already crossed off that day, I'd say, "No, it's already booked." I didn't have to explain further. This helped me keep my balance.

AM: This is fascinating because, of course, our usual thinking in North America tends to be, "You're too moody." The underlying assumption is that we should always be the same.

MB: No, never the same.

AM: So this is part of the variety of personality and of life to which we should become more attuned?

MB: Yes, and to the different phases you go through as a human being. That's why I say the moon is a teacher, the mountain is a teacher, the trees and water are teachers, your body is a teacher. As a woman, your body is a very good teacher because you learn a lot of lessons from it.

Anyway, to go to the end of the moon time, to menopause as it's called, and what happens. As an old lady once explained to me: "The grandmother, she comes and visits you every month to teach you all these things. As you get older, you don't need her as much, so she stops coming. But you miss her, so she comes back and visits every now and then. After fourteen months or so you come to that time when you don't need her anymore, and then you become the grandmother."

That's why I feel that this is a great time; I pay attention, trying to learn from everything that's happening, even the heat waves. At first I said, "What is this all about?" Then this one time when I had a heat wave, I had a most incredible experience, where I felt more and more grounded and connected into the earth. I felt like my feet had grown roots that went right down to the core of the earth, right to the fire in the centre of the earth's belly. My roots went down through my feet to that fire, and that fire came right up through me. I felt the power of that fire at the core of the earth. If you resist, then it's uncomfortable. If you give yourself to it, and let it come through you, you feel that power. Then it passes and you learn. So, yes it's uncomfortable; it's not always convenient or magical. Yet, at the same time, there is teaching in these experiences.

For my film, I want to learn more about those teachings and how people made that transition. Our culture has had rituals for all the different transitions in life, including this one. The only ritual in North American society now for people is a seniors' home. That's not the way it used to be in most Aboriginal and ancient cultures. I want to talk to teachers and elders in different cultures to get some of their stories, teachings and rituals. I also want to use these images, sensations and experiences from my own body to create something like a spiritual poem, a celebration or affirmation. It would be an affirmation of myself, and also of the wisdom that's come before me that I can access and pass on to women in the future, because there's been a gap in what women know about these things.

I think post-menopausal women should run the world. That's their power, and they have the time to do so. But they don't see themselves as having that power, and therefore, they're not doing it.

AM: How else has middle age affected you personally?

MB: I don't think of myself as middle-aged; rather I think of myself as halfway through my life. Middle age has certain connotations in this society. I only began my life in film and video five years ago, and I intend to be productive until I'm ninety. I started noticing change – like, when the grandmother wasn't visiting – about three years ago when I was forty-five. And I haven't had a moon for seven or eight months. So I probably have another five or six months before I know for sure, but I just feel that it's end is near. At first, I felt unsettled. I called the heat waves my 7/11s because at seven in the morning and eleven at night almost like clock-work, I used to get them.

I've also gained weight and slowed down, but that's partly because of my lifestyle the last two years – of travelling and not having a regular life. So I feel the need to be more physical again. I would be more comfortable if I lost the ten to twenty pounds that I've put on. Overall, it's not so much a weight problem as a shift that's occurred in my being. I know that it will change because my life is going to be changing very soon, so this is just a phase.

My attitude has changed mostly for the better because I am more grounded. I feel my direction is established and I'm on my path, where I'm supposed to be. I've always trusted the twists and turns my life has taken that always bring me to different places. I've also become more patient; my sense of time and place is different. When I went to Johnson's Canyon in the Rocky Mountains, that gave me a sense of time. When you see the power of water and the millions of years it took to make that canyon, it teaches patience. What's happening in my body is teaching me a different kind of patience too. Also, my yearning to make this film to affirm my being as a woman comes from a very spiritual place because woman, you know, has been so abused and violated over time and through the centuries. I have been too, in every way, and I need to restore myself as a woman and honour that.

AM: Do you want to talk about the abuse?

MB: Well, there's been institutional abuse and physical abuse, sexual abuse – all of those abuses – a lot of violence in my life: intellectually, emotionally, spiritually. In the church, my spirit was bashed around. I was violated as a child. I was always bashing against systems and situations. The world is a violent place; it's not a safe place for women and children. All of those things I carry in my body. There's a lot of pain in our communities.

All along, much of my work has been about healing. You know, there's this collective memory – it's not just a personal memory – and we always have reminders of it every day. Even though I'm not now being abused personally and have ways to protect myself, I'm still part of the collective identity and feel it. Now my work as an artist and as a woman will put forward images of beauty and affirmation of women, who are the carriers of life and have the power of creation. We have to honour that if we're going to survive as a people.

AM: You have a very strong sense of identification with your community.

MB: I've always been a community animal. My whole life has been lived in groups. I'm the oldest of twelve children. I lived in the bush in an extended family situation, then was the member of a religious community. My life and work have been in the community; that's the nature of my being.

AM: What religious order were you in?

MB: Our Lady of the Missions. It's an order that's mainly on the prairies. My family was poor, so I joined the convent when I was eighteen. I didn't have many other options – to go to school or do anything else – and I knew I didn't want to get married and have twelve kids. But at the time I wasn't conscious of this motivation. When I was thirty-three, I left the order.

After that, I carried on with community work, except that I was freer of institutional constraints and was no longer divided against myself. Money was difficult, but I was used to having little anyway, so it wasn't that hard.

Part of that time was deciding what kind of relationships I wanted and whether or not I wanted to have children. I guess I chose to not have kids because I knew what a commitment they require. In a way, I was just getting my life back again, and I didn't want to give it up for another twenty years. Also, I didn't feel the need to have my own biological children. Children belong to everyone. In our family we have eighteen nieces and nephews. I guess you'd call me a great aunt, but in Cree they call me a little grandmother. So I have lots of children in my life, always have, always will. Because of my age at that time, I felt that certain pressure, but not for long.

In terms of relationships, I felt like a piece of meat for a while because men figured, "Oh, wow, she's available," and all that stuff. It didn't turn me on. I was used to being myself and wasn't prepared to be something other than what I was. It took me a long time to work that one out, but I was strong and knew I didn't want to fit into anybody else's idea of how I was supposed to be. At the same time I questioned and doubted myself because I didn't have the same life experiences as everyone else and didn't value my own. Most of my intimate relationships have been with women because most of my life has been with women; it was more natural for me. Also, most of the men that I met were not men that I wanted to be with or who could see me the way I wanted to be seen. Now I've been out of the convent as long as I was in.

AM: Both in and out of the convent, you did extensive community-based work with Aboriginals and many other groups.

MB: Yes, as far back as the sixties. I worked with Canadian Urban Training, a social action network for about ten years. Most of the work that was being done at that time, particularly in cities, was charity-based. There wasn't anything that was really justice-based, that looked at why things were the way they were, that analyzed poverty and situations and tried to move away from the "do-good" approach to change. So this network started to train people who were working in inner cities to address systemic issues at a much broader level. I worked in numerous areas: with youth on the street, with native women, on literacy projects. The professionals and the members of the community worked together so that the people were able to become experts on their own issues. There were some pretty neat things.

I was also working through the social action office in the Catholic Church at the time, and we were always coming up against systemic barriers that institutions would impose. I worked organizing in the prisons and in northern Manitoba around flooding issues, such as the Churchill River diversion for hydro projects. The people didn't even know what was happening, so I would spend a lot of time in the communities telling people what was going on, then helping them sort out what they wanted to do.

I also worked with a native women's transition centre. In that situation, we wanted to have a place that wasn't crisis-centred and that would make real change – I'm always focused on making real change – and have it as a home where women could support each other through those changes. Self-sufficiency was always the goal. We came up against all the bureaucracies. The City of Winnipeg didn't want that many welfare women under one address. They wanted to institutionalize us; we insisted that the home is a place where people live and care for each other, not an institution where others provide care. They've still got battles, but the centre is still going. Even the women that left still come back and help the others, so that a network was created.

AM: I notice you're not using that currently popular word "empower."

MB: We talk about self-government or self-determination. It's the same thing, I guess: governing yourself, owning yourself and making decisions about your life. That's what has always been at the heart of it all. Not self-government the way the government talks about it, because that's a real-estate deal and their agenda, not ours.

AM: When did you leave your life of community work for video and film?

MB: I was forty years old. I say that I ran away from home and went to Toronto and film school. I was living in Manitoba, which I call home. I ran away in the sense that the personas and roles that I had taken on started to burn out. The work wasn't new and didn't excite me any more; I knew I needed a change. I also needed to do something for myself, my own voice and creation. I'd been trying different things to find my own expression, such as playing guitar and making pottery. I write a lot, always did. I have journals from the sixties to the present. But I felt the need for more. Apart from all the outside work in the community, there were internal needs.

So I thought, "Okay, what am I going to do? What can I do? What's my forum?" I didn't know. Then one day, while I was driving to do a literacy workshop with a co-worker, we talked. "Why don't you go back to school?" she said. "School! I hate school, and besides, what would I take?" I said. When she asked what I would do if I could do anything, I said, "Wow. I would want to be a dancer, but it's kind of late for that. I'm forty years old; my body would never be able to do the things that I would want it to do. It always captures me whenever I see someone really communicate through dance." Then we explored why dance appealed to me: it communicates without words, expresses feelings and movement.

"Well," she said. "You're always telling stories and thinking in images." I didn't think about being a creative person because I just put it into my work, always inventing everything – exercises, popular education and all that stuff. I was doing it before it was "the done thing." "So what about film?" she asked. "Huh!" I replied in surprise. "Well, it's movement, it's images, it's all those things that are you," she said.

We didn't talk about it again. That night I was lying in bed in our hotel room, and every time I thought about it, I would actually smile. I couldn't stop myself from smiling. Then I came up with all the reasons why I couldn't possibly do it. I'm a total techno-peasant, hate technology, all these things. But every time the smile would come back.

Then I tested the idea out on my friends, the way I always do, by throwing it out to see the reaction. "Well, I'm going to film school," I'd say. Nobody was surprised. I was the most surprised. So that's how it happened. I chose to go to Ryerson in Toronto because it has hands-on learning, and I'm that kind of person. When I got to Toronto, I didn't know anybody. I was a student with no commitments, no groups, no nothing.

AM: Quite a change.

MB: It was totally freeing. I thought,"Now if anybody likes me it's because of me. I'm not doing anything for anybody." I had time and space to explore all this new world, and I did for two years.

When I'd had enough of school, I needed to learn and mentor with different people in the way I learn best. For another three years I stayed in Toronto. I got involved, worked on my films, on other people's films and learned as much as I could. And – back to my old self – I got involved in all the cultural action and began organizing. Then I thought, "Toronto can eat me up if I stay here." I was doing less of my own work and more organizing stuff. So I came back to Saskatchewan. Maria Campbell wanted me to come. There was a blockade against clearcutting in northern Saskatchewan, and the elders wanted someone to document the struggle. I got a camera and went and pitched camp at the blockade for three months with the elders.

I stayed in Saskatchewan and, at the request of the community, then ended up becoming a "runner" for the Aboriginal Film and Video Alliance at the Banff Centre for the last two years. The alliance was formed in '91 because we were tired of fighting individually to make films on our terms. Others didn't believe that we could tell stories differently, in our way, and that it would work. So we organized ourselves, supported each other and developed our own network. Then we ended up negotiating with the Banff Centre. That's when I was asked to make a path; that's my gift. People know that about me, so whenever they want somebody to kick a few doors in, you know – open doors and make a new path – they ask me. Now it's time for someone else, and I'm going to be back full-time into my own work.

AM: For years you were out there working with people on the streets, trying to help in a very practical, hands-on way. Do you think that the work you do now with a camera can also help bring about change?

MB: Oh, more than any other way because it is a very powerful medium, and people need to see themselves in other ways. The camera can offer possibilities because it images people in other ways. Imagination: image in nation. Through art, you can put forward possibilities that you can't as well in other forms or actions. And I think the artist has a responsibility to give that back to the community to help the community see itself in new ways and reflect, not just on pain, but on potential. That's what you can do as an artist: you can create those new visions and give them back to the people so they can remember who they are in new ways.

AM: Can you generalize about what motivates you to choose to do a piece?

MB: Necessity. There are things that have to be said or done. I just do what has to be done at that moment in time or in my life. I don't think about it. It's just an intuition, a need. For example, I want to do the film on menopause because I'm in it, and it's important to me. I need to do it – for myself more than anything because I want to affirm myself. It seems that when I'm being true to my own inner voice or need, the work also resonates for other people, and they will get something from it too. As for other work, sometimes people ask me to do it and if I want to or can, then I will. I've said no, too. Sometimes I'm not interested.

AM: From your film and video productions that I have seen, your works look at life from a variety of perspectives: as a human being, as a woman, as an Aboriginal.

MB: Yes. Well, it's a multi-versal world. There's more than one way to look at something.

AM: Right. "Wings of the Same Bird," your video about a feminist conference with representatives from many races and backgrounds has some very touching sequences about inclusiveness. Sometimes feminist groups get railroaded into "thou shall/thou shall not" strictures that people cannot fit into.

MB: That's what I dislike about feminism. It becomes so dictatorial, limits life and creates all these boundaries. It's still patriarchal in its models. So I always try to find ways. Only after we have made room for differences will there be room for everyone. Everybody has something different to offer. My intention in making that video was to let the women speak for themselves about where they are, and not to try to shape their answers. Now that video is being shown mostly to education audiences and at women's festivals.

I'm also experimenting with documenting events from the participant's point of view rather than from the organizer's point of view. Usually, in such documentaries, the organizers find the people that give them the answers they want. For me, a film is a search; you don't know where it's going to go. That's why I have trouble getting money to make my films, because I can't tell them what my film's going to be. And the premises they have for making films are not mine.

AM: Your "Good Grief" piece about the accidental death of your younger brother must have been a very personal effort for you and your family because, in it, they express their feelings about his death.

MB: Making that film was like making medicine for myself and my family, and for making peace with my brother, Danny, who died. Different people were grieving in different ways. One brother made a song. On Valentine's Day I wrote a letter to everybody and said that I wanted to make a video to sort out stuff for myself, and asked if they would do that with me. They said, "Good grief, Marjorie." So that's how it came out. I went back home at Christmas time and shot it on the first anniversary of his death. The process was good for me and for my family.

Once the video was out in public, different people started asking for it, schools and grief groups. It's been interesting to see how the video helps other people.

AM: So you come to create things from very different motivations as well as perspectives?

MB: All the time. One was for an artist I know, another was an event that I was asked to document. My "Bingo" film was my own medicine. I was processing the victim mind. Bingo was a metaphor for life, and the script is around winning and losing, chance and fate.

Documenting events is really interesting, especially if you have a stake in the event. To me it's all about the relationship you have with that subject at that moment and about your interaction with it.

AM: You're not objective?

MB: No, never. I'm biased and proud of it. There's no such thing as objectivity. There's always a point of view and a bias. You think the media is not biased? They call our documentaries biased because they present a differing point of view. Yes, I have a bias; yes I have a stance. I have a position in life, and I'm not ashamed of it.

AM: You've talked about violence, about dealing with it in your personal life, your community and your work. Many women who have such experiences are very angry, but you come across as an essentially gentle person.

MB: No. I have my rage. Now I use it to create with. In the past, I've ranted and raved too, and I was very angry for quite a long time, but it wasn't healthy. I was just hurting. I hurt myself and others, and had no peace. I think my rage has been transformed into courage. It's still rage, and I will never lose it; now it's fuel that propels me in a positive way, rather than in a negative way.

AM: What about the spirituality now? You spent a large part of your life as a religious person.

MB: I don't go to church, that's for sure. I left the institutional church because it was no longer life-giving for me, but I continued to go to women's circles within my own community, to the rituals and sweat lodges and the things that I needed. I tried to find these along the way and people to share them with, and I still do.

I don't embrace any one lifestyle or discipline. I've always integrated whatever my life has given me, and gone on changing. There's not one fixed form. There's something good in everything. I take that with me and leave the rest.

Some of my work now is de-churching people in our community. We need to de-school, de-church, de-colonize, ourselves in so many ways. That's the healing that has to be done if we're going to be truly self-governing and truly own ourselves as people, and restore the circle.

A lot of our communities have traditional people and Christian people. When I was at the blockade in northern Saskatchewan, there were people up on the hill in the evening. They had put up a little shrine to the Virgin Mary and would say their rosary there at night. I went up there and I called on Our Lady of the Blockade. To me, the Virgin Mary is still a grandmother, she's still somebody I can talk to. The church doesn't own her. But I don't talk to her with the rosary.

And then, the next morning, you go right next door on the same hill. There's a teepee, and you do your sweet grass, make your offerings and greet the day. To me, it's not a contradiction. But a lot of people are torn between these things, and the communities are divided. People have to find their own answers. You help people in that way, I guess, by just telling your story, and they tell you theirs. That's how we learn.

AM: What are you interested in doing next?

MB: I have no idea what I'm going to make. Right now my main focus is my women's film. I'm also going to be producing dramas with other people, but I'm not interested in writing dramas yet. There's enough drama in life to last me a while, and to capture the drama of real life, you know – those moments fascinate me. I don't have to pre-plan because there's always enough on my plate. If you're present to your life, it's full of all kinds of things that you can choose.

In the coming year, I'll be teaching two courses at Saskatchewan University. I've taught for many years, but this is the first time at a university. And I've been writing a lot of articles. I just remembered that I'm going to be doing two half-hour documentaries for Global Television's First Nations special. One is about art, culture and community in Saskatchewan. There's also a co-production with Yugoslavia to present an image of contemporary Aboriginal people.

AM: You're going to be very busy!

MB: There are probably other projects that I can't remember right now. My life is like that. I take what's in front of me today and know what's going to be happening sometime in the next few months. I'll do it. If I started to think about everything, I would just get tired.

Denise Grant

KIM CAMPBELL

Kim Campbell's professional life has encompassed political science lecturing in academia, the practice of law, and – building success upon success – elected positions at all three levels of government, culminating in the leadership of the Conservative party and the office of prime minister. Then came the crushing defeat. "Someone recently commented that perhaps the defeat and the survival were more important as examples to women than if I had won, which is certainly seeing a silver lining that I had not observed," she says. As she candidly discusses her professional life and private life, a silver lining does, in fact, become apparent.

KIM CAMPBELL: I think that midlife is a wonderful time because you've fought many of the really difficult battles, such as the great challenge of raising children. And you are who you are; there no longer seem to be infinite possibilities regarding how the rest of your life is going to play out. The most important thing is not to be afraid.

Perhaps one of the great roles that my friend Gregory Lekhtman plays in my life is that he really believes in me. Sometimes when people are hurting me, I have a tendency to want to pull back. I'm just a human being, not a superwoman, and as hurt by malice as anyone else. Gregory will say in his Russian way, "Don't be a scary cat." He means "a scaredy cat."

There are people who would like you not to be who you are, mainly because they're afraid. If you do it, then what does that say about them? You can only live your own life; you can't live anybody else's life, and nobody else will live their life for you.

I love my stepdaughters very much, and when I was thinking of ending my first marriage after nine years, Judy had gotten married, Amy was off in Toronto doing her internship and Pam had gone off to Chicago to do her Ph.D. Although I wanted to make a stable base in what had been a very difficult life for them, I realized that I had to come to terms with whether I could make my life in this marriage. My first husband is a wonderful person in many ways. However, he was happy for me to accommodate the specifics of his life, but he wasn't happy to accommodate my life. It just got to the point where it became soul destroying for me. I realized that when I would be fifty, none of them were going to thank me for staying in a marriage that made me unhappy.

Women tend to be very self-sacrificing, and there are a lot of good reasons for that. I wouldn't say to anybody who's put their own goals on hold to raise children that that's a poor move. It's wonderful, part of our commitment to the world and a life bigger than our own. But it is important to realize that nobody's going to come along when you're eighty and say, "I'm so glad you didn't make waves." "I'm so glad that you didn't make me feel envious or jealous." "I'm so glad that you kept a low profile." And there you're going to be, looking back on your life and saying, "What the hell did I do with it?"

ANDREA MUDRY: You have done much and had much that this world has to offer in terms of the highs and the lows. What gave you strength to make the political ascent and to deal with the defeat?

KC: After the election of 1993, I was hugely disappointed, and in my book, *Time and Chance*, I write quite honestly about it. I've discovered that a political memoir is like a Rorschach blot. It's fascinating to watch how people respond to the book, often in ways that have very little to do with what's in it. Writing the book was very helpful because it enabled me to go back to my political career before I ran for the leadership, and remind myself why I was a candidate.

My support for the Conservative party leadership came from the grass roots of the party. In Canada, there was a huge interest in me and my candidacy. It wasn't something that a group of back-roomers manipulated. If the party establishment did jump on the bandwagon it was because the support clearly was there. In public life there are people who are self-appointed arbiters of opinion, who have very strong views and have a concept about who is going to be in the power structure. But they didn't make me; politically, I had come up differently – from British Columbia, not central Canada. I think there were a lot of people who thought, "Who is this person? If we don't know her, she doesn't exist." And that can be very difficult to deal with.

AM: But you did deal with it, despite the occasional feelings of vertigo and of being out on a limb that you have expressed. What helped you to say, "I'm into this, and I'm pushing on"?

KC: I guess it was the fact that I had support, I believed in myself, and I was sort of fatalistic. I'd think to myself, "If people want to support me to do this, I will do it." I wasn't naive about what that would mean the higher I went – the political stakes and the power stakes are really quite significant – and I did represent a challenge to the status quo in terms of political power.

That's why, in the summer of '92, I thought a lot about the leadership because there was so much rumour and speculation about whether the prime minister would step down. I began to think very seriously about whether I wanted to be prime minister or whether I just liked the idea that people thought I could be. At the end of the day, you have to be able to sort out ego gratification from the reality. I realized that I was there for the right reason: I really wanted to make a difference. I understood some of the issues facing our country and was aware of the deep political malaise that I believe is still haunting us – people's fatigue about government and also their sense of disaffection from it. I used to teach political philosophy. I'm a "big picture" thinker who thinks about these issues and worries about the health of the body politic. That's what drew me into politics.

My period as minister of justice was important because I had three years in a portfolio and was able to make changes, to make a difference. That convinced me, and it was crucial to how I wound up being a leadership candidate with all this support from my caucus. The pundits said, "She doesn't have roots in the party; she won't have support in the caucus." But more than one hundred members of the Conservative caucus supported me, many of whom were 180 degrees from me on issues like abortion, gay rights and gun control.

AM: After the crushing defeat, what gave you strength? You must have had your own personal feelings to deal with plus a lot of people coming at you from various angles.

KC: Oh, it was extraordinary. I think that age, experience and education made a difference. I'd studied politics for a long time and read a great deal. Churchill, who certainly spent a long time in the wilderness, was one of my early heroes. So that was part of me – the intellectual, rational view. Many leaders and parties and movements have spent time in the wilderness, and it's very painful in the short term. But, in the long run, people will look back at the '93 election as part of a temporary realignment in Canada. As always happens, some aspects of the change will remain, but I don't think it's the end of the Conservative party. There is room in the political spectrum for a national party.

I was also surrounded by people who loved me, and there were practical things that had to be done. Even if I had been tempted to indulge, to curl up in the foetal position whimpering, I felt that I owed it to the position to be a strong person. And I was strong. We all have our own survival mechanisms. I think some people were disappointed that I didn't have a nervous breakdown. Well, I didn't. Somebody was asking me the other day, "You must have been very depressed?" I said, "No. I was devastated, I was very disappointed, I was very sad, but I was not depressed."

At first, I wasn't going to take up the fellowship at Harvard until the fall because I wanted to start working on the book. Then I changed my mind, and that was a positive decision because it took me into an environment where people valued what I had to say, what I had to offer. I'd taught for seven years and I'm a good teacher. That very much reinforced my sense of self-worth. I also got out of the country, so I wasn't reading the paper every day and torturing myself. In fact, I've never wallowed in the media. It can throw you off your stride.

On returning home to Canada, I found that people were very friendly to me. They said things like, "Listen, this wasn't your fault, it was an anti-Mulroney vote. Don't even think about it." And they weren't treating me pityingly, which was a very good sign. They would say, "How're you doing? We hear you're at Harvard. Are you having fun?" People still come up to me on the street and want to shake my hand.

AM: You're going to be turning fifty next year. Do you find that you view the world differently with the passing of time?

KC: It's hard to separate age from experience. It has been said that women don't really sort out what they want to do with their lives until they resolve the question of whether they're going to have children. I'm now at the stage where I'm not menopausal yet, but realistically that's an issue that's been dealt with in my life. My parenting has been as a stepparent. And so there is, in a sense, a clearer path in front of me than at thirty-five, when this was still a question in my mind.

AM: Did you decide not to have children?

KC: In my first marriage, I tried to have children and couldn't get pregnant. In fact, one of the things that disillusioned me with my marriage was that my husband would not go to have a simple fertility test to see where the problem was. I was very close to my stepchildren from that marriage. I was friendly with the stepchildren in my second marriage too, but my second husband and I just didn't stay married as long. I was especially close to my stepdaughter Pamela from the time she was seven. That was an important parenting experience for me, not just in terms of the pleasure of working with a little person but also in terms of living out my own lost time.

My mother left our family when I was an adolescent. Later, I came to realize that her decision to leave was in fact a very unselfish one, designed to protect my sister and me. Now I have a very good relationship with my mother. So, in terms of having somebody to socialize me into what older women do, it's very positive. And I also have my grandmother, who went back to teaching at sixty. When I go back and look at my life, suddenly I step back and say, "That was really quite significant because most girls didn't have that experience."

AM: What about physical change?

KC: At forty-nine I'm getting to the age group where I can't take it for granted that youth and hormones will protect me from certain health problems. During the last few years I've put on a lot of weight, and now that the book is done, this is my next challenge. I was very fit, but starting with the referendum campaign in 1992, my exercise time got eroded. In some ways, letting myself put on weight was perhaps a form of rebellion, refusing to yield to expectations. But this body is the vehicle that's going to carry me through, and I'd like to go into old age in good shape.

My mother has some health problems, but she regards the years she's living now as a gift. At the turn of the century many women didn't have those years. She reads and goes to the theatre, and life is not dull to her at all. She wasn't there when my sister and I were adolescents, but she's important to both of us now and has that role as a mother, although she's always respectful of our rights to define it as we want. My sister, who lives in Victoria, does a lot of legal consulting work in Vancouver, and stays with Mom whenever she goes over; they have a wonderful friendship. So I'm conscious of the extent to which health is a very important key to pleasure in life as you get older.

AM: Is marriage still a viable option in your thinking?

KC: Well, I don't rule it out but I think, again, at midlife you have a totally different perspective. My mother was widowed in 1979. She said that was the first time in her life she'd ever lived alone, and she loves it. She doesn't have to answer to anybody else. It's not that she wasn't happily married to my stepfather, but she went from her parents' home to the first marriage, then the second marriage. Betty Friedan, in her book *The Fountain of Age*, talks about older women who live alone quite happily.

I mean, I don't need to be married. I have a significant other, Gregory, in Montreal and he's very devoted. Fortunately, he's also a very independent person. Gregory is a manufacturer and a developer of medical electronic products, a very brilliant and interesting man. Friendship, mutual understanding and support are what's really important in the relationship. Still, it drives him bananas that I travel so much and am ambivalent about any kind of commitment. Maybe to some degree it's also a question of just my frame of mind and emotions coming out of 1993, because I had met Gregory shortly before the election. When he read my book, he thought it was wonderful and he said, "You never told me these things." When we first started seeing each other, I wasn't very talkative about my life, perhaps because I was working it through in my mind. Having gone through the process of writing the book, I've been liberated in some way to be a more social person, a more outgoing and caring person. When you commit to write a book, you carry it around with you all the time and use emotional energy trying to wrestle with how to deal with things in that creative process.

Marriage is not something I rule out. I'm unambiguously heterosexual, although I suppose, as Germaine Greer writes in her magazine articles, you get to midlife and, you know, your hormones give you bit of a break in the sense that you aren't quite as rabid as you were when you were younger. But I like companionship, and think that there's nothing more wonderful than to be with somebody that you feel really understands you, and that you understand and respect.

Just in the last year since returning to Canada I'm enjoying all of my friendships more. In particular I'm feeling that I can be a better friend to people because, for so long, when I was the one that was living this frenetic life, my friends were very supportive and helpful. They made my life possible. Recently, the mother of a friend died. Now I'm in a position to call and see how she is because she certainly deserves that kind of friendship and support. It's nice to be the one who isn't the neediest – not just in emotional but in practical terms – and be the settled person who's there and can respond to somebody else's problems.

AM: What about finances? The media reported that you received $69,000 as a severance pay, but no pension when you left government.

KC: I have no pension. My accountant wrings his hands about this a bit. Now that the book is done, I have to earn a living. Until now, a full-time commitment to anything hasn't been possible. Like anybody else, I have to earn a living. That's something I'm more conscious of: the amount of time left in my life to establish my financial security. Part of me can't imagine ever not working, but more realistically, I will get to that stage, so that is a priority for me now.

At this point, I have a sense that I've done some significant things, and I have options as a public person. For me, the challenge is to figure out what I want to do and to divorce that from other people's sense of what they think I should do. In some ways, having been a prime minister is a bit like having gum on your shoe. I mean, you kind of carry it around with you ...

AM: What a great comparison!

KC: Well, you know, it sticks occasionally, and you find every once in a while that you hit a warm sidewalk and you say, "Oh ..." I don't feel I could flog vegamatics on television. It might be lucrative, and people would know me, but I feel I owe something to having been in the office. That's a bit of a challenge.

I'm not at liberty to talk about all of the options. Some of them I can certainly tell you. I've had offers to go into a law firm, but haven't done that. Practising law does not appeal. I wouldn't mind doing something on a legal consulting basis and government consulting – not so much lobbying government. I'm really quite interested in some of the developing democracies, especially work that's being done to help them develop institutions. I've had a lot of offers to do media work, which interests me because it's part of the public debate.

I'm on the board of International Affairs at Harvard and do a lot of travelling and speaking. So I'm also considering options that would deal with international issues, because international politics was my first career and my first interest.

I care about issues relating to politics and society, and there are a lot of different ways of approaching that: as a consultant working with institutional development and advice, by going overseas to work, even by working with media and public opinion and the public discourse in my own country.

I like to do things that stretch me. A job that doesn't faintly terrify you when you start is probably not worth doing.

AM: A lot of people don't think like that.

KC: Well, if it's still scaring you a year later, chances are you're over your head. Recently, I read about the identification of the risk-taking gene. It was found that some people – those who do bungey jumping and drive a gazillion miles an hour – sometimes have this special gene for risk taking. I am a risk taker, but not the bungey-jumping sort. It is important for me to set challenges and goals. That's what makes my adrenaline pump.

AM: Do you tend to plan your career moves ahead or do things "just happen," or is it a combination of the two?

KC: There's some interesting writing about how women's career paths look different from men's career paths, often because we defer to familial considerations. For example, when I went to graduate school, I had hoped to have an academic career. But I married somebody who was a full professor at the University of British Columbia, and the university did not want another Soviet specialist, and Simon Fraser University didn't either. There wasn't any place else I could go, and I wasn't mobile.

So, very often with women it isn't just a matter that they lack direction. They have direction but can't always go in the direction that they want to go.

There are certain types of things that give me pleasure and make me feel that I'm making a contribution, make me feel that what I'm doing is worthwhile. There are a lot of different ways to do that. I love teaching, but I'm not interested in writing for an academic audience, and I'm not really keen to go back and set syllabuses, exams and essay papers. I think I'm much better used now doing some of the stuff I've been doing at Harvard and the University of California, where I go as a distinguished visitor to talk about various subjects. In California, I spoke on the state of the post–Cold War world. I also talked to groups about women and politics. That, to me, is a much better use of what I have to offer now.

I used to say to students that the secret to happiness is to find what you like doing, and can do, and do it. So many people choose jobs that they think will provide a good living. But they won't be stars at it because their heart won't be in it. *(Note: Shortly after this conversation, Prime Minister Chrétien appointed Kim Campbell consul-general in Los Angeles.)*

AM: Looking back on your political life, what are you most proud of?

KC: I could point to different pieces of legislation, such as getting the British Columbia claims process going when I was the junior minister of Indian affairs; that was extremely important for the province. But I would say I'm most proud of simply mainstreaming a lot of women's issues and raising up a notch the normality of women as participants in the political process.

At a recent reception in Ottawa to celebrate the donation of my papers to the archives, a number of officials attended who had worked with me when I was minister in Justice and in Indian Affairs. One of them said, "Kim Campbell transformed the views of a lot of men about women in government." Working together we had accomplished an enormous amount, and they were pleased to have had me as a minister who had the political will to take legislation through concerning issues such as sexual assault, gun control, mentally disordered offenders and electronic surveillance.

Those kinds of things change the way people think about women in politics. It's not a dramatic revolution, but it is an important step that makes it easier for the next woman to come along to do the job without having to apologize for being a woman or for including women *qua* women – as one says in the law – in the policy process.

I also think it was important to show that a deliberative, respectful approach to policy making in Parliament can work – that you can create policy that approximates the national interest in a way that is very democratic, that respects the fact that each member of Parliament is in fact elected.

In my experiences as a provincial legislator, travelling the province on a variety of task forces, I came to appreciate the importance of hearing from people who are going to be affected by what you're doing and the extent to which people are articulate when they're talking about what they really know. That's such a fundamental part of my democratic vision. Or, going back to the fact that I started as a municipal politician, where you work in complete intimacy with the people you serve – that was such an important part of the vision that I brought.

Judy Rosener writes about women and "interactive" styles of leadership, and I realized that describes my style of leadership. For example, it describes the way I was able to take very contentious legislation, such as the gun-control legislation, through my caucus. Interactive leadership entails consensus building and understanding that you have to kind of tack to get someplace, instead of just barging straight ahead in a command-and-control type of leadership. Both are good and both are effective, but each works optimally in certain kinds of circumstances. In policy making, where you need to empower people and you need to foster creativity, interactive leadership is very effective.

AM: You have said that policy needs to be brought more in line with women's lives today. What can be done to help bring this about?

KC: There just aren't enough women policy makers. I think we're slowly being able to speak in our own voices, and that's crucial. It's not enough just to be there. The first generation of women in the legal profession, for example, were tolerated if they were ersatz men. You have to get beyond that to being able to be who you are and bring that reality into the discussion. I tried to do that, and that's why Justice was such a bully pulpit; I wasn't a one-issue minister so I couldn't just be dismissed. I could say, "Look, we're not a minority group." But numbers are important.

It does take time to reprogram people's expectations and to win the right to be who you are. We're all subliminally conditioned to expect certain kinds of people to do a job, and when somebody comes along who doesn't match those expectations – the shape and timbre of voice and way of expressing – we react, feeling that there's something not quite right there. That, I believe, is why women sometimes don't support other women whom they intellectually consider competent.

AM: Absolutely. I've certainly become aware of my own conditioning and try to deal with it.

KC: Yes, I was conditioned too.

The fact that I had such a high approval rating as prime minister in December '93 suggests that a lot of Canadians were in fact prepared to accept a woman as prime minister. So I was at least able to push that barrier a bit. I'm not sure that official opinion-dom was prepared. I think they were not quite sure what to do with this, and that's why the "Gidget goes to Ottawa" comments developed. The only way you can identify those barriers, make them visible and begin to give them names is to be part of the development of policy, and to insist on articulating women's reality.

Somebody asked me, "What are the three things I can do as a woman?" I said, "Write a cheque for a woman candidate; read the literature to help understand some of the things that you're confronting; then just be as uppity as hell, and don't take no for an answer." That's easy to say, but I really do think it is the real challenge. Men are themselves; that is why we would never expect a man to speak for all men because we expect that men are free to articulate the variety of their experiences.

Women are not so free. That's why, for the sexual assault legislation, for example, it was so important to talk to groups of women who had very particular insights into the whole issue, to empower them and to listen to what they had to tell us.

Speaking more broadly, I would say that society changes, so we have to be forever vigilant. I don't have an excessive faith in constitutionalism because the courts' interpretation of the constitution is very much a reflection of the values of the time. For example, the Supreme Court of the United States interpreted the constitution in the early '70s to guarantee a woman certain rights to abortion. Here we are in the 1990s where the constitution is the same, but different judges may decide the issue otherwise. I don't believe that history is always moving onward and upward; societies do regress. Constitutional principles are no substitute for the political and social will to support certain values.

AM: I'm curious about the famous picture of you, bare shouldered, holding your robes in front of you. I understand that you have explained it as a representation of the person and the role.

KC: In 1989 Barbara Woodley was doing a series of portraits for a book to celebrate Canadian women, and she asked to include me. After some discussion, where I refused to be photographed with a cello and Barbara said she already had a shot of Beverley McLachlin in legal robes, we decided to shoot me holding my Q.C. robes. The picture is not even faintly titillating. When it was exhibited in Vancouver, everyone thought it was wonderful. Like all good art, the picture was serendipitous.

Other pictures in the book show Margaret Sommerville with her legs curled up and her feet bare and Sharon Wood, who climbed Mount Everest, eight months pregnant with her climbing rope wrapped around her body. There's a quirkiness and originality about the pictures. When you see my portrait in that context, it makes a lot of sense.

AM: Your picture is beautiful. But I'm thinking of you as a politician vis-à-vis the general public, which I am sure for most politicians is a real pain at times, because you do have to be politic. And sometimes you weren't. It wasn't just the picture, but other things too – almost as if you didn't have patience: "Dammit, why can't I do this? Why can't I be me?"

KC: I never pretended I'd only said "Fuddle Duddle" in the House of Commons. I didn't do pirouettes behind the Queen. I didn't go out with movie stars. What did I do? I let a photographer work with me to create an original and interesting picture.

AM: Well, you also did make comments here and there that hit the headlines.

KC: Well, I did a little bit of stand-up comedy. You know, I'm a person. Who do you think is going to get to be prime minister? Somebody who's a mouse? The reason why people have been attracted to support me politically over the years is because they felt I was a person. And how can I be a humane person if I have no sense of humour? I mean, God spare me from people with no sense of humour; they terrify me. I can laugh at myself.

When I think of the things that men have gotten away with. I was never a Bill Vander Zalm – talk about shooting from ye olde lip and nothing much coming out. I never said, "There's no whore like an old whore." I don't think I ever said anything that was outrageous or mean-spirited. Again, I think the level of acceptability for women is very different, and I don't see why a woman can't be as original and humorous as a man.

One of my American friends who read my book said that this is a book about somebody who had always tried to be a human being in politics. I think that's true. Perhaps, if there's one way I'm not cut out to be a politician it is that I wasn't prepared to make certain compromises; I wasn't prepared to be something I wasn't. On the one hand, I think I had a very good feel for what the issues were and a very strong vision of democracy and the energy and the courage to put up with the guck to make things happen. But I wasn't prepared to pretend to be something I'm not.

PATRICIA GRAY

Complex and sometimes controversial, **Patricia Gray** is looking forward to rediscovering the world with her husband now that their children are grown and she has finally succeeded in establishing the Canadian Animal Distress Network. Patricia's concern for animals began in early childhood in Indonesia; she now lives in Prince Edward Island.

The period of midlife gets a mixed review from Patricia. But she unequivocally welcomes what she describes as a newfound freedom — "the feeling that says, 'Hey, I am who I am; I like who I am; and I am content to be who I am.'"

ANDREA MUDRY: It becomes obvious from the paintings, photography and other objects around your home that it is nature, and not just distressed animals, that plays a central part in your life.

PATRICIA GRAY: Absolutely. Well, you notice that the house is filled with plants, and I don't know if you saw the tree that I have in my living room. I must have greenery around. It could be because of my youth in the Far East, where everything was always lush, green and growing. Animals too, I must have a cat or dog – something furry – around me, and anything that has to do with the outdoors, even rocks. I just love – and feel a real connection to – these things. If I were to tell you that trees actually communicate, you'd probably say, "This lady is mad."

AM: If you're a whale-hugger, why not a tree-hugger!

PG: Yes! Exactly. My trees and all the things that you see in the garden, we planted seven years ago. When we came to this house there were a few big trees, and that was all, so we planted the rest. They are just my pets. I walk around the garden, talk to them, and they seem to respond. Meanwhile, the neighbours shake their heads and say, "Oh, boy. She's not planting another tree!" I suppose this is a bit of an eccentricity. If I admit it, I usually get off the hook.

Albert Schweitzer wrote a wonderful paper called "Reverence for Life." He talked about bending over to pick up a worm from concrete and helping it into the mud. That's the kind of thing I now do without thinking. Ten or fifteen years ago, it was so easy to swat a fly or brush something away without thinking. But then I made a conscious effort. After a while it became something that was natural, and I could never go back to doing anything against another creature callously. I just couldn't; it's become a way of life, a religion. Even when I go to pick a plant or a flower, I make sure that there are several flowers left so that the plant can fulfil its destiny by seeding itself. Otherwise, what's the point? However, I'm not a fanatic. If you need to kill for food, it's justified. But killing because it's fashionable to wear a hide, for example, is just a waste.

People ridicule me for my beliefs. Sometimes my family ridicules me. It can be very difficult, but I also find that it's so much easier to live my life this way because I am not in conflict within myself, and I really don't have to explain myself to other people. This is the wonderful freedom of realizing that you don't have to justify why you are, who you are and what you are doing. Because you believe in it, people realize you have that conviction, and it causes a stir in the company of others. It's just a knowing, and for some unknown reason it just comes out of you, it's all around you. People tune in right away. It's incredible – it really is.

AM: How else have you changed over the years?

PG: About two years ago, I had time to look in the mirror and suddenly realized how old I was: the wrinkles starting to form around my eyes, my face not quite as young as it used to be. But to tell you the truth, I have a lot of hobbies. I have a terrific zest for life; everything to me is interesting.

I come at the subject of age from different angles. My Russian grandmother lived with our family for fifteen years, and I viewed old age with fear because of her. She was always depressed about something. She and Dostoyevski probably had a lot in common. But, then again, she was displaced. She had lost everything in Russia and was forced to live with our family because her husband had died. She was a very unhappy person.

I was really afraid of middle age too. My mother had a very difficult time through menopause. I would classify it as a nervous breakdown. She also developed breast cancer and had a mastectomy. It was very frightening seeing what happened to her. Menopause was always the big bogeyman that was there in the future.

The last couple of years I've started to go into it, but I've been so busy. First, my father died of lung cancer in British Columbia, and I was there nursing him for a good two months before he died. That was traumatic. Then my father-in-law died, in the same year, in England; we had to go there to look after him. So death started to become quite prominent in my thinking. Recently, my husband has experienced some ill health, and he's just retired, so that's another readjustment. I haven't really had time to think about me or what's going on.

Perhaps this is the age when these things happen. I no longer fear it; I have made up my mind that it's not going to get me down because I am going to stay busy. The seven kids are mainly gone now. Half of them are in B.C., one in Toronto, and the others are in Calgary and New Brunswick.

AM: What ages are they?

PG: They range in age from twenty to thirty and are mainly independent now. When the children left home it was extremely difficult for me, like losing part of my body, my mind. I had things to do, but I wandered around the house and was just lost. It was terrible, especially when the youngest ones left. But then they keep coming back. I just get used to it and they're back again.

Now my life is with my husband, David, and it's a readjustment. We have a boat and just bought a big truck that we're fitting up for camping.

We've got the whole world ahead of us and we want to travel, probably to British Columbia this fall, then England next year, and we want to tour North America. I want to continue with my animal network, and I have a very good group of people to take over when I'm not here. After five years, I think I deserve to be able to leave the network for a while. Maybe we'll even trade this house off for a forty-foot boat. I don't know. But that's the kind of thing we're planning.

We are both interested in photography. We love photography. He paints, I paint. I'm a geologist. I studied for three years and could spend a whole day just looking at rocks. I've got bowls of them everywhere in the house. I've got a lot of interests. Touch wood, unless my health lets me down, I have no fear. I'm very positive about these changes.

AM: Have your perceptions changed with time?

PG: Yes, now I live for today. I don't really think of tomorrow that much anymore.

And I used to be afraid of everything, so terribly shy. Now I find that there is a calmness inside that never existed before. I was always in a turmoil – hyper and temperamental. When I look back and remember the experiences and all the things that I've been through, somehow or other this inner voice seems to be more comforting. I seem to be able to face things a lot more calmly than I used to do.

And I must admit that I trust myself more than I used to be able to. Before, I was very unsure; I always felt that I had to lean on somebody. When my husband went to the hospital this time, he was away for three weeks. I was completely alone for the first time in my whole life, other than when I went away to school as a child. My children weren't here. There were just the dog, the cat and me.

I was amazed. I actually enjoyed it. I enjoyed the quiet, and when I came back from the hospital, it was my house. The house sort of hugged me: it was all familiar, and I enjoyed my own company. When you have raised a large family, you never have any peace or a quiet place for yourself, other than when you go a mile down the road without telling anybody where you're going. So it was a luxury, I enjoyed it, and I have to say that it was the first time I actually grew up.

AM: In what sense?

PG: Well, I got to know myself, which I hadn't done in the past. I was able to think, and I couldn't rely on David to make my decisions for me. David is an all-encompassing person who likes to take charge, and I've always leaned on him. We've been married thirty-one years; I came into marriage very young at seventeen. Mind you, I have travelled on my own.

I guess, too, it was the fear that maybe one day I would be alone. How would I cope? When things like this happen, it's a real eye-opener. I realized that I can stand on my own two feet.

AM: It's interesting to hear you say this because you've been in the public arena for years, actively promoting animal welfare from the local to the international level.

PG: Yes, but David was always there. He is one of my greatest supporters and has always backed me, right from the beginning.

AM: Do you think your international upbringing has affected your attitude towards aging?

PG: Oriental women don't seem to go through what we go through. I mean, I think they hide it very well. But then these people have a different perception of age, a respect for age that we don't seem to have. We have a youth culture. Living here, I have never been allowed to grow old gracefully because I've got young children. They'll say, "Hey, Mom, come on, get with it." So I am brought up by my socks. But I guess what you say is absolutely right. Being raised in the Orient, my perception of middle age is different from the North American and European view, for the simple reason that, yes, they view old age as something to look forward to. For them, old age means wisdom, respect, and that you have finally arrived. That's it, really.

But as I've said, I have mixed feelings about aging too. I really regret the loss of energy and vigour that comes with getting older. I also regret the fact that if you have experienced something before, and you know the outcome is negative, you are very reluctant to try again. Youth has no idea what the outcome is going to be, and so will try anything. I am very, very sorry about the loss of innocence. Now I'm overly cautious, just don't want to try something because I know it isn't going to work, whereas in the old days I would have tried anything, and I loved that feeling. I also loved the feeling of having a youthful body and being able to keep up without my knees hurting and my back hurting. Things like that. But, with t'ai chi and exercise I can still manage — when I have time to do it. I try to do all the things that one is supposed to do, but it's very difficult to fit it into a day, especially when I'm pressed for time. So I try.

AM: Yes. It's hard to find time for everything — especially exercise!

PG: One of the things I've noticed is that if I go to my doctor with a problem, he usually wants to give me a pill, which I'm totally against. So I smile at him very nicely, put the prescription in my pocket and chuck it. I feel strongly about the fact that doctors do not support women when they're going through difficult periods. The moment you're depressed, they put you on Prozac or something. That could be another book: *Women Against the Medical Profession.*

If I'm going through a depressed period, the best thing is to get my mind off it. I try desperately hard. When you are in a depressed state, you can't read a book, you can't settle to read anything. I listen to music or go for a walk. I would tell anyone to get out of the house, get fresh air, stay active. Winter is very hard if you're confined to the house. While you're trying to think rationally, your body doesn't want to respond. The best thing to do is to meet it halfway and try to do positive things. The only health problem that brings me to a standstill is migraine headaches, mainly due to barometric pressure. I get very bad ones; then all I can do is stop. That could be part of menopause, too.

AM: Has it happened to you recently?

PG: They have been increasing, lately. But then again it could be stress, too. There are a lot of factors: my husband retiring, my children coming back and forth. Several of them have moved to the West Coast in the last couple of months. Sure, that brings on a migraine very easily.

AM: You must feel very strongly about animals to put the time and energy that you have into developing the distress network.

PG: I do. I feel very strongly about the marine environment, as well as animals, because it has featured prominently in my life. When I was raised in the Far East, most of the places I lived were island communities surrounded by water. I remember when I was around eight years old, my mother took me to a marketplace in Indonesia. Lying on the wharf there was what I took to be a huge fish. A man came along with a knife, cut the fish's belly open and inside was a baby fish.

It was only when I grew up that I realized that what I actually witnessed was a dolphin that had been landed, and there was, in fact, a baby dolphin in its belly. That was probably my earliest recollection of seeing a marine mammal and feeling that awful, devastating sorrow from seeing the animal just lying there. I remember looking at its eyes, and I couldn't get over the fact that the eyes were so human-like. I guess that's where it all started.

Animals always have been my friends. I was an only child, raised by parents who were very busy with their social life as well as their business life. Most of my playmates were animals. I had squirrels, baby owls and an animal like a polecat as pets, as well as cats and dogs. I used to climb right to the top of coconut trees to rescue baby birds. So it started right from the time when I was very, very young.

AM: How did your involvement with the stranded mammals begin?

PG: When we first emigrated to Canada in 1968, we ended up in British Columbia, where I heard about the East Coast seals and seal hunts. We eventually moved to Prince Edward Island, and in the spring of 1981, we heard that seals had come down from the island's national park and that the Department of Fisheries and Oceans was going to issue licences to people on the island to hunt them. Two of my children persuaded me to take them to see the seals.

When we arrived at the national park there were cars everywhere. We could hear the baby seals crying from the ice flows; it sounded like a nursery. The scenery looked idyllic, with the wonderful pink hues of the ice and snow and the sun coming up. Then, all of a sudden, I could hear the boom, boom of the clubs coming down. We drove up to the area where we saw a crowd, got out and walked along the shoreline. We could see carcasses and patches of blood everywhere on the ice. People were just standing around watching, some with expressions of absolute horror. Other people were saying, "Hey, well, this is normal, this is nature."

All of a sudden, my peripheral vision disappeared. It was as if I developed tunnel vision; I could only see straight ahead. And I could hear the banging of the clubs in the distance. Inside my head a voice said, "You can never let this ever happen again. You have to do something." It was a spiritual occurrence. After that, I joined the International Fund for Animal Welfare (IFAW) as Atlantic coordinator at their invitation, and was soon lobbying government and travelling internationally as a representative. I got to know a lot of people in various countries: Australia, New Zealand, Europe and North America.

Then in 1984, in an effort to stop the seal hunts, the IFAW asked Europeans to boycott Canadian fish products. The results for me and my family were devastating. Here we were up in Souris. Teachers and students began to harass my seven children at school. My husband was working for Manpower; the minister in Ottawa told him I was persona non grata with the government and that he was not to get involved in the seal issue. The RCMP tailed my movements on the island, my phone was bugged, my letters were opened, and I was threatened with blackmail.

AM: That's all heavy duty.

PG: Yes. Some Souris families were totally reliant on the local fish plant for income. Finally, I could not justify putting those families out of work, making them suffer for my ideals. All the time, I had a nagging thought that using those means to accomplish my ends was just not the way to go. Rather, you should educate people and think in the long term.

At that point, my husband took a position with the Department of Veterans' Affairs, we were transferred to Ontario for a few years, and I left the IFAW. In Ontario I wrote articles on wildlife for various publications, including European magazines, and did some broadcasting. Meanwhile, there was a moratorium on the seal hunt, and the European market banned the importation of seal pelts. When we returned to the Maritimes, I continued to document seal slaughters and incidents of stranded mammals.

Then, in the spring of 1989, my thirteen-year-old daughter was diagnosed with cancer. The prognosis was good, but that year was fairly chaotic for us. For some unknown reason, I had this pressing desire to write down a contingency plan and put a stranding network into place. I remember that my daughter would lie on the couch and I'd be on the floor with my papers spread out all around, talking to her and using my contacts around the world to gain information. We were really excited about this. By the fall of 1989 she was cured and back at school and I had a contingency plan.

I circulated the plan to all my acquaintances and to the various government departments. However, they didn't pay much attention until I subsequently coordinated the rescue of six sperm whales that were stranded on the northern end of the island. Then, working with people I knew, including veterinarians from the Atlantic Veterinary College, we formed the Canadian Animal Distress Network. It took me ages to come up with that name. The CADN was very important to me because CDN on a car in a foreign country means Canadian, so CADN represents Canada for me.

AM: What are your plans for the network's future?

PG: My dream is that this organization will be national and will deal with terrestrial as well as marine animals. It will respond to all animals, such as the wolves in the Yukon and British Columbia and the bears in Ontario that are being illegally hunted for their gall bladders and paws.

In the early 1990s, the network's board of directors wanted to put the lid on things for a little while. It's only this year that the Oil Spill Network is actually becoming activated. All of a sudden, the Canadian Coastguard approached us for our expertise and volunteers. And we are getting involved with terrestrial animals. One of our directors, a pathologist, is extremely interested in birds of prey. So the whole thing now is evolving, and we are gaining support from groups in other countries. Australia, New Zealand and the United States are leaders in this field.

Our major objective is to establish volunteer response teams and adequate facilities to care for suffering wild animals until we can return them to their natural environment. We want to accomplish this through education and cooperation with other agencies.

Our work is useful in various ways. Marine mammals are the canaries of the ocean. When we open them up to do autopsies, we find heavy metals and all sorts of things. Since they are at the top of the food chain, such materials occur in the fish stock too, and will eventually find their way into humans.

We live in one of the most beautiful countries in the world. I hate to say it, but many Canadians do not appreciate what they have here. Unfortunately, if we don't develop laws to protect wildlife as well as marine mammals, we are going to find that people are just going to come in here and take it all away from us. Canada is worth fighting for. We have to get by with next to nothing in funding because we have no support from the Canadian government at all.

AM: You've been involved in this struggle for many years, and have had a lot of pain and uncertainty in the process. Now it seems that your efforts have flourished into a recognizable entity.

PG: Absolutely. What you find is that there is a pattern, and if you look back in your life, you begin to see that pattern right through. It's only when things do come together that you can actually have that insight to look back and see how it flowed.

Probably the greatest plus is the feeling of accomplishment. If I ever feel low, and if I feel my self-esteem is suffering, I look back on the things I have accomplished.

AM: I understand that you've also had many different jobs over the years.

PG: Yes, I worked part-time and sometimes full-time for many years, and some of the jobs were awful: grocery clerk, janitorial work. As immigrants, we had a pretty rough time getting ourselves established. We started with one dollar and twenty-five cents in Canada, and built ourselves up. The Canadian government lured people to this country under false pretences. My husband was a naval officer in the Royal Navy in England, but there were no jobs once we got here, and no information. However, the people that we came across were often fantastic and helpful.

And, of course, raising a large family is very expensive. Would I go through it again? No. I certainly would want to have all my children, but I wouldn't advise anyone to have a large family today unless they have a lot of money. Since I was the only child of an executive of a large American company, it was a big realization about life when I couldn't buy exactly what I wanted for my children. It hurt to see them having to do without. However, our children tell us that having a tight family unit and knowing we were always there for them greatly made up for the material things they didn't have.

I would like to tell you about my oldest daughter's second son, Lia, who has Down's syndrome, because he has brought our whole family together in such an amazing way. All of us have an inherent fear of having a child and something going wrong, but my daughter has come out of it wonderfully. When this little boy comes to visit, all of us grow and learn something.

AM: In what way?

PG: It's his innocence, his humour, his total exuberance. He is comical in the things he does, and just watching him grow and seeing him try to fit into our world is amazing. Of course we had our fears about how badly he's affected. We now realize that he's not "affected" by anything. He is just him. He is a little boy with this situation which is Down's syndrome, a little human being. Trying to bring him up to our level is the wrong way of looking at it. You just accept him at every stage as he comes along. If you follow him around and just watch him for a day, you, too, would begin to see the world in a different light, and realize that he has no concept of fear, mistrust or stress. He is a totally content little being. If you hold him, you get instantaneous peace. He is so trusting of people, and it's been a terrific experience for us, and it's something I want to share.

AM: I've read Jean Vanier's writings about such special people, but to hear you speak as a grandmother is something else.

In closing, is there anything else you would like to say?

PG: The only thing I would say to other women is, be content with who you are. Once I arrived at that point and began to like myself, everything else fell into place. I think most of us were born with this insecurity, this feeling that we are inferior and don't live up to our potential. We don't get the chance to because there's always somebody pushing us around. This is especially true of our generation, not so much the younger generation, which has had more freedom. But for us, if we didn't have a dominant father, we had a dominant mother, or we had somebody else telling us that we "couldn't": "You can't do what you want to do because it's not right," or "Women don't do those things."

Also be proud that you are a woman. Women should understand the power that they have. If they would only see what they can do and how they can influence things, I don't think we'd have the problems we have. Many women don't have the confidence to use their power, but women can change a lot of things. Lots!

M Y R N A   K O S T A S H

A provocative and compassionate writer, **Myrna Kostash** has produced numerous articles, scripts and four non-fiction books – *All of Baba's Children, Long Way from Home, No Kidding* and *Bloodlines*. Her major themes reflect several of our society's issues during the last three decades: social justice, feminism and ethnicity.

The recipient of writing awards and a former chair of the Writers' Union of Canada, Myrna is now concerned about the future of publishing in Canada as well as her own writing future. She continues to write, travel and live with gusto. Myrna was born and currently lives in Edmonton, Alberta.

ANDREA MUDRY: You have been intensely concerned about politics and social issues since the 1960s. Did you ever consider becoming a political activist instead of a writer?

MYRNA KOSTASH: It took me a long time to get over feeling guilty about not being a political activist; it wasn't until I accepted the fact that being a writer was a form of activism. Not everybody can organize rallies, and not everybody can write. So we should each do whatever we can. It's all towards the same end.

For a very long time I struggled with this question of how to integrate political and literary concerns. If you're too politically engaged or committed, does that distort your writing? On the other hand, if you're overly concerned with literary values, isn't that kind of petty bourgeois and counter-revolutionary? I realize now that even though I deeply lament the temporary decline of the left, the fact is it was still a powerful environment for what I was doing. I was really stricken by questions about how you could serve the revolution by being a middle-class, freelance writer. You know, who cares about how you felt about anything? The important thing was to squelch your own individual voice and to find out how the people feel.

Now I'm free of such concerns. In a sense, the left isn't around to make those points. By the same token, I think it was really important that I was shaped in part by that environment because it gave me a sense of engagement and passionate attachment to ideas and things beyond my own life, which I think is very sadly missing in a lot of writing now: that sense of the urgency of other people's lives, the urgency of the rest of the world, not just your own.

AM: What do you think the ideas and idealism of the sixties mean to us today?

MK: Even at the end of the seventies, when I was writing a book about the sixties called *Long Way from Home,* I assumed that, in that decade, we represented the beginning of some new wave of political consciousness. I believed that the baby-boom generation had left-wingers and social activists who would continue in this huge bulge of sheer numbers, and our concerns would continue to be very important. I now realize that assumption was misbegotten. In fact, that experience of our youth represented the end of something. We were the last of a kind of romantic generation, rather than the beginning of a new revolution or generation.

AM: You are focusing on the politics.

MK: Yes. In other words, the new right has almost had a kind of universal success in taking over the political agenda and defining it, particularly in terms of the young people who came after us. It may be normal that the generations – parents and their children – are opposed to each other politically. I don't know. But I had assumed that we had set an agenda for the next generation, and that has turned out not to be so.

Now our own children look back at the politics of the sixties and make fun of us. They also accuse a more liberal generation of having squandered the public purse, and accuse the women's movement of being hysterical and anti-male.

AM: Where do you get that impression?

MK: Who gets to write the main editorials and columns in the *Globe and Mail,* or *Saturday Night,* or *Chatelaine?* You know, the popular mass media. I agree, this is not to say that there's a kind of monolithic generation out there. I know that there are more progressive people too.

And, of course, some young people today are nostalgic for the sixties. It seems very strange that fifty-something rock and roll stars, such as the Rolling Stones, are still considered great. I don't know how to explain both the endurance of such sixties "contributions" – if you like – and the absolute contempt with which the political agenda is now held. It seems that the reaction to my book, *Long Way From Home,* was affected by such contempt. The book was nostalgic for the sixties, and it was published in 1980, just as we were about to go into the Reagan years.

AM: That book has a lot of good material and relates the ideas and events of the sixties in Canada to what was happening in the States and elsewhere.

MK: Well, particularly since nobody else has gone back to do a proper look at it. It remains one of the few books, if not the only one, that is a general overview of that period of Canadian society.

To answer your original question, I now, in my middle age, can look a bit bemusedly at the sixties and at what we thought was going to happen after us. Although we were not successful in writing a political agenda for the eighties and nineties, nevertheless important questions got raised – which I think get raised by every radical generation, not just the sixties. This includes issues of public life, public concern: how are we going to make this a more just and equitable world; how are we going to guarantee fairness in human relations; what's the best route to human liberation?

I remember when I was young and thinking, "Just wait until we get our hands on the levers of power. Boy, are things going to look different."

Well, in fact a lot of much younger people have their hands on the levers of power now. I have a very vivid memory of being twenty-something and being really frustrated with the world of my elders – you know, that whole mentality portrayed in Bob Dylan's song "Ballad of a Thin Man." The notion was that the Mr. Joneses of the world – the middle-aged men in suits – just didn't get it. Well, now I have that feeling about the twenty-somethings in suits – that they just don't get it. You know, it's still some jerk in a suit who doesn't get it, except this time ...

AM: You're the sandwich generation alright!

MK: I continue to be hip, no matter what! It's the people after me now who are no longer hip.

AM: How do you think that the feminism of the 1960s is meaningful in our lives today?

MK: After writing *No Kidding*, a book about today's teenage girls, I was struck by the fact that girls and women seem to think about maturity in a much more hopeful way than males do. Of course, this is a broad generalization. I noted in my book that, for men, the stereotype around masculine maturity is like the shutting down of your dreams, it's the putting your nose to the grindstone, taking on the mortgage, being responsible for a wife and kids – the whole closing down of male adventure. So the male adventure is the adolescent one, the "on the road," free-wheeling Bob Dylan adventure, the unmarried male on his horse riding off to the revolution.

For women, I think it's exactly the opposite, especially thanks to feminism. It's that you can look forward to maturity as the opening up of all these possibilities. In a sense, the most closed, restricted period of your life is when you're young, especially given the controls there are on young women and their independence. Women look forward to being grown up because it is as grown-ups that they're going to be smartest, most independent, most autonomous.

In a sense the sixties was full of very romantic ideas. I mean, people didn't think about being married and having families. In that sense, it was a youth movement. It wasn't meant to be about middle-aged people in mid-career. There's a good reason why revolutions come from students and the young. They're the ones with the time! For them it's all possible.

I also want to say something on behalf of the much-maligned sexual revolution. I'm very aware, of course, that now the sexual experiences of twenty-year-olds is very different. I'm also aware that the women's movement of the seventies was very critical of the sexual revolution of the sixties, believing that it was actually bad for women. But I am, again, one of those who benefited from it. Although we all had to learn all kinds of things about sexuality after that, nevertheless I have had profoundly different sexual experiences than my mother. Profoundly. If you compare our lives in other respects, there is not nearly as dramatic a difference. She was an educated women for her time, a teacher and a community activist, et cetera. I would say sexuality is the single most important thing that separated us from our mothers. For all its problems, the sexual revolution gave permission to us as young women to, first of all, have sex and then to actually enjoy it. And it was also quite a romantic movement – although not all the experiences were romantic – surrounded by music, dope, men in long hair. It was a very sensual environment as well, the idea of being a free spirit, a child of nature. I think these things were all very liberating for women.

AM: How do you see feminism assisting mature women now in dealing with their futures?

MK: I think something happens to women when there's a whole period of time after the years normally alloted to child-rearing. In my late forties when I was thinking about turning fifty – which I dreaded and I don't like being fifty, I must say – I began to see my life as a series of three eras. The first era, a period of life where the main knowledge comes out of an experiential relationship with the world, I called erotic. Then the second period I saw as encountering the world intellectually. The third and last period is what I call meditative or reflective. As an older person you find your place in the great metaphysical pattern of things. So: sensual, intellectual, spiritual.

Given this extra third of life that women have gained, it means there is a chance to have that spiritual dimension. I don't know whether that has anything much to do with feminism. I think feminism will inform the kind of spiritual search you have.

AM: What else happened to you personally when you were turning fifty?

MK: Well, I decided that I have maybe twenty good years to plan for. Beyond that, I'd be pretty lucky. Twenty years can go very quickly as you and I know. I mean, it wasn't that long ago I was thirty. I've mapped out these twenty years to ensure they don't just get frittered away. I see them as a series of five-year plans and have identified one thing I wanted to get done in each of the five years. Right now I'm trying to figure out ways to live in Toronto or in some European centre. Then, the next five years, I would like to go off to some little island or fishing village and have that kind of an experience. And then I would like to go to university to study an entirely new subject for a time. Finally, I'd like to volunteer for some cause or other. So, if I can get those four things done over the next twenty years, I will consider myself not to have squandered this last third of my life.

Someone pointed out that these plans have nothing to do with the writing, and I decided that was because it's understood that I'm going to write. I don't necessarily know what about, but I will probably always write something. I don't have to stake that out. What I do have to stake out are those things that will arise on my "deathbed test." You know, when I'm lying there saying, "Damn, I never did go to New York, or I never did study Arabic."

AM: Why a stint as a volunteer?

MK: It relates to that other earlier struggle, which I suppose one never does really finally resolve: "So who cares if you're writing. Get out there and do something!"

It would be very easy to just spend the rest of my life in Edmonton. I mean, God knows, I've got a rhythm, a routine, a community and so on. And I don't want to be on my deathbed saying, "Oh damn, I never left Edmonton." I'd like to live in another kind of city. I've also had deeply satisfying experiences living in very small places, such as a little village.

I've also realized that you have to really juggle money because you're running a bet against yourself about how long you're going to live. It would be a damn shame to have piled up a bunch of money that you're keeping for your old age only to discover you don't get an old age. In the meantime, you've denied yourself things and not spent any money.

As I get older, I've also noticed that I'm getting bigger and bigger, no matter what I do. So sometimes I think, "Well, I'm going to be one of those big mamas – what the hell." I do what I'm supposed to do: eat low-fat foods, exercise three times a week. It doesn't make any difference. I haven't gone through menopause yet. My doctor keeps telling me this is what it's all about. When you're finished menopause, you find your body again, he says. I was never particularly fetishistic about my body to begin with, so I'm not really all that sensitive to the changes. As long as I can keep walking around, am in good health and get my writing done, then I'm fine. Now I'm almost completely grey and have dyed my hair since I was forty; I can't face a full head of grey hair yet.

I'm acutely aware of the fact I have no one to pass my stuff on to in terms of the memorabilia of my life, not to mention the stuff that I got from my grandmother and my mother. There is absolutely no one. My sister doesn't have children either. So there's a real block right there. And

I feel keenly the absence of that next generation to tell the stories to. I console myself I guess by saying, "Well, my books become my way of addressing future generations," which is true if they stay in print.

AM: They are your children in a way.

MK: That's true. I look at the prospect of an old age where there are no younger people around. I can see now what a consolation I am to my mother, who is eighty. It's a big part of her quality of life that she has good relations with her daughters. There will be no one who has that relationship with me. Of course I also see that there's no guarantee that, having children, you're going to have any of those goodies either.

So, is this such a crucial thing here? I was married once for three years in the seventies. I have never been tempted to repeat the experience.

AM: Tell me about the marriage.

MK: There's not much to tell. I was just starting out as a writer and he was at Ryerson, wanting to be a filmmaker. One day I just decided, "I must be crazy, I don't want this." So we separated on my thirtieth birthday. It's been a long time. I've since lost track of him, but I think of him very fondly.

Later I had a long-term relationship with a younger man; we lived together. I broke it up and felt completely liberated as soon as I decided that. So it's very clear to me I'm not the marrying kind. I don't want a husband. But I very much resent the fact that, as a middle-aged woman, I'm increasingly invisible to men as an object of desire. I'm acutely aware that I'm moving to a part of my life where I may have to give up the idea of ever having a lover again.

AM: So soon?

MK: Surprise me, okay. I'm ready to be surprised, but I'm getting myself psyched up for this.

People are wonderful, and no matter what new environment I'm in, I'll invariably make three or four new friends to add to the roster of interesting people in my life. And that makes it harder and harder to fit a man in there somewhere, you know. In other words, my life is so full – with wonderful people and writing and intellectual challenges – that I forget that I don't have a man. It's a bit like the cartoon that was reproduced on greeting cards depicting a female figure sitting bolt upright in bed with a conversation balloon above her saying, "Oh, my God. I forgot to have children!" I feel like that from time to time: "Oh, my God. I forgot to find a man!"

AM: I guess we all have to make choices.

MK: Yes. I was acutely aware many years ago that if I had to choose between love and writing well, I would always write well before I'd fall in love.

AM: That's a hard choice to make.

MK: I sometimes applied the deathbed test: if I were on my deathbed looking back on having made a choice to get into a relationship as opposed to getting on with some writing project, I'd kick myself. I know that a lot of women would say, "Well, men don't have to choose." Actually, I'm not sure that they don't. They may have the outward trappings of a family life, but I certainly hear from a lot of women that their husbands are virtually absent. So I think that when men are on some kind of creative project, they're not available to the ordinary give and take of human relations. It goes for women too. It's just that we don't have a society in which women, such as myself, would be taken care of by men who give their lives over to making sure that Myrna is left undisturbed in order to get her work done, like the wives of some writers I know. They put a little tray with lunch outside the door so as not to disturb the great thinker within.

AM: How did you become a writer?

MK: I grew up in a very liberal-thinking household in Edmonton. My parents were school teachers. My mother never stopped growing and is very intrigued by the world. My father especially encouraged me in my reading and writing. I was always writing something – you know, diaries and journals and so on.

Both of my parents were children of Ukrainian immigrants, and I grew up very much inside that whole mythology of the western Canadian pioneer experience, visiting the homestead and being told stories of the pioneers, their sacrifices and all that kind of stuff. In that sense, I feel very rooted. As a girl, I went to Ukrainian institutions: the Ukrainian Church, Sunday school and Saturday school and dance classes and all of that. As an adolescent, I kicked over the traces. I was surprised that the Ukrainian world was not interested in the stuff that I was increasingly interested in, events of my generation beginning with the civil rights movement, rock and roll.

In 1965 I left Edmonton to do graduate school in the United States and Toronto. It was in the United States that I encountered all the sixties politics and culture. I was completely transformed by my encounter with the new left and hippy culture and then, eventually, by the women's movement. My field was Russian literature. I ended up getting a master's degree at the University of Toronto in 1969.

Then I took off for Europe and in the course of two years got this image of myself as a writer. I went off to Spain with a little coil-bound notebook from W.H. Smith in London and a couple of ball-point pens. The fact was that I had nothing to say yet, and I hadn't found my genre, so I did a lot of meaningless scribbling. But the idea was planted. Actually, it was from England that I sold my first Canadian magazine story to *Saturday Night* magazine in 1970. I was very heavily influenced by the new journalism that was being encouraged in Canadian magazines. So it was a perfect fit. I returned to Canada, to Toronto, assuming that I could get hired on by *Saturday Night* magazine as one of their writers. Bob Fulford was the editor then, and he patiently explained to me how magazines are done by freelance writers. That's how I found out about freelance and that that's what I was going to be, writing for different magazines. By 1975 I had a column in *Maclean's*.

AM: Yes, during International Women's Year.

MK: I really got to be known as a writer there and in *Chatelaine* magazine. Within three or four years of starting out, I was a national magazine writer. Altogether, my development as a writer was a gradual process, and I'm very thankful for having the opportunity to hold off until I was in my late twenties to really make a commitment. I feel so sorry for young people who feel they have to make lifetime choices in their early twenties – it's awful.

Then, in 1975, I decided to apply for a grant to write a book. Most of us who'd been writing for magazines felt very frustrated by the fact that our work just disappeared every month. I was determined to write something that would stay between hard covers. When I cast about for something to write about, I came up with this idea of writing about Ukrainian-Canadians in Alberta. I don't know why; I hadn't thought about them for ten years. So I packed my bags and went to Alberta, thinking I was going to do my research there, then come back to Toronto. Twenty years later, I'm still living there.

Alberta turned out to be a very powerful experience: making contact again with Ukrainian-Canadians in the West, being celebrated by them for what I was doing as a writer, causing a huge controversy in some quarters with that first book, *All of Baba's Children*, then finding Ukrainian-Canadians who had experienced the very same things as I had in the last ten years. They too had gone through the new left, gone through the women's movement. And there they all were in Edmonton in the mid-seventies, largely because of the Canadian Institute of Ukrainian Studies opening up at the university.

I fell in with this group of people, who were then graduate students or whatever and who are now doing all kinds of things. Some of us are helping in Ukraine, others are involved in a bilingual project with the Edmonton School Board, some are writers. But there was this very, very important moment when we came together as ethnics, as leftists, as feminists. It was probably the single most important moment of my life. That's when I realized all those things could come together. So I stayed on as part of a group of people of my generation who had decided not to go to New York or Toronto or Vancouver, but to stay in Edmonton and make their films, publish their books, open their art galleries – whatever it was: the New West, if you like.

I got really interested in being western Canadian. It was part of that whole Canadian nationalism, of turning your back on America. I had to find myself as a Canadian – find my voice as a Canadian. There was also that whole sense of a project that we had together about discovering our Canadian stories.

Then I got lured away by the East European issue. This is where coming from a Ukrainian background always means that you're a little bit different. Once I took up Ukraine as an interest, I got sucked into something which is very different from the rest of the life of my generation.

Unfortunately, the white ethnic agenda is no longer considered important. The question of colour intervened, and many ethnics got lumped in with whites generally. I was looking forward to what second- and third-generation ethnics were all going to be saying next about our ethnicity as Greeks or Poles or whatever. The differences among the white ethnics, I think, are very important, but they are not on the agenda right now. It will probably come back.

AM: Where do you see your writing going in the future?

MK: This is a sore subject because it all depends on where Canadian publishing goes. It's in a crisis. It's always in a crisis, but for the first time since I became a professional writer in the early seventies, I face the very real prospect of not being able to sell books, or maybe even get them published. And this is a recurring theme among some of my other colleagues. Just as we are about to do the best writing of our lives, we are going to find it very difficult to get published. It's a combination of what's happening in international publishing and a growing monopolization of the media by the few corporate players, plus the fact that you cannot count on Canadian readers to value you.

So, I don't know. There will always be, I suppose, room for a certain kind of journalism. Many times I've encountered writers in Eastern

Europe who described their situation in the hopeless terms of being able to write only for the desk drawer. And of course they meant because communism didn't allow them to write and to be published. Well, I feel like I'm going to be in exactly the same situation in the middle of a totally capitalist world.

I'm working on a project about political obsession right now which I'm hopeful will get a publisher, if only a small one. That's in the works, and I'm going to get it done.

Also, it seems that there is still a role for a person with certain kinds of tools like me, who can help a community get its message out, even if it isn't my community. That's the kind of role I played when I was chairing the Writers' Union of Canada because I was a non-WASP person among the various racial groups.

AM: Engagement with ideas has fuelled your writing. Have your ideas changed much over the years, in terms of politics for example?

MK: Not so much change as endless adaptation to new stuff. Like, right now, I'm trying to make some sense of this whole post-modern critique. It's very important for us who came through the sixties and seventies movements to understand that there's a whole new world of critical perspective on what we do, and that we can't just dismiss it out-of-hand as being gibberish and jargon. Certainly, as a feminist, I had to go through a number of changes because of how the women's movement evolved. And when I went to Eastern Europe, my thinking as a leftist was enormously affected by encountering the world of so-called socialism.

In meeting members of my generation in Eastern Europe who had been students in the sixties, I found them completely unsympathetic with the Western new left of the sixties. This was very startling. It was the first time I realized that there was another way of looking at that sixties generation other than just admiring it. But I have my own sort of disappointments about what's happened to Eastern Europe since then.

Regarding political changes in Eastern Europe, it's important to make distinctions about what in fact has been discredited. Certain kinds of political practice have been discredited, certain kinds of political claims from the left have been discredited. But wherever there is a distinction among classes, unfair exploitation, growing misery of one part of the population as against the growing wealth of another, you are always going to have the need of some analysis – a critique of capitalism. There's a sense of urgency around it as well. Even here we need someone to step forward and say, "Hey, wait a second."

I like to think of my politics as having some basic ground, some nonnegotiable ground; certainly, my values as a writer are the same way. I'm an adaptable person. I don't just batten down the hatches and say, "Well, this is my position. I'll stick to it no matter what." In fact, I find some of the most exciting moments of my life are the ones in which I'm seriously challenged. The old gears turn ... *eerch* – like this – and I think, "Oh, do I really have to do this?" Yet it's very exciting to realize that you're starting off on some new intellectual journey or adventure.

AM: Do you want to add any closing thoughts?

MK: My father died this summer at the age of eighty-eight. He had a very good life and was much loved. So there was no sense of any kind of tragedy involved in his death, just a sense of missing somebody terribly. I was quite impressed towards the last months of his life by the fact that he seemed to be disengaging. There was very little that we could bring from the outside world that would engage him; he already seemed to have his eyes turned inward towards the life to come or whatever it is that happens after that. Of course, when you contemplate your death, as a younger person or even as a middle-aged person, you think, "I'm not ready." That experience impressed me with the idea that perhaps there is a time you reach in your life span where it is possible to think of leaving this beautiful planet without the awful sense of being torn away.

It's given me as well a kind of perspective with which to see the issues that agitate me normally on a day-to-day basis, such as, "Oh, my God, what's going to happen to Ukraine?" or "Which way is feminism going?" One of the benefits of getting older is that while those things can still remain important, you also begin to frame them in something like cosmic time, and with a certain kind of wonderment and astonishment about the span of a human life.

Also, I have a sense of astonishment about being somebody who's got to the age of fifty, and I feel a certain tenderness towards other people in my condition – all of us who have turned fifty right about now. How did we get here? Isn't it amazing that some of us are grandparents already? Why, my goodness, just the other day I was still going to discothèques and flirting with boys or something, and there's this sense of, "Oh, so this is what it means, that time passes, that other generations will eventually take over." And you have a right, I think, to feel nostalgic. Nostalgia often gets attacked as a useless emotion, a self-indulgent emotion. But I think that by the time you're fifty, you have more of your life behind you than ahead of you, and the past does become your achievement. That is what you did, that is the track of where you were. You have a right to look at it and remember it, recall it, even idealize it.

BETH KELLETT

When **Beth Kellett** first agreed to meet and discuss her encounter with breast cancer, she cautioned that her experience had happened seven years earlier and was becoming peripheral to her life. Soon after, she discovered a recurrence of the cancer. She still agreed to our meeting, which took place in Regina a few days before her second surgery. "Initially, I thought, 'I'm just an ordinary person, and have nothing to tell you,'" explained Beth, who is a mother of four sons and trained as a nurse. "Then I decided to go ahead because all of us are ordinary, but we all have something to contribute.'"

BETH KELLETT: You get into your forties and realize that's not old at all; fifty isn't old. Really, I haven't had to deal with very much middle-age stuff. Now I'm being forced to do it. Before this recurrence of the cancer, I knew menopause was coming and expected that symptoms would be appearing in the next little while. Now my concern is about having the sudden onset of a surgical menopause when my ovaries are removed, and then I guess I'll feel middle-aged. But as much as I know that I'm going to have negative feelings, I'll deal with them and get over it. I know I'll still just be who I am. You know, I'll be a forty-six-year-old menopausal me. I don't know if you understand what I'm saying there.

ANDREA MUDRY: I do. I think I do.

BK: That I'll still be me, and I'll still be just the age that I am.

AM: I think your sense of your own identity has really been tried ...

BK: Yes.

AM: ... and you've claimed it.

BK: Everything in our lives makes up who we are. This is part of who I am, and I can't change it. Seven years ago when I had my first surgery, I was struggling to come to terms with this. I didn't want to be this mastectomy person. I wanted the Beth I knew before, but I couldn't be. There's no going back; you can't change it.

AM: How did you first become aware of a problem back then?

BK: I just discovered a lump one day. And, as with my luck, it was on a Friday before the May long weekend. I couldn't imagine that it would be anything ominous but managed to get an appointment with my doctor very quickly. He didn't think that it was anything, but wasn't sure. So he referred me to a Regina surgeon who was able to see me that very same day. She immediately did a physical exam and took a history. I think right at that point, she realized what she was dealing with. She did a fine needle biopsy and sent me for blood work and a chest X-ray and mammogram – the whole works.

After the exam, when she told me to get my clothes on and then come to see her, I realized for the first time that maybe this was something serious. She told me that she was concerned about a malignancy and made her recommendations. Since it was a relatively large tumour and some of it was behind the nipple, she recommended a mastectomy rather than a lumpectomy. Then she asked me to come back to see her that afternoon, after she had finished with the tests.

I remember walking from her office to my husband's office crying, and his classic denial when I told him. He said, "Oh, she didn't really say that." By later in the afternoon, the surgeon had talked to the radiologist about the mammograms, and those results were suspicious along with everything else that she had seen. I had Alan with me that time so he could hear for himself what she was saying. That was obviously traumatic. I just felt it couldn't happen to me: I was healthy and I was fit.

AM: You certainly look athletic and healthy.

BK: I appreciated the fact that decisions could be made quickly. I was in a situation where it was highly suspicious because of the results from the mammogram and needle biopsy, but we didn't have a definitive diagnosis. I could have gone in for an excisional biopsy, had the definitive diagnosis, and then gone back for the mastectomy. But I opted for the one-step procedure: they did the biopsy, and when the frozen sections came back malignant, they immediately did the mastectomy. I first saw the surgeon on a Thursday. I was in hospital the following Wednesday and had the mastectomy Thursday. It took one week in all.

The physical recovery from the mastectomy was nothing. I was in hospital for five or six days and didn't have a great deal of pain. But emotionally it was very difficult. I'd lost a breast; that was really devastating. So many women I know who have had breast cancer were mainly concerned with the cancer. I don't know whether it was my nursing background or whether I didn't expect the cancer to be a major problem for me because there was none in the lymph nodes, but the mastectomy was the most devastating – the loss of the breast. It changed my body image. The breast is so closely tied to who we are as women. My aunt, who is in her seventies and had a mastectomy a couple of years after I did, said she always thought it must be worse for a married woman. I had to disagree with her because we are all people – we're all the same.

There's the rational side that tells you what is true, but then there's an emotional side; you have to struggle to get these two sides to balance out. I felt old and asexual, and had just a real struggle to get through that.

My sexual life hasn't changed. I know that my husband loves me just the same as he always has; in one sense, that was the biggest reassurance I could have had. I remember feeling when I first came home from the hospital, "How could things ever be the same?" The first night home from hospital that we made love was just the best gift that Alan could have given to me. It was like saying, "I still love you. It doesn't matter." Some women, unfortunately, are married to real jerks who don't feel that way, who can't see past the body. I can't understand how you can have a marriage if that's all there is.

AM: I've heard that this can be a problem for either partner or both.

BK: This could be so. It probably affected me more than it did my husband. Fortunately, it didn't bother him, because then it could have been very difficult. Eventually, I think I would have come round anyway, but it was certainly nice to have his reassurance.

In time, I began to think, "Yeah. So what? The breast is gone." During the day you're the same because you're clothed, and you know you look the same as anybody else. But at night and in the morning, when you're dressing, it's difficult. I guess that's partially why I opted for the reconstruction and implant. It was like not being whole because I had to add something to my body – a prosthesis. A reconstructed breast certainly doesn't look like the real breast, but it's close enough. So, I worried that the mastectomy would affect me sexually; in fact, it worried me more than it affected me. But, as I said, I got beyond that.

AM: Of course, implants have since become controversial. What did it entail?

BK: I started about a year after the mastectomy, and it was done in three stages. First of all, I had a tissue expander put in. A few months later the implant was put in, and then I went on to have a third step done on the nipple and aureole. I have a silicone implant, which is the one that there's been a lot of to-do about with complaints about leakage of the silicone. I've not had any problem with mine and don't regret doing it.

AM: You didn't have chemotherapy or radiation?

BK: No. I guess treatments have changed. At that time, they weren't doing chemo routinely if they took a sample of your lymph nodes and the results were negative and showed no cancer, as was my situation. Now I know women with negative nodes who are having chemo. Radiation was basically used for lumpectomies, to kill any missed cancer cells.

It occurred to me to get a second opinion, but I didn't doubt that the pathology was correct and that there was a malignancy. Another surgeon might have suggested a lumpectomy, although I really think that the surgeon I had would have done a lumpectomy if at all possible. As I said, the tumour itself was large in comparison to the amount of breast tissue, and because it was partly behind the nipple, I would have lost the nipple anyway. So cosmetically it wouldn't have been good.

AM: Did your nursing background help you through all of this?

BK: Clinically I knew what was going to happen, but then there's the emotional side, and that's not protected. Certainly, it was beneficial to be knowledgeable about how the medical society functions and about hospital routines.

AM: How did you cope during those early days after surgery?

BK: My surgery was in June, and initially I was okay, a little down. Then in September I was really depressed. Apparently that three-month lapse is fairly typical. I really feel that it was God's grace that got me through it. For one thing I had met Jackie, a neighbour, about a week before I discovered the lump, and I believe that she was a gift from God. She's just a very understanding person and an excellent listener. Certainly, my husband was a great support. But Alan doesn't talk very easily about his feelings, and he sometimes feels threatened to hear about my feelings. So it's really good to have somebody else to talk to as well. I also did a lot of reading, everything I could find on the subject. And my spiritual side really helped.

AM: That's part of your history and your family history.

BK: Yes. My parents were ministers in the Salvation Army, so it's been my church home from when I was little, and I still do work for the church. So often, you can have a faith in God and lead your life normally, but until there is a crisis, you don't really realize what this faith in God is doing for you. It's like, "Okay, God, you say you're here with me. Show it." It was a time of real spiritual growth and confirmation for me.

I spent a lot of time with my Bible, a lot of time praying, and I had a lot of support from my Christian friends. All those spiritual promises that I had been taught as a child, they were all just fulfilled. Maybe it's hard to understand for a non-believer. I had a real awareness that God was there, that yes, He does love me.

I believe He can choose to intervene for me. If not, He will give me the grace to manage. We live in a crummy world; there's lots of sickness and suffering and misery, but that doesn't alter the fact that God cares for me and that He was there for me. It was a real palpable feeling: "I understand and care. I love you and I'm with you even though you feel miserable and abandoned. I haven't abandoned you." It was a struggle. Everybody struggles, whether they are believing Christians or not. Then I came to a real peace.

AM: Do you have a sense of how women manage who lack your religious faith?

BK: I don't know. I think they find other ways to cope, but it may be harder and take longer. Some people just shove it out of the way, and it never gets dealt with. Basically it's a grieving process, and as with any other kind of grief, some people go through the stages and process well, while others go into denial. You pay for it later if you don't acknowledge real feelings.

One of the best ways of dealing with anything is to talk about it. That's why I wanted to read, find out about as much as I could, then talk about it. For a lot of older women, it's very difficult to talk about very personal things.

AM: Did you join any support groups?

BK: Initially none were available. Jean, a woman I already knew, visited as a representative from Reach to Recovery. She brought items such as pamphlets of information, an exercise guide and temporary prostheses. Later, I got involved in Reach to Recovery as well and I did hospital visits. Then we got a support group going for any breast cancer patients who wanted to attend. It ended up being more of an information group, rather than a support group. We had various speakers in, such as a plastic surgeon to talk about reconstruction and a dietitian to speak about diet.

Now there's a weekly support group that is really an emotional support group run by one of the medical social workers from the cancer clinic. It changes as more women are diagnosed and as some finish their treatment or don't need it anymore.

AM: In my reading, I came across the story of a woman who died in her nineties, and only then was it discovered that she'd had a dual mastectomy.

BK: It's very isolating not having anybody to talk to. Perhaps some older women feel they shouldn't talk because they're older and breasts aren't important to older women. Well, of course they are. I guess it's more than just age, it's also the culture. Now more women are able to talk and open up. That's how we learn.

What I found really amazing is that at the time it happens, you feel so alone because you don't know anybody else who's had this. Then, all of a sudden, people come out of the woodwork. Older ladies in the church would say, "I had my surgery forty years ago." A mother on David's hockey team told Alan that she'd had a mastectomy about three or four years before. No one would have ever known, yet there's so much of it out there.

In time, my life settled down and we went on happily for more than seven years. My sons, who are now twenty-three, twenty-one, eighteen and thirteen, were still young then, and I was busy at home. I really enjoy and value being at home as a mother – not that I don't value a woman who works outside the home. We haven't had much extra money through all the years of moving around Canada for my husband's government job and having the children. But we had enough financial stability that I was able to stay home. Not all women have that choice. I like to be at home and know what's going on in everyone's life, make sure everyone is eating right – just be there to make a house a home.

Then a couple of months ago I discovered a lump just below the reconstructed area. I was concerned, but my doctor and surgeon didn't think it was anything. The lump wasn't on the incision line, where most recurrences show. My surgeon thought that it might be some scar tissue that had to do with the reconstructive plastic surgery or silicone leakage, and sent me back to the plastic surgeon for a biopsy. And he didn't think it was going to be anything either. Nobody did. So we were all really taken aback when it turned out to be a recurrence.

AM: I bet.

BK: My surgeon was the one who actually phoned me to tell me there was a recurrence, and that was just before the long Easter weekend. Those long weekends – they do it to you all the time. So then I waited through this long weekend – it was a really, really long weekend – until I got in to see her, and we talked about all that would have to be done. I had to have a bone scan, a liver scan, some blood work, chest X-rays and a mammogram. All those tests had to be done again. And I'll be having surgery. Everything else was negative in the test results, so that's good for right now.

We've set the surgery date for Monday of next week. Because my tumour is positive for hormone receptors, which means that it depends on estrogen, I've agreed to have my ovaries removed at the same time. Everything will be done in one surgery; then I'll only have one recovery period. So I'll have three surgeons: my general surgeon, plastic surgeon and gynaecologist.

AM: They're going to be operating on two sites?

BK: Yes. My gynaecologist will do an oophorectomy first and remove the ovaries. That will only be small incisions through the umbilicus and subpubic and two little incision on the side. Then my plastic surgeon and my general surgeon will do the breast: remove the implant and take muscle. I'm not sure how much she'll have to take. She doesn't think it will be a lot area-wise, but the cancer was going into the muscle. Then afterwards I'll have a course of radiation. As I said, the surgical menopause concerns me most. I'm forty-five and haven't been having any menopausal symptoms yet. Now it will happen suddenly and therefore my symptoms may be that much more severe.

AM: What are you expecting?

BK: My gynaecologist says by the time I see him post-op, I'll be experiencing hot flashes and vaginal dryness. I don't really suffer a great deal from PMS, but I do know that my mood swings are cyclical, so I expect that I will have some emotional disturbances. I do have bouts of depression, and I wouldn't be surprised if I have those kinds of periods because it's going to be a sudden onset.

Of course, I can't take hormone replacements because of hormonal positive cancer. I tend to be a natural type of person and might not have taken it anyway: if the natural process of the body is to be without estrogen after a certain age, then that might be the right way. However, I realize hormone replacement has many benefits from cardiac to skeletal.

I'm starting to explore avenues outside of conventional medicine for relief of menopausal symptoms, such as vitamin E, ginseng tea and acupuncture.

AM: Will you go through a reconstruction again, or have you got that far in your thinking?

BK: Probably not. Now I'll be living with breast cancer, whereas before, we did the mastectomy and I thought I would never live with it again. I think I will live happily and be well adjusted, but it's a major factor in my life now. Also, after radiation, the skin is damaged and less elastic. I don't know whether I'd have enough to accommodate an implant. Other than that, I could go with a tram method, where they do a hip to hip incision, take muscle and fat and tunnel up to make a breast. It's very good cosmetically but is very major surgery. At this point, I don't think I want more surgery.

AM: I read an article where a woman was arguing against using any replacement for the breast at all.

BK: The first time around I wanted to be able to do that, a way of saying, "This is who I am." But it just didn't fit with who I was really. Clothes obviously hang better if you've got two breasts, you know. Before, there were many days in the summer that I wouldn't wear a prosthesis because of the heat, but I always would when I went out. Al would say, "Why put it on? Why don't you just go the way you are? Nobody else notices." I'm not big breasted, but health-wise, it's important for heavy-breasted women to wear a prosthesis because breast tissue is heavy. If you're lopsided, back problems can result.

AM: What is your long-term prognosis?

BK: Well, my risk of a recurrence has certainly increased; there's no doubt about that. Hopefully, I'll be one of those lucky ones and this will be the only recurrence. As much as the likelihood is increased, it's not a major concern of mine right now. I know I can handle the surgery. I had my tubes tied using laparoscopy, so I know what I'm facing there. I know what I'm facing in the chest area. I'm not anticipating any major problems, and it can be years and years you know, and we'll deal with that later.

AM: Sounds like you've constructed a way to deal with it.

BK: Well, when you are first handed a diagnosis of cancer, it's awful. You have to face your own mortality. You start wondering what will happen to the kids, and all of those kinds of things. I've already done that before. Yes. I had cancer, I dealt with it then, had many happy, healthy years, and I have many happy, healthy years ahead of me again as far as I'm concerned.

I never, ever thought I'd have a recurrence. I mean, this just blew me away. Eventually you get to trust your body again. At first you don't. Every time you've got an ache or a pain, you think, "It's back!" Then you get to trust your body again. I really never thought that I'd deal with this again. I was wrong.

AM: Do you feel at all that your body betrayed you?

BK: No. I certainly didn't think it would happen, but a recurrence was always a possibility. My chance of another recurrence or metastasis is much greater now, and if that happens I'll deal with it then.

I've learned that each day really is a gift; so let's enjoy the day that we've got. Whether it's a terminal disease or being hit by a car, none of us are promised it won't happen. And so I've got today, and I'll enjoy today. Each day has its own troubles, its own joys, so I cope with the joys and the troubles that the day presents.

One lesson that I learned the first time round is that life is wonderful and we cling to it. Crises fade away with the passage of time, and you forget what you've learned. I want to remember that there are joys every day and to really be thankful for all that we have. Sometimes it's still hard, as I go around picking up messes after my kids, thinking that when they leave home, I'll have a clean house. If we wish away today, we don't enjoy what we have today.

A crucible experience can be hell – a kind of trial by fire – and you don't want to be experiencing it. But I believe that we discover depths to ourselves we didn't know. The difficulty could be financial, health or family problems, the death of a spouse – all the things that we as humans encounter. How we come through those difficult times makes us who we are.

AM: Beyond the surgery and all of this, do you have any special plans for the future?

BK: Everything will basically carry on pretty much as they are right now. For the last few years, I've been working part-time for the government, which leaves enough time for home and my involvements with church and friends. We don't live a fast-paced life. Our sons are getting older, so we don't have a lot of the extra-curricular activities that we used to do with them. I like to spend quiet evenings at home.

Actually, I and a couple of friends at work bemoan the fact that we have these boring lives and don't do anything exciting. But really, my life is just fine the way it is. I'm really quite happy.

As I said earlier, I've really become a "live in the present" person. I've got kids that I want to finish seeing grow up. Our oldest, Matt, is going very seriously with a girl right now. I'd like to see them get married. But I don't live in dread that I won't, as I did when I was first diagnosed. So I'll raise my kids and watch them start productive lives. I don't really have any major plans.

POSTSCRIPT: As *World Enough and Time* goes to press, about a year after our conversation in Regina, Beth Kellett reports that she is managing well. The second surgery went as planned, and she suffered no side effects from the subsequent radiation treatments.

"The prospect of premature menopause intimidated me because I thought I could have every possible symptom," she says. "I was especially worried about my emotional state because I can get depressed easily. But emotionally I've been fine. However, the awful hot flashes haven't let up. I haven't tried much alternative medication because I tend to want to do things naturally. In our North American culture, we've medicalized menopause. It is a normal occurrence, although for me it's been surgical, so I'm trying to just go with it, accept the hot flashes and hope they won't go on for too long."

"Before my second surgery, I understood that once you've had a metastasis your chances of further recurrences are increased." Beth says. "But now, from further reading, I think that, with my kind of recurrence, the additional surgery and radiation may have taken care of it. I certainly don't live in fear."

ROBERTA BONDAR

For **Roberta Bondar**, midlife has only served to sharpen an already keen sense of commitment and urgency. In her view, the 1992 flight aboard the space shuttle *Discovery* was just the beginning of her career as an explorer. After the transforming experience of viewing the Earth from space, Roberta says she has returned "to really explore this as a planet." And exploring it she is, as a scientist and an artist.

Although she has succeeded in a number of traditionally male domains, Roberta continues to address the inequities women can face. "You have to deal with reality, speak about such issues, and get them clarified, get them on the table," she says.

ROBERTA BONDAR: I think that when you hit the age of fifty, you suddenly realize there's more behind than ahead of you in terms of acquiring new knowledge and having the physical ability to do the same kinds of things you've always done. You suddenly realize you don't have forever. At least that was the case with me. I think when you're younger, there's always this road so long ahead of you; there's time to waste doing frivolous things.

Right now I don't want to waste any time; I don't want to waste a day; I don't want to waste an erg of energy; I don't want to waste one second, one minute. I want to accomplish more than I've accomplished before. I certainly want to be efficient about it, and – even more so than before – I don't want to be involved in a lot of things that are going to cause me stress.

It's like eating. My attitude towards eating is, "Am I going to eat this chocolate bar because I'm hungry; am I going to eat it because I like it; am I going to eat it because I've got 270 calories to spend today that I haven't spent?" Now I look upon everything I do with my energies and say, "Is this how I want to be using the energy that I have, or am I going to use it a different way?" I've always said, "Do things that make you happy." For me now, it's not just happiness, it's feeling fulfilled, that I really have done a good job with this particular day.

ANDREA MUDRY: So you have a heightened awareness of your objectives in making choices, your options and your activities.

RB: I've always had an awareness, because my motto has always been to have a sense of where you are. But what I'm not willing to do now is to compromise that. It's one thing to have an awareness, and it's another one not to compromise that vision of yourself in a practical sense. Of course, we all have to make concessions on a day to day basis sometimes, because of some personal, political or job-related matters.

I haven't noticed much in the way of physical changes with time. Well, I wear bi-focals; that's probably the main thing. I've worn glasses all my life, so it's not that much of a problem except that I have to make sure that I get the right segment through a pair of binoculars or a camera lens. I guess I don't really think about it to tell you the truth.

I haven't noticed any loss of energy, although I think I'm probably better at conserving my energy now. I have the confidence to tell people when I don't want to do something. The demands on me now are even greater than they were pre-flight, and so now I have a very disciplined way of looking at certain activities people want me to do and I say, "I do this. I don't do that."

Now I seem to deal with children differently than I did before the flight, and it's probably because I'm grandparent age. I don't know. As I get older, I really do take it very much to heart that I don't have my own children and that I'm influencing many more people. It can just take one visit to a school. I still get notes from people who heard me talk years ago, telling me that they did x, y, or z as a result.

AM: What are some examples?

RB: In Calgary at a book signing, a woman in her late thirties said to me, "You know, Dr. Bondar, this is my first trip outside of Banff since my surgery." I said, "Your surgery?" "Yes," she said. "I've just had a brain tumour removed, and it helped to keep me going when I knew that you were coming." What could I say!

I'll give you another example that is important because it shows how soft I am. A lot of people think of astronauts as being very macho. And I certainly can be as disciplined, straight and scientific as need be, but not always. For my homecoming to Sault Ste. Marie, people filled the Memorial Gardens, which holds about five thousand people, three times. It was incredible, the most emotional experience of my life – more than the launch, more than the landing.

Anyway, they had the mikes on the floor and anybody could go up and ask me a question after I had shown my film from the voyage. This little girl, who was about ten, came up in a coat and boots and wearing thick glasses. She got to the microphone and said, "Tell me, Dr. Bondar, what's it like to be loved by everybody?"

Well, there I was on the stage, with everyone starting to scream, "We love Roberta," and I'm standing there, with TVOntario's camera right on my face. I'm thinking, "I'm going to lose it right here in front of all these people, I'm going to start bawling." That was probably the moment when I really understood what an impact I had and I was going to have for the rest of my life.

People have told me that I'm Amelia Earhart, and my answer to them is, "Not quite. I'm alive." It's the idea of being a historic figure in your own time. We don't discover new lands in Canada: there are very few things we can do in terms of being an explorer and still be a Canadian. That, to me, is what it's all about – and being alive and being recognized for it. To me, it's extraordinary.

AM: Is there a down side to the fame?

RB: The down side is that you become so obvious to people that if you do something or say something, you're on centre stage. If you were some-one else, nobody would pay attention.

AM: How do you respond to that? You must have developed a kind of *modus operandi* to deal with it.

RB: I must say that it's still discouraging. So, you have to look in other parts of your life for relief. Right now, for me photography is one of the big areas; sports medicine is another. And my support systems are great, with friends who are constantly reinforcing me. I think that, as a woman, you have to have some intrinsic things that you do. And I say "as a woman" because I really do feel that women still have a real tough time. I think that we're kidding ourselves if we think that life is easier for most women now. For women in a professional area, you have to have some-thing that's really, really strong inside you.

Recently, I was off for two months at a photo college in the United States, in Santa Barbara. I went out on field trips, and got an A in the course. Many of the people there were professional photographers, and it just means that I'm at the same level, which makes me feel very good about myself. That's how I cope, by doing things and looking forward.

AM: So it's having interests and also good friends who don't have unre-alistic expectations of you as a sort of heroine and historic figure.

RB: My friends have expectations of me as a bright individual and friend. And they don't want to see me letting other people waste my energies, because I have a lot of energy, a lot of drive and a lot of things to do yet in life. They really don't like to see that being teased away.

I'm also writing a book called *Women Beyond Earth* that deals with female adventurers. Basically, I decided that sometimes people don't take women seriously as adventurers. You know, it's viewed as some sort of public relations ploy. You walk in a room, and if there are a man and woman who have climbed to the top of Mount Everest, people always gravitate to the male, never to the female. It's as if women are not seri-ous; only men can do this stuff.

I got a little bit annoyed with all this nonsense, and I said, "Oh, heck. I'm going to write as a woman who's flown in space. I'm probably one of the few people who can write a book about the women in various countries who have flown in space – what moulded them, their opinions about certain issues." I've interviewed about fifteen of the women, some of the original American women, including Sally Ride, the first American woman in space, and the only British woman and Japanese woman in space. We're talking small numbers here. I'm hoping to have it finished by this fall.

AM: What, specifically, fascinated you about space travel in the first place?

RB: Last night I was unwrapping a box of books and came across the first science fiction book that my mom bought me. Also my aunt worked at NASA and used to send me posters and crests. I was always into mechano sets and speed: I wanted to be a bird, I wanted to fly a plane – and I did get my pilot's licence. Space travel seemed a very romantic, adventurous thing to do. I'm into adventure and fun. The more danger, the more I like it.

I'm just fascinated at night – I go out looking at the skies and am very philosophical. When I was young, this feeling would come over me that I was going to go into space some day. I really felt that I was going to be doing something different. In high school, I felt so different from the other students. It was very uncanny and something I never really lost track of, so that if I was going into something and felt, "This is not it," I would back away.

AM: Is age an issue for women going into space?

RB: No, it's not, mainly because astronauts are usually in the middle-age group. They have to be to have enough experience to qualify. Shannon Lucid, the American woman who's on the Mir space station right now, is around fifty-four. She's one of the original group of females who joined NASA back in the late '70s; now she's a grandmother, and she's been up in space more than any other woman.

AM: You take such an interest in women's issues. Do you have a word for women at midlife?

RB: It's a very individual matter. What I've always tried to do – and not always been 100 percent successful – is to have a sense of where I'm at. For example, first of all, you have to have this reality check. If you always wanted to do something, then you need to try to do it. But there may be problems – logistical, financial. For example, if you always wanted to be a veterinarian but can't afford the years of study, perhaps you should look at another aspect of the dream, such as doing work for the Humane Society. I always wanted to be an astronaut, but until 1983 it was impossible. And if I'd had that as my only goal, I'd have gone to the States and applied to the American program.

So I think you have to have a bit of a reality check and have a sense of what's possible. At midlife, people are usually in situations where they can't just cut and run. If children are still at home, for example, that is a responsibility that has to be considered.

AM: In *Touching the Earth*, the book you wrote about your space trip, you mentioned that, in going into space, you finally felt free of a "life-time of coping with issues of role and gender."

RB: That was a bit of a teaser.

AM: I'm teased. What were you thinking of?

RB: I'll give you some examples. My parents respected my sister and me as people, as individuals, but the whole of society was not structured that way. The society of the 1950s said that women belonged in pink, frilly dresses and were not allowed to run around in church basements. Now when I'm speaking, especially to women's groups, I ask, "How many of you have said to a little girl, 'Oh, that's not ladylike,' or 'You don't run around'?" Then I say, "Now who's exploring the world?" That's the kind of biasing I was taught, and that's what I was alluding to.

Many specific instances have happened throughout my life. When I was in grade eight, we had to write a test; the highest person got to be captain of the school crossing guards, and the second place got to be lieutenant. So I wrote the test and got the highest mark, but the policeman who came to make the announcement said, "Well, Roberta had the highest mark, but Tommy got the second highest mark and, since he's a boy, he'll be captain and Roberta will be lieutenant." This was so unpleasant that I almost started crying in class, but I controlled myself.

So that was the first time. After that, there was an uncle who always took male relatives – boy cousins and so on – out on his boat. My sister and I were always left behind. My dad tried to make up for it; he bought us fishing poles and took us fishing off the rocks. I was starting to get the idea that being a woman was not the ideal thing in life – that if you were a man, the world was open to you. And yet, I didn't want to be unhappy with myself because, I thought, "I am what I am." I mean, what am I going to do? I'm not going to have a sex change just because I think that men have more opportunities than me.

Then when I got into high school, it was the same thing. The boys always had money going into more of their gym equipment or they were more encouraged to do things. If a boy was going to be a doctor, everybody made a fuss about him, but women were never encouraged to go into a professional career.

"I want to be an astronaut." I remember saying that to a relative, who laughed at me and said, "Oh, you should just marry a rich executive at the steel plant or be a secretary." This was the attitude. So it was really tough.

And then, when I got into university and especially medical school and beyond, it was – and it still is – very, very hard for women, even though a large percentage of the class is now female. In residency, I hit one of the meccas of male chauvinism. In neurology, I was never encouraged or given any kind of mentorship at all, and I had a Ph.D. in neurobiology. So it was always a fight against an establishment and the status quo.

AM: It takes a long time for attitudes to change.

RB: It didn't get me down. I became stronger, persisted and succeeded. But I think it's important to talk about these things. As a result of my experiences, I better understand what people go through on the basis of race and culture. And I've tried saying something about that in my first book because it's important to me for people to respect other individuals as human beings. It is, to me, a disgrace in society when we don't. So, I think the whole gender issue affected my mindset, but I was relatively untouched by it. Yet, when I think of some of the things that have happened to women: we just have to think of the December 6th shooting at L'École polytechnique in Montreal. It's very chilling.

AM: What were some of the influences in your life that gave you the independence and self-assurance to persist?

RB: For myself as a woman, it was important to be part of co-ed groups and, more importantly, female groups. In the Anglican Church they had junior auxiliary and girls' auxiliary, and then I belonged to the Family Y, which is both men and women, and we had a girls' basketball team. One of the really important organizations was Girl Guides, which I belonged to for eighteen years.

Until we hit adolescence, we're all fairly self-assured. Then we become very sensitized to the world around us, to what our friends think about us. I wasn't that popular socially in school, and chose to do a lot of athletics. To me, this whole biological change thing wasn't a major issue. I was going through that period, but I had a mind that was very excited by things: I liked to learn new things and acquire new information and have fun doing it. I was really up to my eyes in all kinds of activities – archery, track and field, basketball, coaching kids – that were building this confidence that I had about myself and what I could do because I was getting a lot of good feedback.

I also developed quite a bit of self-confidence because of a job I got as a result of being in a science fair. After reading Rachel Carson's *Silent Spring,* I was totally taken with the effects of DDT on the environment. I entered a project in the fair that led to a summer job offer from a local lab to help with insect research. I was there for six summers and made enough money for my education and to get a pilot's license. Besides getting to work with real scientists, I was also able to work independently, and actually saw the science being applied. I'm technical, very goal-oriented, and like getting results.

It certainly helped that my parents were very supportive, although my dad has died. Even now, if I feel down, I call my mom up and she will see something positive in whatever it is that happens. She says, "Well, dear, you know ...," and she goes on and tells me something else, and usually by the end of the phone call we're really laughing. Parents are in a unique position to share that kind of warmth with a child. It doesn't matter if the offspring is five or fifty, you can still share that bond. This doesn't mean that you have to spill the beans or do everything with your parents.

Because of my parents I have a very generous heart and would fly around the world to help a friend. That's why I wrote that book about my space trip. It's not a money maker for me. It's nothing other than me trying to share with the people who put all their tax dollars behind me because I know that this was important to them.

AM: You have four academic degrees. What motivated you in your academic choices as you moved from an undergraduate science degree to a master's degree in pathology, to a doctorate in neurobiology, and then to a degree as a medical doctor?

RB: Well, I always wanted to be a doctor. When I was a kid, I wanted to be a scientist, an astronaut and a doctor. I didn't think I'd ever be a doctor for many reasons: only boys were encouraged to go into medicine; there was no medical person in the family; I didn't study and therefore didn't have high marks or a scholarship.

So when I began at the University of Guelph, my idea was I was going to be a physical education teacher or a science teacher. When I took ill in my third year, Sue Corey, a zoology professor, took me under her wing. She hired me as a part-time technician in her laboratory, and I loved working with microscopes. I'd had one at home since grade eight. I took every course I could in the veterinary college that related to physiology and pathology; although I had no intention of being a veterinarian, I was still thinking about medical school. At Western, I did my master's degree in pathology, which is in a medical faculty.

Then I became engaged to a chap who was going to Ryerson and moved to Toronto. I was actually thinking about doing pharmacology and becoming a pharmacist. Then it hit me: I was getting caught up. I suddenly realized what I was doing and said, "This is not right for me. I really want to be in medicine and I'm not there yet." So I started my

Ph.D. at the University of Toronto. I broke off my engagement and eventually got accepted into McMaster Medical School.

AM: So through all of this you knew that you really wanted to study medicine? Was the marriage something that was just in the way of this aim?

RB: Well, it was in a way, insofar as I knew that this person would never be happy with me because I was too driven. And I did not want to have that on my plate – going through with a marriage and then knowing it was not going to end up well.

AM: And from medicine you eventually went on to become an astronaut. In your book you describe how your experience in space has altered your perceptions in various ways. You wrote, "The huge physical presence that I see below will endure long after I and my kind are gone."

RB: Yes. We are very short-term thinkers. Our year is 365 days because the seasons change, and we think of the year as being long. But this is a window in time in which we, as life forms, can exist on this planet. We will not exist forever. The window is only open for a short period of time. We don't know for how long, but it is not forever. It has not been forever.

And from space flight, I think I understood for the first time what being on a planet really means, what being dependent on living things on this planet really means. Because when you are up there, you can't get away from the sight of Earth. You can't just walk out of the movie theatre and go to the bathroom or get some popcorn. You are faced with this when you look out the window, and you are faced with it day in, day out, day in, day out. You're living in this tin can, and there's all these Earth-derived things around you. There is no escape from the reality. There's nothing else around that would sustain you.

I don't see how anybody could not be touched by that realization. And that is different from looking at the beauty of this thing below us. I want to stress the distinction between looking at the planet as this beautiful world that's below us, with its wonderful mountains and turquoise seas, and the issue of looking at Earth being all alone and us being alone.

AM: That's an awesome thought. How did you deal with fear in space? I believe at some point you said that it's not appropriate to show fear.

RB: It's not just inappropriate to *show*, it's not appropriate to *have* fear. I don't know how many people have asked me, "Were you afraid a lot, did you think of the *Challenger?*" Well, they see themselves going into this seething rocket with all this dynamite underneath that could blow up any second, but they don't see us as trained professionals. We go there because we're trained. Some people flying in space are not trained professionally. The first woman from Britain who flew basically won a lottery and got to fly with the Russians. You take a chance on people like that.

But for the average person who has been selected by an astronaut program, whether it's Europe, Japan, Canada or the States, there are certain expectations of that individual: that they can work in small environments, that they have interpersonal skills. Then, once you get into the program, you start dealing with more and more complex situations and more dangerous things.

I was an airplane pilot by 1968 and joined the space program in 1983, so that early on I had the ability to cope with danger. People talk about fearing fear itself, and that's kind of a neat phrase. I think what it means is that when you are afraid of something, you are no longer focused or in control or disciplined, and the last thing that you want to be in a space situation is undisciplined, unfocused and uncontrolled.

You don't want to be an Air Canada pilot with fear if one engine goes out. Maybe afterwards, the pilot could say, "You know, I had some pangs." If there is a little corner of fear, it has to be in a box and you have to move it away. That is not the time to deal with it because your life and others' lives are in the balance.

AM: What are you putting your energy into now?

RB: Mainly my photography, sports medicine and my speaking engagements. The research work is ticking along. I'm in the middle of a phase of a research grant that was peer reviewed, looking at how we recover from being de-conditioned in space flight, and trying to use the technology and insight we have gained to look at patients on Earth who suffer from diseases with the same kinds of symptoms.

The space flight made me different than most other people in the world, and I believe that I can best explore the changes that I feel on a more artistic basis. Photography is my passion; it's my way of being an artist. Through it, I'd like to show people what I see on this planet.

I'm still an astronaut because I've flown. But I don't see the space flight as the pinnacle; I just see it as the separation point – from what was before the flight in terms of preparation, and what is after the flight.

Now I'm back on Earth and exploring. I'm looking at the environment and what type of creatures inhabit it, and I'm observing as a scientist. I'm doing many things now that make sense. I mean, from the viewpoint of wondering why we're here and what we're doing in life, think about it – we're just really treading water until we die. We are born and we're going to die; those are the only two given things. And we have to do something that's going to give us something emotionally good because, otherwise, well, we don't like crying a lot, you know.

So, for me, the photography is a very, very important issue. It's a very technical, precise way to be very artistic.

AM: What about your work for the Friends of the Environment Foundation?

RB: The work that I do for that Canada Trust Foundation is an education role as I see it. There are many, many issues, and I'm just dealing with the major issues of how to think about the environment.

The most important point is that we are not stewards of the environment. I hate that term. We are part of the environment. Somehow, as human beings, we always feel that we are such a super-species that we can isolate ourselves away from everything, but we are part of the environment. Secondly, environment has to be a good word. David Suzuki draws it black all the time. It shouldn't be, it should be a very uplifting word because we're a part of it. And we shouldn't be ashamed that we are changing the environment. We just have to understand our interactions and how it's impacting other things.

Our problem is that we develop so much technology, but we don't seem to develop ways of getting rid of its waste. Animals get rid of themselves because of beetles munching up dead bodies. But there's nothing munching up our pop cans. So I think my contribution is mainly the educational role of talking about some of those issues.

When I speak to people of any age about the space program or the environment, I often incorporate the photography. I'd like to be a sort of Yousuf Karsh of the environment.

JACQUELINE VÉZINA

"Mega" is a fitting adjective to describe **Jacqueline Vézina**'s imagination and creations. Her company, Les Productions Jacqueline Vézina Inc., annually produces four of Quebec's major exhibitions. Le Salon des Femmes, a rendez-vous where women can make contacts, exchange information and discover new products and services offered by women, has been a popular Montreal event for more than a quarter of a century. Les Fêtes Gourmandes Internationales de Montréal annually attracts more than half a million people, and is the best known of her three exhibitions that feature food and agriculture.

Having achieved considerable success in the external world, Jacqueline has embarked on an internal journey, which is altering her life.

JACQUELINE VÉZINA: I don't describe myself as a business woman. In introducing me, people say, "We present to you, Madame Jacqueline Vézina, one of the major people doing business in Quebec." But that's nothing to me; it's not the title I like to have. I am a creator. Money for me is nothing. I spend money for my ideas – to create. I'm like a show business person.

When you are creating something with other people, it's deep, it's interesting, because people who are creators are very special people. We are not the same as everybody. You cannot be pretentious when you are a real artist or a real creator because it's a talent that was given to you for now. Will you have it tomorrow? Will you have ideas? You don't know. You don't have a diploma saying I'm a doctor, I'm a psychologist, I'm a lawyer, I'm an engineer, and I give you the proof of what I know.

ANDREA MUDRY: You depend on yourself.

JV: I am depending on "now." Will I have a good idea today? Will I do it well? I'm always starting and starting, and I hope tomorrow it will be the same. It's a gift that was given to me. I don't know where it comes from. I have special feelings for things and for how to do them. That's it.

I think that creation is the most important thing in life. Everybody can create at a different level, in a different way. Everybody cannot be a painter or an actor or a sculptor. But if you open yourself to creation, to your imagination, you start to be like a kid and say, "Oh, today, for my children, I will have a special meal. I'm going to put some pretty earrings on my cake. I'm also going to put two flowers or I'm going to put small tools." These are crazy things, but now you are creating! You're doing things differently, and that is fun in life. What kills people and couples is doing always the routine, where you don't invent things. I think we should all do better in this regard.

The Salon des Femmes at Place Bonaventure that you saw yesterday, I created it – the setting, the dancers, everything. I'm a show business person because my start in life was on television. I had my own show for children on CBC-TV. I was writing the script and was on once every week for five years.

After that, I worked in a musical on television. That's where I learned, where I started using my imagination. To be frank with you, I never studied art, I have no diploma from university. I am an autodidact. Is it the same word in English?

AM: Yes, exactly: a self-taught person. How did you begin producing large exhibits?

JV: I started with a festival for records and music in a big hall. I created that event, and all the record companies were there with the artists autographing the disks. For the close, I created a big gala to give some trophies to the best productions of the year. For five years CBC televised the show at La Place des Arts.

AM: How did you feel then? Did you have a sense that this exhibition was extraordinary?

JV: No. I was just creating and not realizing what I was doing. I was so involved in the work. It was so difficult to do every day and to think of everything. It's a funny question you're asking me because I was never happy at any of my events. It was always so hard. You have deadlines: the public is coming in for the opening the next day, and you have to work all night, always running.

That's why I never sat in a chair and said, "This is my event. This is my creation." There was always something wrong that I wanted to do better. Even when the show was on, every night I was having a meeting with my crew – the group of people working around me. Say, just for example, the Salon des Femmes. We started the first show, and I said, "No, no, no!" The lights, the sound, it was not what I wanted. So, after the first show I said, "Okay. Everybody in my office. Big meeting. Take your pencils, take your pads to write. We're changing the whole show and redoing it. What was at the end, we put it elsewhere. We are cutting this number and putting in another." I did that, and the day after it was super. For me, I had to see it on stage. In show business, it's always like that. You have the premiere, and then everybody sits and corrects a lot of things. So it becomes better, better, best. That's the way I am.

AM: Is there an exhibition that you especially enjoy?

JV: Les Fêtes Gourmandes. It is incredible. The foods of different countries are represented and all the products that are used for different kinds of food preparation. It's a fiesta, a real happening, with singers, dancers and music at the Expo '67 site, on Île Notre-Dame, right across from Montreal. Around the island there's a little canal all lit up. People are happy – they are singing and laughing. You have romantic couples; you have families; you have business people at lunch. Others come at night and they leave at midnight or one in the morning. It's super, super – very much a wonderful atmosphere.

It's all Quebec agricultural products because Montreal has been a city of international cuisine since Expo '67. Many of the chefs from different countries in the Expo pavilions decided to stay and open restaurants in Montreal.

I like big attendances – big shows. I cannot do something in a theatre just for a thousand people.

AM: Wow! You don't like to be called a business woman, but you must possess a rare combination of creativity plus the ability to see things through. And this would include the ability to choose and to delegate to people who can look after the numerous details, from renting spaces to organizing hygiene and safety for these vast shows.

JV: It's life that gave me experience. I can do anything – pass the broom on the floor, paint some walls. At the end, if it was not ready, I would say, "Okay, let's do it – all of us."

AM: So you just learned by the seat of your pants. You must have made some mistakes along the way, eh?

JV: Yes, business mistakes.

AM: What was the worst one?

JV: The worst one was last year at my Salon des Femmes. I'd been producing it for twenty-five years and it was a big success, but I wanted something new. So last year I said, "Okay, I will be new in a certain way. I'm going to change the name." I called it Les Folleries. It's a French expression – Follerie – that means "crazy things." So I called it that way. Then I asked all the exhibitors to be costumed like Charlie Chaplin. They agreed. So we had hundreds of Charlie Chaplins – women and men – with the little moustache, the hat, the cane, the little white blouse and tie. I built a stage like Broadway with Charlie Chaplins in wood that were thirty feet high. And I lit the stage. You should have seen it.

I lost $265,000. It cost me that just for my crazy idea, but I wanted to do it. People didn't recognize that it was the annual Salon des Femmes. And because I was working so much with all my ideas about Charlie Chaplin, I didn't work much on my publicity. But I was so happy, and I didn't mind. Okay, I lose money. So what? I created something. It was so beautiful.

AM: You have been doing these exhibitions for quite a while now, and I wonder if you want to do something else?

JV: I'm not sure. I'm at a passage in my life, and I will take a little while thinking about it in silence. And I'm starting to change things. This international trade exhibition for agricultural machinery that is on today, it's a big show with representatives from thirty countries. It belongs to me because I bought it from the government. Yet this year I didn't work on it as much as before. I have an experienced director and people who help him. And also for La Salon des Femmes, I worked, but not too much. I have an experienced crew and they respect me. I am a perfectionist. They know how I think, and they work the same as I do. If they can go farther, I am happy.

So I don't want to create new events for the moment. I just want to stabilize my business, and I will see what else I want to create. I don't know.

AM: Are there things you enjoy doing when you're not working?

JV: Well, I do. When I create, it's for my business. Just for example, what I do at a wood shop of mine, creating very interesting personages – cartoons for some of the exhibitions, like the Charlie Chaplins. You should see the cartoons. I find the ideas and I create there. When I arrive home, whoosh, I'm in my bed.

AM: So work-related activities have taken up much of your energy?

JV: Yes. I live in the Laurentian mountains, and when I arrive home, I like to look at the trees, the lake, and I rest. I also like to go to good restaurants. Friends – I have a few, but good ones.

I like people, but they take too much of my energy because they want me to be like that image of a business woman. Everybody knows me in Quebec. I can go three hundred miles from here, and they will know me. They use me as an example. "That's a working woman and she has so much energy," they say. The men give me as an example and the women say, "Help us because we try to be like you." But now I am a little bit tired and want to say to people, "I cannot give you what I was giving you in the past because I discovered quality of life, and I discovered myself."

For five years I have seen a psychologist. I'm discovering that I'm not a machine. Now I have more a life of my own. To be frank with you, it happened to me because I had a love affair that failed. And it was not the first one. Every time they love me, but at a certain time they say, "We cannot continue like this. You're not there; you're not with me." The last one was the hardest one for me. I was living with someone for nine years, and when it stopped, I said, "I have to do something."

At that time, I started delegating at the office because I had that big problem. Now I appreciate it so much, that I can delegate.

My therapy was marvellous for me, and I am not finished. I want to go farther. I've changed a lot in five years in my way of living and thinking. I am searching for more truth everywhere and am not much interested by artificial things.

I also changed a very important thing in my life. I was helping others too much and forgetting myself. I was like someone on a mission, helping everybody who had problems. Even in the metro, in the streets, I was giving all that I had in my pockets to people who were asking.

I was so sensitive to people having problems because I had so many problems in my life. My parents were dysfunctional people who destroyed themselves, and I was trying to be the opposite of them.

AM: What happened?

JV: They were a couple that did not love each other. They had three children, and I was the oldest one. My father was a druggist. His father was a doctor. So, my father was near medication. He went for an operation, and when he left the hospital he started to take drugs – morphine. And my mother did too. It was difficult for us. We had a crazy life. They killed themselves very fast – in their thirties. My mother died when I was nineteen, five years after my father.

So I wanted to be the opposite of them. I had such a big drive. We say in French, *la survie*. You want to live, survive. That's why I create. I was happier for that, but I was not near my feelings enough.

AM: So you got more in touch with yourself.

JV: Yes. Now I am more able to love and to "be there."

There was another thing in my love affair that was a problem. I was thinking that I was nothing in life unless I was creating and being a big success, having money and being known – things like that. Without that I felt little, like a little mosquito. So I was always producing big events, thinking people loved me for that. But five years ago I was left because I was "never there." Now I am in touch with my feelings, and I know that I have needs. Before I was just giving, giving, giving. So this is my big change. That's it.

When I'm in touch with nature, that's where I recover. That's why I live in the country, and I also have an apartment in Florida on a little island in the Palm Beach County. When I have enough, I go there. I go on the beach. The sea is very quiet.

I also travel all around Europe very much. I've never been to the Orient. Maybe I will. But what I want the most is contact with nature. That I need. I like the city but not for long. You go there and you fight for your life. You see shows, you see museums, but all that is part of what you need in life to succeed. When I go away to be in touch with my feelings, I stay quiet.

Nature is so wonderful, it's alive. It's the biggest show you can see, especially in Quebec. We have four seasons. Each season has something different, and I observe a lot in nature. In the winter, everything is dead;

everything is white. Then, at a certain moment in spring, it starts with little green things on the trees and then, wow – you know what I mean?

AM: Yes, I do.

JV: And I like to swim. In winter I go to a place near my house with a little river and a sauna. I go in the river with the frost and all the snow and ice. I feel so good after that, and I have a good massage.

Now that we are talking about it, I have a feeling why I like the country. It's because when I was young and life was so horrible in my family – my mother and father destroying themselves, having fights – I wanted to go away. And I had an uncle who was a gentleman farmer. He did not farm himself, he engaged a farmer. My uncle brought me with him for a year when I was twelve or thirteen because I was dying as a kid in the middle of such struggles. It saved my life.

We went skiing together. He had some lumberjacks working for him. So, every day we were going on the trails to see how they work and to bring them some coffee. I was also going three or four miles to the village with my skis to get the mail. I was in nature all the seasons.

My uncle was a poet. At night he would sit on the balcony with me, explaining to me all the stars and about the animals, about the trees, the flowers. And it saved my life. All summer I went there with my brother and my sister. It was marvellous. There were some chickens, some cows, some horses. My uncle was a real gentleman. He was special, so it gave me a lot. I lived in the country then, and I never forgot it because it saved my life. Every summer, many weekends he asked us to come.

So that's why I think I like the country. And I also work with agriculture in these exhibitions. I believe in those people who are working with nature because they give us energy with good foods and they help us to build houses with the wood. It is very important for a country to produce its own food.

When I was young, at Christmas morning I remember asking my brother to let me play with his plastic farm – with all the animals and buildings. Now I really do work with agriculture. It's strange, isn't it?

So this is it. I read a lot of psychology. I think it's very important to know ourselves and know others and their reactions.

AM: I think that the more you know and understand yourself, the more you can know others.

JV: Yes. And we women, I think today we are learning about ourselves and are able to know others better.

Me, I didn't live a life like other women. To be honest with you, I never had much to share with women. I have no kids, no husband. I had success young and made money. I worked with men – obtaining sponsors, selling ideas – because they had the money.

Now women are getting involved in business, and I work more with them. This year, I associated myself with the Association des Femmes d'Affaires du Québec for the Salon des Femmes. They helped me and my crew a lot. At the opening, I said, "This year, you are all with me, and I feel so pleased about that. We shall never be alone now. We shall get together, and help each other, be associated in all kinds of things."

There is a big difference with women of today and twenty-five years ago. When I organized the first Salon des Femmes years ago, I was reaching the women alone in their houses, in their silence with their kids. They were alone, and I created that event to help bring them together to exchange and talk. Then women started to go to work, to study. And now I think the revolution is not the same. We did it. Now feminism is no more something for collectivity, for all the women. Now feminism is an individual thing. If we want to go further for our rights or anything, we have to fight by ourselves in our families, in our work. That's where we are now, I think.

And there's another problem. We women wanted to be autonomous: to work and to have a family. But now the "superwoman" is panting from too much to do.

I think women are more intelligent and are saying, "Okay. We want to be autonomous, we want to have money, authority, success, power. But we are killing ourselves because at the same time, we also want family – kids, a husband or a lover." It's very difficult, especially now, living in a recession when it's so hard to earn money.

So I think the values of women – men also – are changing. Money will no longer be so important. If we have to choose, we will choose to have less money but more pleasure, the good feeling of being at peace, being happy with the ones we love. We balance now the money, the work, the power, the success, and we don't want to pay too high a price by sacrificing our private lives. That's where I am, and I am not the only one. I can see it all around me.

I think we have passed through a lot of complexities, and we no longer feel guilty if this or that is not perfect, or wonder, "What do they think of me?"

AM: Do you think that age has something to do with this attitude?

JV: I'm not so sure. No, no, no. The young generation, young women, are thinking like this, and more than we are because they have kids, they have a lover. I see it at the office. They say, "Well, I have to go because my husband is waiting. He has a meeting tonight." Or they say, "I have to be there for the kids," or "Tonight I'm going to the theatre." Another night she will stay, but that night there's nothing that can keep her. She has to go.

And I think the women of middle age are marvellous women, marvellous. They are connected with themselves and the rest of the world, enjoying life. And I feel like that too. I am a connected woman. I like beauty, money, success, the country, poetry.

For me, spirituality is to be connected with your soul more and more. If you are connected in this way, it is impossible that you are not connected with everything around you – people, nature, progress. *Oui.* For me, the spirituality in my life is my connection with other human beings, and the silence is important.

It's funny, but I'll tell you something. I am a woman who creates events, and my ideas are always in advance. But I never read newspapers or magazines. And I don't much look at television. Yet I am advanced in my ways of thinking and doing things and creating. It's the way you're connected to the earth and your soul and your feelings that is important. I think we can go and get everything there – in ourselves and in others. I like to speak of deep things, not the latest movie. I like to speak of evolution – of my personal evolution and the evolution of other people. All my relations are connected with that. My best friend is a psychologist, a marvellous man. I am friends with comedians, actors, creators.

AM: And has the new you met a man who can appreciate you?

JV: Maybe. I don't want to talk too much now. But I will say, for the first time in my life, I will fight for a relationship. I realized that I would always fight in my work. There was nothing to stop me. I could do anything: see the Pope, see the prime minister. I fought all my life. But for my love affairs, for my feelings, I was not fighting, never. If somebody didn't want me, I went away. Now I know that I will get another one because I'm ready.

Peter Caton

LINDA SILVER DRANOFF

"**L**ife is unfair." Many are willing simply to accept this statement as true. **Linda Silver Dranoff**'s life and career as a lawyer have centred on evening up the odds, and she encourages others to join the fight.

Linda is known for her reputation as an effective practising lawyer, which includes precedent-setting work in the area of family law, her activities for law reform, and her media work and public appearances which offer the public access to an understanding of the law. For eighteen years she has been the adviser featured in *Chatelaine*'s "Ask a Lawyer" column. She is also the author of three books: *Every Woman's Guide to the Law, Women in Canadian Law* (a history), and her latest, *Everyone's Guide to the Law: A Handbook for Canadians* (HarperCollins, 1997).

ANDREA MUDRY: What do you see as the major issues that women have to face at midlife ?

LINDA SILVER DRANOFF: The crucial issue is financial independence, which involves many other issues, such as unequal pay, inequitable employment opportunities, inadequate divorce settlements, and lifestyle choices that don't give women the same set of skills as men for both the investing and the earning of money.

It's up to women, from as early an age as they become aware of it, to make sure that they arrange for their own financial security in their later life. It's really foolhardy for women to rely upon anyone else to take care of them at any stage in their lives, but particularly in their later years. I don't mean to say that interdependence is not appropriate and desirable, but not dependence. Women really have to smarten up about such issues.

One woman came to me as a client for a divorce and said she remembered hearing me speak fifteen years earlier. I had said that every woman should have her own savings account because if she has all her money in her husband's name or in joint accounts, she doesn't have any sense of security or protection. And any woman contemplating marriage should have a marriage contract with built-in financial protections. This woman told me that she then went home and told her husband she wanted an account. Fortunately, he listened to her. Much later, the marriage broke down, and she at least had some money in the bank as a cushion. But even if a woman just decides to take a vacation, she should have the financial capacity to do so. It's very important.

AM: What do you see as major ways of gaining that independence?

LSD: Getting a proper education is a major way to gain financial independence. It's never too late to get education or training to do something that can earn a reasonable living. The biological clock is a reality; the career clock isn't.

When I thought of going for legal training for five years, some years after getting an undergraduate degree, I worried that I was too old and it was too late to do it. But then I realized that I would be five years older in five years anyway; I might as well have something to show for it. I had to try. That was a time when everyone thought a person had to go through and complete their education all at once. That's changed. Nowadays many people understand that a person can be educated or re-educated at any stage in life. However, some women have told me that they're "too old" at fifty. And I wondered to myself why – at fifty – would anyone think herself too old?

I think it's never too late to do anything you want to do if you have the intellectual and emotional capacity and you do not have physical or financial limitations. Some people are only limited by the limitations they place on themselves.

AM: True. In your book *Every Woman's Guide to the Law,* you say that control of one's life is the essence of equality.

LSD: When I talk about the need for women to be educated and to have money in their own names, what I'm really saying is that they should take control of their own lives – that if they're dependent on anyone else, they will not have the opportunity to be equal. The essence of equality is to be a fully independent, autonomous being in our society, which is accomplished by being in charge of your own life. Too many women aren't.

One reason for this lack of independence is biological. I think it's very difficult for many women to be in charge of their own lives and to be mothers. The childbearing and child-raising responsibility sometimes impedes our freedom to become educated – especially if a woman gets pregnant at an early age – or to earn a good income. This responsibility can further affect women in later life because of the impact on job opportunities, seniority and pensions. One of the important changes our society must make to help women of childbearing age is to provide for proper day-care services. I don't think that women will ever be fully equal without day-care services, because how can you really take charge of your own life unless you've got some kind of support system in place to help you take care of your children? No woman can have a free mind at whatever work she does unless she knows that her children are taken care of.

AM: Financial independence covers a big area. Are there other issues for women at midlife?

LSD: Women find it difficult to balance a satisfying family life with challenging work, community interests and time for the self, and this is a constant struggle. It's a tightrope I am constantly walking.

AM: You've been involved in women's issues for several decades. When did this interest begin?

LSD: I guess I've always had what are now described as feminist views. To me, it's all about fairness. I never understood why women were excluded and sidelined from life's centre stage.

My first recollection of an active involvement in any issue that today some might call feminist was back in 1959, when I was an undergraduate at the University of Toronto. John F. Kennedy, then a senator, was debating Stephen Lewis, who was a student at that time. Women were not going to be allowed to attend, and a group of us considered it very unfair, especially since it was expected that John F. Kennedy would be the next president of the United States, which of course turned out to be true.

At that time, Hart House was for men only, and one debate a year was open to women. So our group arranged a meeting with the head of Hart House at that time, Warden Joe McCulley, and made our request in a very civilized manner. "Why not have the one debate a year be this one because we would really like to attend," we said. And I can picture him to this day, looking at us with an expression of amusement on his face as if to say, "There, there, dears. What makes this the one that we should deign to permit you to participate in?" His answer was no, and so we women picketed Hart House in the rain while the debate was going on. That we did this was so surprising it made the *Toronto Telegram* and the *Toronto Star* and other news media the next day.

As part of our lobby campaign, I remember writing a letter to the editor of the *Varsity*, the student newspaper, and the last line of my letter said, "WOMEN OF THE WORLD, UNITE." The issue for me was that it wasn't fair.

AM: What exactly wasn't fair?

LSD: It wasn't fair that women should not be permitted in Hart House, period. That rule did change some years later. Secondly, it wasn't fair that women should be refused admission to that significant debate. That is what feminism is all about – fairness. It's about the right to choose. That wasn't fair, although in 1959 no one I knew was talking about women as having any special rights. I think that a sense of inequity must have existed among women for all time. When it wasn't a movement, it was little groups here and there with strong feelings. The more of us there are fighting these battles, the more chance that there will be some change.

As for Hart House, they opened the next monthly debate to women; I can't remember who spoke. The men sat in front and the women were requested to sit in the back behind a rope – in other words, to be seen but not heard. I attended with a few sympathetic women and men.

The fellow who was the chair or the moderator of the evening thought this whole thing was a big joke. At the discussion period after the debate, I stood up and asked to be recognized as part of the discussion, just like the men were. They refused to acknowledge me. I remember standing there and being so nervous, just standing there. The custom was to stand up until recognized. The moderator said, "Women are here on sufferance only. So sit down and leave us alone. We have to let you in once a year, but that's all you're going to get." That wasn't acceptable to me, so I stood my ground, nervous as anything. Finally, they let me be heard. I made my comments and felt that I had shown them that we just weren't going to accept that treatment.

AM: In the early sixties, I had an English class at the University of Toronto that was split in half alphabetically because it was too large for one lecturer; one half was taught by the famous Marshall McLuhan and the other half was taught by a rather boring lecturer. So everybody crowded into McLuhan's class until the administration said, "You will not receive a final mark if you do not attend your designated class." We all knuckled under. I've looked back and thought that if that had happened later in the sixties, we would have protested because protest was common by that time. But in 1959 you and a group of other women did protest. You showed your feelings; you didn't just have them.

LSD: That may be so, but while I was strong enough to challenge the rules about who should attend the Hart House debates, I wasn't strong enough to challenge the unwritten rule at that time that women did not go to law school.

AM: How did you finally get to law school?

LSD: After getting an undergraduate degree, I married, lived and worked in New York and had a daughter. When I divorced, I returned to Toronto. Then it was a matter of deciding what to do. And I decided that since I in effect had a second chance, I was going to make the best use of it. That meant doing what I really wanted to do, rather than taking second best and doing what I thought I should do or what seemed practical to do. As a single parent with a two-year-old daughter, it sure wasn't practical to decide to study law for five years, but what a thrill it was when I graduated and my daughter ran to me and gave me a big hug just after I was handed my diploma. I had no role models and did not even know, or know of, any lawyer who was a woman. It certainly was not a career that was expected of me. I just felt that law was the career that best suited my talents, interests and goals. And I guess, thinking about it, that the whole issue of fairness was involved. I perceived law as being an instrument to create fairness. I still do!

AM: Your career seems to have had a definite, although not exclusive, focus on family law and issues of concern to women. At what point did that really begin taking shape for you?

LSD: It wasn't that I had a long-term plan. I always followed my interests, and opportunities arose. One of those interests was writing. I've given expression to that interest by writing articles and books that explain law to people and take it out of the realm of being a secret code for the initiated.

AM: In 1972, when you were still in law school, you published an article about how women lawyers were viewed by the profession and how they viewed themselves.

LSD: Yes. I wanted to find out what I'd have to face in practising law once I graduated. At that time, of the three hundred students at Osgoode Hall Law School, only fourteen were women. So it was a fair question for me to ask: "What am I going to face out there?" But I didn't know anybody to ask. So, for a seminar course on the legal profession, I wrote a paper on women in the profession. The paper included a survey I prepared and sent to all Toronto women lawyers, and then I did a survey analysis. The survey asked about discrimination in the profession in terms of work assignment, pay and opportunity. I wondered how women combined being a parent with practising law. The paper got an A and the *Law Journal* printed it, and I thought it would help me to know what to expect from my life in the law.

From a professional point of view, my involvement with women's issues really arose out of that article. I was asked to speak about it as part of a panel at the first National Conference on Women and the Law in 1974, the year I was called to the bar. Then I became involved in the lobby effort to reform family law after a group of women lawyers asked me to join them in preparing a summary of the four-volume *Ontario Law Reform Commission Report* on family law that had just been issued. Until that time, Ontario family law had not provided for any sharing of property and assets between husband and wife after marriage breakdown. Laws basically provided only for support of spouses and children, custody and access.

One thing led to another. When our summary of the *Law Reform Commission Report* came out, I was asked to participate in the government discussion process to change family law. It was very clear to me that it was an issue I wanted to be involved in, so I said yes. In law school I had studied the divorce case *Thompson & Thompson*, where the wife had contributed to work on the family farm all her life but was not granted any share of the farm assets. I was absolutely appalled that the law would leave a woman in such a situation. This case predated and was similar to the famous 1974 *Murdoch* case, where the Supreme Court of Canada denied the wife entitlement to any assets. The *Murdoch* case was seen across the country as a great injustice; it resulted in change to the family laws and led to the 1978 Family Law Reform Act in Ontario. The changes provided for sharing of family assets such as the family home, car and cottage, but not of investment and business assets and pensions, which usually belonged to the man.

AM: I understand that since then you've been involved in a number of precedent-setting cases in family law and have worked to reform the legislation too.

LSD: A number of my cases set precedents and thereby established new law. For example, after the Family Law Reform Act came in in 1978, I read the legislation itself as allowing an opportunity, in the right circumstances, of getting a woman 50 percent of everything and not just family assets. It seemed to me that that's how it was worded and that was the intention in the statute. But the courts were very reluctant to take that step. They didn't mind giving the woman half of a cottage and half of a boat, but the guy's business, his pension, stocks and bonds were seen as his.

In one of the cases that I had at that time – the *Leatherdale* case – I made the pitch at trial that the wife should get 50 percent of everything. Basically, they were a middle-class couple. He was a Bell Canada worker with a pension; they had a house and some stocks and bonds which they were saving for their retirement. The trial judge agreed with me and made an order that she would get one half of everything. The husband then appealed to the Court of Appeal, and he won.

So, I took the case to the Supreme Court of Canada and won the principle that a woman's financial contribution to the marriage entitled her to a share of the investment, business and pension assets. Unfortunately, her homemaking contribution was ignored, and that bothered me. Once that decision was handed down, I formed a committee of leading interested citizens and lawyers, and started a campaign to change the law in Ontario. This eventually resulted in Ontario's 1986 Family Law Act, which says straight out that the value of the assets accumulated during the marriage by the couple should be split 50/50 with certain exceptions. All the other provinces have similar laws in effect now.

So much of what I did in the practice of law to try to improve things for people evolved as the need became obvious, from the clients who came to me for help. Each case taught me what the law should evolve into.

AM: How has the Family Law Act actually worked out in practice in the courts? My own separation and divorce took place in the early 1980s. At the time, I was appalled at the stingy legal attitude to my contributions as a wife and mother. I started to write about it to warn other women, but then the new act came in and it included many of the changes that seemed necessary.

LSD: I don't think it's worked out precisely as I would have liked, but it has been a definite improvement overall. Any legislation is open to interpretation. If the interpreters of that legislation see fairness differently than I might see it, then the decisions might not be what I would agree with. For example, when the act initially came in and provided women a full share of property rights, the courts and lawyers started to say, "Well, once she gets property, she doesn't need as much support or time-limited support will do. She doesn't need to have the house to live in with the children. Give her 50/50, but she can go support herself, now or in two or three years."

AM: So they would tell a fifty-five-year-old woman who had raised a family and never worked outside the home to go get a job and totally support herself?

LSD: That's exactly right. There were a lot of cases happening through the 1980s where women were getting little or no support and should have. That trend has finally been redressed by direction of the Supreme Court of Canada. The law right now provides for basically 50/50 sharing of assets and for lifelong support where necessary. So it has finally been refocused in the right direction.

When you're younger, you think that a change in the law is going to make an overnight change, but it doesn't happen like that. There's a change in attitude, and then there's a gradual change in the right direction. I think that's what's happened in family law, but it's taken really all the years I've been practising law to see that change evolve.

Even then, there are people who try to ignore the law. In one of my cases, during a thirty-year marriage the wife had helped build a business, worked alongside her husband and even had some of the property in her name. Yet her husband tried every which way he could to use the legal system as a club so that she would not be able to get what was coming to her. I carried the case for years until we finally got it into trial, and we fortunately got a good decision. Even so, the husband continued to use the legal system by appealing the judgment.

I've come to understand that you must work hard and be prepared. Then if you're lucky, you get justice for people; if you're persistent, you get justice for people. But it isn't automatic. You have to fight for it even within the system. This whole process of achieving fairness is a process — it's just that.

AM: In the course of your career, have you been much affected by sexism?

LSD: Without any doubt. I've felt it in the practice of law right from the very beginning, even though it was subtle and not necessarily direct. The survey I had done on women in the legal profession only prepared me in a general way. The subtle ways in which discrimination against women in the profession expressed itself in practice took me by surprise. Very early in my career, certain lawyers where I practised made things very difficult for me. It led to my conclusion that I would not be allowed to progress in someone else's organization and that even if I worked hard and smart in such an organization, not only would I not advance, but I would be stepped on. As a result, I decided to go into practice for myself right from the very beginning. I was called to the bar on a Friday, and on the following Monday, my "shingle" went out. Thankfully, on the Sunday night before I opened my practice, a man in the apartment building where I lived called me and asked, "Are you a lawyer yet?" I said, "In fact I'm starting tomorrow." He asked, "Are you going to do divorces, because I need a divorce." I said, "You've got it."

Since then, I've had clients among both men and women, but I probably have more women clients. I think you have to know both sides. Sometimes a male in a litigation situation is the one who's really in the position of the underdog. More often it's the women who are not being treated fairly, but it happens with men too.

Practising on my own was not just a response to discrimination, but a positive decision too. It was a way I could be in charge of my own life and career, and have the time to devote to my daughter, without having to answer to bosses who did not understand and were not willing to accommodate my priorities. In those days, day care was not readily available, and I came to know first-hand how tough it is for working mothers. So, universal and accessible day care has been an issue I have worked for.

I've been fortunate in that the field I chose for myself had that option of being my own boss. While I am subject to all the same restrictions and rules that anyone in our complex society faces, I have had the relative freedom, being self-employed, to follow my interests – to get involved as an activist as well as a lawyer in community, women's and legal issues. And to take time to write.

AM: What has motivated your concern for fairness and equity?

LSD: I guess I'm in search of a society that works for people, that takes into account real human needs and at the same time works on a practical level. I just feel that I have a responsibility to do what I can. If you see a problem and you think you have a solution, then it's your responsibility to offer your views.

I believe that there's a lot of people in our communities with very good ideas who shrug their shoulders and don't come forward. If they just chose to participate in the community around them, they would have an awful lot to contribute. When I go out into the community and speak to people, I find that so many have such good sense, real common sense, but they don't think that it's their role or that they can make a difference. One person can make a real difference. I learned that in working with others on the Family Law Act, trying to get the law changed in the 1980s. If you do the right thing and you're in the right place at the right time saying the right thing, it's quite amazing the impact that you can have.

AM: You certainly seem to have contributed to helping women lawyers within the legal profession and heightening sensitivity within the profession to women's issues.

LSD: I spearheaded a feminist legal analysis section at the Canadian Bar Association Ontario. I saw the need, got it organized and served three years as chair, and it is now being run by some twenty excellent lawyers who are from every kind of firm, every field of practice.

We put the feminist perspective forward in legal briefs on changes in legislation, and we advance the academic exploration of feminist issues in law, such as sexual assault, emerging issues in the civil and criminal justice system, midwifery and the law, reproductive technologies, international law, contracts and so on.

But this was not something I planned, it just evolved. It was something that came along. Looking back, I see that this was not unusual for me. From time to time in my life, I seem to think something will be a great idea, decide to do it, and even if later it becomes clear that it is going to take much more time than I anticipated, I don't let that stop me.

AM: What else is happening in your life at middle age?

LSD: I don't like the terminology and therefore don't want to be defined that way. I'm a person with certain life experiences. Obviously, having lived a certain number of years, I've had more life experiences than someone younger, but I often think these labels tend to be used to diminish people and to pigeonhole them.

AM: I appreciate your point and have certainly thought about the whole question of terminology. I'm using terms such as "midlife" and "middle age" so that other people can recognize and identify with a specific period in life, and I don't intend to pigeonhole. In fact, the women I've talked to for the book are all unique individuals, all so different. Is it better to ask how it feels at this point in life, looking back and looking forward?

LSD: What we are is closer to death than to birth. We may have done more than we still have time to do. But we don't know. How can we be middle-aged when we don't know how long we have to live? That may be middle-aged statistically, but someone's middle age is in the middle of their own life, and nobody knows how long that's going to be. I don't know, I just think you have to live each day as well and as joyfully as you can, make as much of a contribution as you can, and let the days after that take care of themselves.

AM: Is your life any different at this stage?

LSD: My delightful daughter, to whom I am very close, has grown up and is independent, and has brought me a son-in-law to enjoy. I remarried seven years ago and now have a wonderful loving husband, who encourages me in all my ventures. And his own children and grandchildren have welcomed me as part of their family. I have a special family and good friends. I have been blessed to experience life's joys, even if everything came in a different order than I expected, and even if I had to work hard for my successes. Sometimes, you have to let things evolve and let life surprise you.

AM: What has been your perception of aging? Is your experience of it any different from other women you know or women in your family?

LSD: I don't think about it. It isn't an issue for me. Maintaining health and energy is more relevant, and I try to pay attention to my health, and take responsibility for it.

AM: What about the future then?

LSD: I'm certainly a person who doesn't really think in terms of retirement. I have a full private practice and plan to continue it. I plan to keep contributing to the evolution of the law. For example, I recently wrote newspaper articles on changes to support enforcement and child support planned by governments, about which I had concerns. I have just written a challenging book requiring enormous effort, *Everyone's Guide to the Law: A Handbook for Canadians,* and I expect to continue to write as well. I'll keep following my interests, and who knows where that will take me? I am going to let life surprise me!

CHARLOTTE
WILSON HAMMOND

In the 1970s, **Charlotte Wilson Hammond** and her family joined the "back to the land" movement, leaving the core of downtown Toronto for the seclusion of Clam Harbour, Nova Scotia. The move dramatically affected her life and her art, which now frequently employs nature and landscape in exploring themes of life, death and regeneration. An arts advocate, Charlotte has learned to fight for the arts as a member – and a founding member – of numerous organizations, such as the Canadian Conference of the Arts. Over the years, she has also learned to fight for the recognition of her own works.

ANDREA MUDRY: Age is a theme in some of your works. When did age begin to be a consideration for you?

CHARLOTTE WILSON HAMMOND: People tell me that when I was turning forty, I got quite weird beforehand. Around that time I had a show that was initially titled "Body Image/Self Image." A group of us –various women artists – we were all fascinated by how we perceive ourselves. We really have completely bizarre images of how we are – and usually inaccurate as well. The first self-portrait I did for it had this old, haggard kind of witch-like look. Then I jested, saying, "There is life after forty," and gradually the second and third portraits of myself became much more positive.

It hit me more when I was turning fifty and went through a very strange space. Part of it was the realization that I've been here in Clam Harbour for some twenty-odd years. Twenty more years and I'd be in my seventies. The realization that my life was more than half over was quite shocking to me. I talked to women who were really positive about being fifty and felt that there was an energy that started to happen around that age. So that was kind of a hopeful sign.

AM: Fifty certainly seems to be a pivotal point for many people.

CWH: But then I had a twenty-year retrospective show, which had been five years in the making at the Art Gallery of Nova Scotia. Unfortunately, the show didn't tour, and a number of other things didn't happen. One of the worst was that because the most recent work in the show was so delicate and light, it was extremely hard to photograph. It's always important to have a photographic record of your work for grant purposes and such.

The period after the show, right around the time I turned fifty, was really horrible. I had a huge depression and didn't work for almost a year, which has never happened to me before.

The show had been the largest opening they'd ever had at the gallery, except for their grand opening. I felt that I had such support, and it was just a series of political crap that it didn't tour. The big thing for Maritime artists – for any regional artist – is to try and get the work to move out of the region. And Toronto is so dominant. Most of the art magazines come out of Toronto, and it's a case of who writes and about whom et cetera – all of that political stuff.

Bitterness is an occupational hazard for artists. You put so much of yourself into the work. I've known people who ruined their lives because they get so hostile and paranoid that they just couldn't go on. You have to work through all of that and say, "This is what I'm doing, and what I've going to do, and I know it's important." My husband, Gordon, showed me an article where Robertson Davies said that, as a storyteller, his important audience is his readers, not the critics.

I've come to the conclusion that my work is valid and I am a senior artist; I know that inside myself. But when you're faced with rejection, it's really hard to maintain that egomaniacal attitude. And that's what I have to work at.

AM: Having faith in yourself.

CWH: Exactly. There were also a number of deaths around this time. My stepfather drove here from Toronto with my mother. One day, when we came back from the beach, we found him holding his head. He was diagnosed with a brain tumour and was dead in a few days. Then my half-brother died of a massive heart attack in his mid-forties. We'd had a fight when he'd visited us here just beforehand. I felt terrible and had to spend time understanding my own feelings.

So, the longer I didn't work, the harder it became to start again. The show ended in March, and in the summer I did a lot of gardening – I generally don't work in the studio in the summer anyway. After that, I read numerous mystery stories. I talked to one friend, a sculptor, who was going through a lot of stuff too. And I talked to Gordon. He's a friend as well as a lover, and tremendously supportive. I guess I just finally worked through it.

AM: Then what happened?

CWH: Then I started very slowly working on the show that I've just had at St. Mary's University Art Gallery. I started working on small things in small increments; gradually they started to fit together and grow. It was interesting that, from the very beginning, I was really clear about what I was doing in terms of my feelings about it.

Often when I do work, I never think of the title for a show but this time, the title – "Intimate Communion" – came really quickly to me. It has a lot to do with gardening and my connection with the earth, and growth, death and decay. It has to do with having friends die and realizing the impermanence of life and how we have to take care of the earth. When I say spirituality, I probably sound new ageish. I'm not. However, I do feel a really profound connection. If I have any religion – so-called religion – it probably has to do with some of the more ancient practices in religions, with paying attention to what comes out of the earth and what goes back into the earth.

I started to come to that through my daughter Thea, who was majoring in religious studies at St. Mary's University. We talked about Christianity and its original meaning before it became institutionalized. That's why I've always avoided organized religion. Everywhere, in any kind of organized religion, there's always a corruption of the initial seed of truth. We also talked about some of the more ancient religions – pre-Christian, pre-monotheistic religions – about how some of the ancient practices really paid attention to all aspects of life. If they cut down a tree, they said a prayer to the tree or they made an offering.

And I found that in my own life, as I gardened, I had an awareness. If I was transplanting and had a couple of plants left over, I felt really awful. Instead of throwing the leftovers away, I stuck them somewhere. So I began to really pay attention to what it was I was doing in the garden. It became a spiritual release for me. And I found, while I was gardening, just turning things over and making shapes and doing stuff, the relationship of gardening to painting became clearer and clearer.

AM: How so?

CWH: I mean, when I'm working in the studio, if I get into a certain head-space, I'm not aware of anything but my work. I might have "Morningside" on CBC Radio, but I don't hear it. And when I'm gardening, the same thing happens. I'm just into it. Perhaps it's certain brain waves. It's tremendously soothing yet stimulating at the same time.

And then, practically speaking, I pick a lot of flowers for the house. When they died, I started throwing them in a basket, where they were drying out. When the time came, I just started using that dried material, almost as paint. Much of this was intuitive. I mean, I wasn't saying, "Now I'm going to do a painting about daffodils." But I was using the daffodils as line and as shape and form, and doing this layering process with the Japanese paper, gel, inks and finally oil paint. I was building surfaces. It was almost like I was going back into abstract painting, which I hadn't done for a long, long time. So the whole thing evolved over a four-year process.

It became really clear to me that what I wanted to do was to somehow convey to the viewer the feeling I get when I sit in a space and look at the ocean, at seaweed, or I look down at the earth here and see all the shapes, the spaces and the incredible organization of nature.

An artist, Rita McKeough, wrote a poem for the show's catalogue, and articulated what I feel just bang-on.

AM: For me, this part of her poem expresses some of what you've just been describing:

*layering fragments   pieces of organic material   it looks like skin
layering it   sticking it back together   order   constructing
something
from what you have torn apart   disorder   ordering nature
reconstructing a body   a sensual land   stabilizing intimacy
reconstructing a spiritual self.*

CWH: When she delivered the poem for the catalogue, I just wept because it was so exactly right.

AM: How did the show go?

CWH: Very well. I had two main goals aside from the work. One was to have the show written about critically and the other was to have it tour because last year I applied for my first A grant from the Canada Council. And, once you apply for an A grant, you can't go back to a B grant. I didn't get it, but if I apply every year, I believe that eventually I will. Part of my problem is that I haven't had a lot of national coverage.

These goals haven't been realized yet, but I'm still hoping, and we have interest from galleries in other provinces. Meanwhile, the show was very gratifying to me. People in the academic community really responded to it, as well as ordinary, non-gallery-type people, and they responded very similarly. It moved a lot of people.

AM: What else is happening at this point in your life?

CWH: Well, I certainly think about age at times. For me, the whole thing of getting older physically seems to be epitomized in the feeling that I look like my mother. She's really attractive, so that's not the problem. It's just that I can see that she's older, and I'm not supposed to be.

So I have this big struggle with my hair, which is quite grey, and I dye it red. This summer I'm starting to let it grow in to see what it looks like grey. But as soon as I look in a mirror, I see my mother's face and my grandmother's face.

This seems like an aside, but it ties in with everything. When I knew we were going to be talking, I began thinking about women that had influenced me, strong women in my life, and I feel I'm from a really matriarchal family.

AM: How so?

CWH: My grandfather died when my mother was sixteen, so my mother was brought up by my grandmother in a female society. Then my real father died when I was two, and my grandmother, my mother and I were all very, very close. My grandmother just thought I was wonderful. She started painting in her fifties, and we took art classes together. My mother, who went to École des Beaux Arts in Montreal and became a potter, married early, had a fairly miserable marriage and was an alcoholic until twenty-five years ago. But despite the fact that my mom doesn't have a really positive self-image – and she'll be the first to say it – underneath she's very strong and a feminist – maybe without realizing it. She and my grandmother imparted this kind of strength.

So, despite the fact that I grew up thinking that marriage will solve all my problems and that we'd live happily ever after and all that 1950s crap, I think I also grew up a feminist. It took me a few years to get that all sorted out in my head. I always felt that if I decided I could do something I could do it. Whereas, I have friends now who are still struggling with that. They may know they can do things, but they just have terrible self-images.

AM: What's an example?

CWH: I have a friend, a performance artist, who is extremely bright and talented in so many ways. She lives alone and is completely self-sufficient. But she can't phone up and complain to the bank if they have messed up her account, for instance. She doesn't realize that she projects an image of strength. Rather, she sees herself as a wimpy person. It's bizarre. Miserable things have happened to her in her life – abuse and all that stuff. Now, at fifty, she's slowly coming out of it.

I'm also beginning to understand the immediacy of things. Earlier, we were talking about deaths. There's been a number of deaths, more than the ones I've described to you, which has made me realize that you've got to "do," that you can't put things off. You can't say, "Well I really want to talk to that person, but I'm too busy now so I'll wait another year to visit." Sorry, they may not be here six months from now, or you may not be here.

Despite the fact that I smoke, I've really become conscious and concerned about my physical self. I do t'ai chi and try to exercise every morning. I'm very bad at those sorts of things. I took stretch and strengthening at Halifax Dance when I was 167 pounds and started to lose weight at that time, but I really wanted to feel better. It was hard work but provided the catalyst I needed to do it at home too.

When you're young, you feel that you're invincible and will live forever. Then, as you get older, you realize the vulnerability of everybody – and I think having children does that to you too. I know people who are almost frantic about the passing of time. A painter friend who's in her seventies, it's almost as though she can't slow down. I want to do both: produce and really enjoy too.

And then there's the empty nest syndrome. I always self-confidently proclaimed it wouldn't bother me when the children left. "I'm liberated, and I have my work to do." That was my attitude. But with each one that left, I missed them tremendously. It was hard. I wasn't different.

AM: Your work indicates a sensual person. Has that changed over the years?

CWH: My daughter is always teasing me about seeing the erotic in everything. I am a fairly erotic, sensual person, although as I get older there isn't that drive. I was having a conversation with a friend of mine who's a lesbian, and she now just wants to be considered an individual; she doesn't want to be labelled. I was thinking about my own sexuality in those terms and decided that if I wanted to describe my own sexuality, I wouldn't say I was a heterosexual or a lesbian, I would say I'm monogamous.

I have quite a few lesbian friends, and when you first have a friendship with somebody – if you really like them – you're often quite physically attracted to them as well. That's always been true of me, whether they're men or women, although I've never had a lesbian relationship. So, describing myself as monogamous would not rule out the possibility that I might someday have a relationship with a woman.

I remember in the sixties, when people were sleeping around and extolling sex for sex's sake, it was considered really important that you could enjoy sex with almost anybody, like you would enjoy a good meal. I tried it, but it didn't work. I have to be in a relationship and really care about somebody. Gordon and I have been together for a long time; we had our twenty-fifth anniversary last year, and it's still passionate, although you don't have the raging hormones that you did at twenty.

Sex, for me, is also part of communication. If we're not communicating because Gordon is so busy, I'm busy – sometimes we barely see each other – then we have to get away. That's sad because we both love this place, and we're trying to work towards treating it as a get-away, to say "Okay, now we're going to have a vacation, only it's going to be here." It's really hard to just pull out the wine and not answer the phone, not mow the lawn. So yes, sex is still really important, and I think my work is very sensual at times.

AM: What motivates you in your work? It's so totally involving.

CWH: From very early on, I always drew and drew and drew. It's genetic, I really think so, because I know a lot of artists who had a grandparent or other relative that painted. I wanted to go to art school, but my parents insisted on secretarial school.

When I got married and moved to Indiana, I took courses in literature, creative writing and basic fine art painting and drawing. And I read Betty Friedan. It was like a revelation, although it was nothing that I didn't know: it was all there, just needing to be activated.

Around the age of twenty-four, I made a decision that I was going to be an artist. From then on, everything was geared towards that. I left my ex-husband and went back to Toronto with my two sons, Geoff and Ken.

AM: Did you feel you couldn't grow in the marriage?

CWH: Oh, no. We probably never should have married. We were too young. I was way too dependent, with this vision of "happily ever after." Every relationship I had in those years, I was looking for my father. And so I'd enter into these relationships where men would dominate, and I would be insecure.

At Indiana I had a wonderful friend I used to often talk to, an older woman. Finally, she said to me, "I'm not going to talk to you any more, because you come here so freaked out, and you lay everything out, then you're okay and you carry on for another week. I suggest that you see a specialist." That was a hard thing for somebody to say – and a wonderful thing.

So I went to this psychiatrist. For an hour, he sat there, saying nothing, and I went blah, blah, blah, blah. At the end of that hour, I knew that I had to leave my husband, and I did.

I went to Toronto, where I eventually met Gordon. After living out in Don Mills in ghastly government housing and taking some terrible painting course from a teacher who taught by method, I heard about the Three Schools on Bloor and Brunswick. I went there to model and to study. Then I moved to downtown Toronto and lived there for a number of years.

AM: How did Clam Harbour enter the picture?

CWH: In the seventies there was a "back to the land" movement, when all sorts of people were going off to farms. I remember Matt Cohen and Suzie Bricker bought a farm in Kingston; others went out west to British Columbia and so on. Gordon and I were living on McPherson Avenue, just above Yorkville, and we decided to move too. We looked at Greece, looked at Scotland, thought about the West Coast, but since my grandmother was still alive, we wanted to be where she could visit. Eventually, Gordon and a friend came down to Nova Scotia – which had cheap land and rave reviews – and by luck found this place – an old hotel with outbuildings and two hundred acres.

So we bought an old chocolate-bar truck, painted a face on the front of it and put bunks in it for us all. Geoff was ten, Ken would have been seven, and Thea was just turning two. Gordon had his beard and long hair; I had my long dresses and granny glasses. People here must have thought we were really weird. My kids tell me that the first day I took them to school I had on a long dress and carried a cigarette in a cigarette holder. *I mean!*

We respect the local people. A lot of come-from-aways come in and try and change everything. The lifestyle and work of the people here are really valuable, although things are changing, of course. But we feel accepted. Sure there's the odd rumour that I have an inheritance or that we're selling the house. When I did a male nude series, that raised quite a few eyebrows. But I think people are really proud that they have an artist in their community.

When I had my first show, the Clam Harbour Collection, at Mount St. Vincent Art Gallery, we got a small grant and had a bus pick up the residents from around this area and take them to the gallery.

AM: Great move.

CWH: People who had never been in a gallery came to the show, including a lot of fishermen. I found out later some of them are mad photographers – taking pictures of the sunrise, the water. And they have that sense of space. Even though my work was quite abstract, they really related to the space of the work. Yeah, it was really neat.

AM: Coming here must have had quite an effect on your work. Your environment here is so powerful and different from the city. You're in the countryside, beside the ocean, with your animals and gardens.

CWH: I literally didn't see the house until we moved here because Gordon had found it. After we arrived, well – you know when you have flying dreams and you're skimming over the edges of the tops of the trees with this wonderful feeling? – I felt like that. I just felt like my soul and my spirit had been loosened and also planted at the same time. And I've never felt any differently in all the years I've been here. It's just the right place.

When we left Toronto, I instinctively knew that I needed to be alone in the sense of not being in the city with a zillion friends and the phone going all the time. I get very involved with people and relationships to the point where it's not good for me because I've only got so much time. This was my saving grace. If I'm feeling depressed, I can just go for a walk on the beach with the dog. You can't go for a walk with a big dog named Parsnip and not smile. This place is so for me; it's so soothing yet exciting and stimulating.

There are times in the late winter, probably April, when it's beautiful anywhere else in Canada, but here everything is kind of grey to beige, and not even an interesting beige. I'd just like to miss that entire month. But then spring starts to happen and the sap starts to move.

When I started trying to work outdoors, the expanse is so phenomenal that I didn't know where to focus, because I wanted to just encompass it all. So I started using a wash that would limit the space and then I focused in on certain areas of ocean or sky or whatever. I produced a whole series of watercolours and some smaller oil paintings, but then the work just got enormous – six by eight feet, big heavy stretchers. Poor Gordon. I had my studio upstairs, and when the work was done, we couldn't bring it downstairs. He had to cut a door onto the roof in order to lower it down. So he's always encouraging me to work smaller.

My work has been going back and forth between representational work – usually drawings – to fairly abstract paintings. Sometimes in working, I get to a point where I know that I've come to the end of that trail, and then I have to branch off. My way of branching off tends to be to work in different ways.

AM: Yes. Your work has varied greatly in terms of the objects – nudes, landscapes, flowers, animals as well as abstracts – and also in terms of technique and style. You've even produced a video.

CWH: Yet there is the thread of what I'm interested in and what I'm trying to address. At this point, I think my main themes have to do with life, death and regeneration. Ten years from now it may be different. The work is also an exploration of me and a self-referencing. So it's what we were saying earlier, that at certain junctures in your life, you get back in touch with yourself – where you look in the mirror to see who you are, or you change at forty and you change at fifty, or you have children and you change. It's that – a very literal way of looking at myself – but it's also much more. I go inside of flesh, inside the body. Rita McKeough saw that in her poem about the collection. A lot of her work has to do with the body and inside the body – actual organs and workings as a kind of metaphor for life.

AM: Aside from your art, what are the plans for the future?

CWH: Garden, garden, garden. Gordon and I have our own business. He does museum displays and all kinds of corporate identity stuff. I'm just a partner. The business used to be in the back room, then it moved to the end of the driveway, now it's in a huge building. Gordon is working too hard – last night until ten, then off this morning at seven-thirty.

He's five years younger than me, but he has high blood pressure, and he needs some time.

I just want to be rich and famous! Seriously, I want to make some money and alleviate some of his stress. We're a profit-sharing company and are now considering an employee buyout, which would leave us with less than half of the shares of our company. Gordon does everything really well, from dealing with people, to design, to hands-on carpentry. What we need is a clone.

The bottom line is he needs to work less, and I would like to make a living at my work. I'd certainly be happy with an A grant that gave me $35,000 and a chance to add to the coffers. Clam Harbour seems ready for a small gallery. We get a huge amount of traffic to the beach on weekends, and tourists want to buy something from the area other than plastic lobsters. We're also thinking of building two self-contained places where people could come, be private and have beautiful surroundings.

We're sort of looking towards our retirement. Of course, we'll never really retire, we're not in that mode. Gordon wants to work on the woodlot, do more fishing, finish renovating the house. So that's what we're trying to work towards. It seems that the kids are all pretty well settled. Although my mother says it never ends.

HEATHER BUNKOWSKY

The need for people to dare and dare again is an idea that often arises in **Heather Bunkowsky**'s conversation. From repairing farm machinery to helping the needy at home and abroad, her own ability to extend herself continues unabated.

Heather lives and farms a few miles from her birthplace in southern Manitoba, where she and her sister assisted their widowed mother in becoming one of the first women in the province to head up a family farm. Heather, her husband, Bob, and their six children created a family singing group that has performed across Canada and in Germany.

HEATHER BUNKOWSKY: I love the freedom of farming and working outside. Nearly every day I can do something new or different, such as treating the grain seed, seeding, servicing the equipment. The other day I had to go out to burn some of the wood and straw left from spring flooding. And last fall we got an open all-terrain vehicle that I love to ride. When I was a teenager, I always thought, "Oh, it would be great to ride a motorcycle." So, this is the closest thing I have to a motorcycle. Recently, I was driving down the road on this new four-wheeler and just started laughing out loud. I said, "Well, thank you God for the opportunity to do this; it's just great!"

So many things like that can happen when you allow yourself to learn new things. A couple of years ago, I was frustrated about not being able to fix some of our farm machinery, so I took a welding course. I was the only woman in that course, and I found it very challenging, but I learned a lot. Even though I don't practise welding much now, I know how to do it.

I always loved the farm. When I was young, my father and I were very close; we worked outside on the farm while my mother and only sister, Cynthia, worked in the house. My father was like my best friend. When I was thirteen, my world really fell apart because he died of a heart attack one day, right in front of me. That was a very traumatic time in my life.

ANDREA MUDRY: What happened after your father died?

HB: My mother decided to keep on farming. She was really quite a pioneer in that she was one of the first women to farm on her own. She was also the first woman director on the local school board and got very involved in politics. My mother is a very independent, assertive woman. I think she got that from her own mother, who became a widow when she was seventy-five and at that age tried to keep her farm going. Mother has a grade eleven education, which was good in those days, but she loved the farm and wasn't afraid of work. I think, too, she was afraid to move to the city and raise two teenagers by herself.

We had 480 acres at the time, and our struggles to get a hired man just didn't work out. So, my sister and I learned how to run the machinery while mother did the trucking and all the hard, physical labour.

Growing up without a father was difficult a lot of the time. My dad was thirty-two when he and mother married, and forty-eight when he died. "Well, they'd been married sixteen years," I thought at the time, as if that's quite a while. Now, I think life is just beginning at that age. Oh, I missed him. He would have been such a support in my life.

When I was finishing grade twelve, I thought of being a missionary and wrote away to a lot of Lutheran colleges. I was very gung-ho. But then I started looking across the field at Bob, a neighbour, and began to think there was something for me there. The way I had my first date with Bob was very unusual. We had always been neighbours; that was all. I used to go there to use their phone because we didn't have one at home. However, this one Saturday night I had a date, and he came along when, as usual, I brought flowers to the church. When we were coming out of the church, my date opened the door for me, and just then Bob came gliding past. His friend jumped out of their car, pulled me into it, and they drove off with me, leaving my date standing there. Then Bob took me to his home. He said to his mother, "I always looked on this little neighbour girl. She is my new friend." That was how we started courting, and we got married when I was nineteen.

I had always said I wanted a large family of twelve children. Well, needless to say, I didn't have twelve, but I got halfway there with five girls and a boy. Six is a lot. Raising the kids was a real joy and a blessing for both of us, although sometimes we'd think, "Oh, we can't handle another one." I don't even know how to explain it, but I always knew there was a purpose for each one.

AM: Most of your children haven't gone into farming. Why is that?

HB: The girls have taken up teaching, social work and policy analysis work for the government. Heidi and her husband, Jamie, were getting into farming, but he died a few years ago when he fell off a silo. Our whole family just loved Jamie. He was born and raised in London, Ontario, and was a city guy, but he kept saying he wanted to farm, and started to do it. Heidi just jumped full force into farming too. They were poor, but they were having such a good time. Life was definitely hard for us all without Jamie.

Our son, William, is just graduating from high school this year – he's giving the valedictory address – and may take up farming when he finishes his schooling.

I think they haven't taken up farming for different reasons. Generally, the men our daughters married weren't farmers. And then there's the economics and uncertainty of farming. Really, there is so much uncertainty. We have to depend on the weather so much. We've had drought and a tornado, and in 1984 two hailstorms really set us back for a while. And now farming depends so much on the politics. It seems more and more that we're dependent on American policy and what they're going to do to our markets – that really affects us a lot.

AM: Over the years, you developed a band with your children called Family Spectrum that has travelled all over the country and beyond. How did that happen?

HB: Music was always part of my family's background. Bob played the guitar with a group; then he moved to drums because they needed a drummer.

When the children came, I usually enjoyed having them around doing things. Sometimes, with our house full of kids, one would be playing the stereo, two fighting, one crying and Bob would be practising his drums in the basement. At times I thought, "This is enough to drive a person crazy." That was before we built an addition and had just the small part of the house. One day, Lisa ran to her father in the basement and said, "Dad, Mom is out on the road walking." Well, he came up right away and yelled out the window, "What's the matter? Why are you walking?" I said, "I just have to walk for a minute to get my sanity back because it was so noisy in the house." But then, our church got a group together for a musical, and we all ...

AM: You started making music together, rather than noise separately!

HB: Yes. Bob would line the kids up on chairs, because they were little, and then he taught them how to sing harmony. We travelled all over with this musical and had a very good time. There were nineteen in our diverse group: singles, married people and kids. When our pastor moved away, it ended. But we kept singing as a family, and over time developed as a group playing different kinds of music – pop, country, gospel. When William, the youngest, was born, he actually slept in a guitar case lots of times. In 1982 we had a twenty-one-day tour in Germany where we played in churches, schools, on a ship on the Rhine, and at the consulate general's house in Düsseldorf.

AM: Do you all play instruments as well as sing?

HB: Yes. Angela plays flute, Heidi plays keyboard, Lisa plays all kinds of guitars, Lorelei plays bass guitar, Shannon plays keyboard and William plays drums. Once, when we needed a drummer, I worked hard and surprised myself and probably everyone else by learning to play the drums.

During the 1980s, we made three albums that we sold while performing at concerts and fairs in various places, such as Saskatchewan and Alberta. Once we were invited to perform at Toronto's Canadian National Exhibition, but that was for two weeks at harvest time, so we didn't go. Now the group is changing because some of our children have other commitments, but we still play.

AM: What is so pleasurable about the musical group that you make room for it despite what must be an extraordinarily busy farming schedule?

HB: People have always said, "You must have so much fun." We do enjoy playing, but it's not just fun. A lot of hard work goes into getting ready, sometimes a lot of arguments, real battles. We resolve these battles by having a meeting and giving everybody a chance to say exactly how they feel and what they think without any judgment being put on it.

That's the way we always operate – by the democratic process. As you can imagine, we have diverse tastes in music; some prefer pop, some country, and some gospel. We always vote on questions like what music we will learn, whether to accept an invitation to perform. And the majority rules, no matter what.

AM: Does "the majority rules" go for other aspects of family life or just for your music?

HB: It goes for other aspects too, because the kids were a really big part of our mixed farming operation, which is now more than nineteen hundred acres – we own half of it and rent the rest. We grow a variety of crops – oats, barley, canola, flax, peas, and this year for the first time, fava beans.

From the time they were small, the kids had to work hard. But that responsibility meant that we also listened to their opinion about the operation, about whether we should plant more trees or whatever. We always gave them the opportunity to make some money by taking on a special responsibility, such as raising chickens or pigs. My daughter Lorelei helped out in the house because Bobby and I didn't have hired men. I work out in the field just like a man does, and service the machinery, which takes a lot of time.

AM: You've had a lot of changes in your life, especially lately with the children leaving home. Have you been changing too?

HB: Spiritually I feel that I have matured a lot over the years, especially in the global sense. My world was pretty small when I was young; as a teenager, I didn't think much about my global family. When I got older and had my children, I started to realize how important all families are. Whether you live in the poorest place or the wealthiest place, you love your children and they mean a lot to you. This realization brought home a sense to me that because I have been given much, I have a great responsibility to share. Whether it is with money, grain or knowledge, if I can help, I will try to do so. There are so many times when we feel so helpless and say, "Well, what can one little person do?"

Just as an example, some time ago, the situation in Rwanda was on the news. It just overwhelmed me to see those mothers with their babies, suffering and starving. When we were at church, we got a letter requesting help from the Canadian Lutheran World Relief. We were sitting in the church at offering time. All of a sudden, I poked Bob beside me and then my daughter Lisa in front of me. "We've got to put on a concert in the park," I said. "Well, we have to do it within ten days because harvest time is coming," Lisa warned.

So we started right away to make arrangements to use a tiny centennial park in Rosenort. The next day, we decided we should also have food for the people and sell it to make more money. Okay! So we made posters. Then neighbours came to help and we made piles of food – four hundred hamburgers – although we didn't have a clue what was going to happen. We put up signs on the highway. It was really quite funny when I think about it. I just said, "Lord, I don't know what we're doing but we'll leave this in your hands." And we did, we really did. People came, we put on the concert, and when all was said and done, we gave the money to the Canadian Foodgrains Bank representative who was there that night. We were just dumbfounded because there was $11,400. Who would have ever thought!

AM: How many people showed up?

HB: I think there was about four hundred or so. But then there were off-shoots. First of all the *Winnipeg Free Press* got word that this had happened – that this country hicktown had raised this kind of money out of the blue. Then the two TV stations, CBC and CTV, got hold of the story, and people responded by sending in all this extra money to the Canadian Foodgrains Bank. Then the development agency, CIDA, matched that times four, so it worked out to over $60,000 in the end.

We just need that little push to step out and do such things, whereas so many times we'll say, "Well, it won't make any difference," or "I can't do this." There's a saying: "Anybody who hasn't had a failure is an amateur." I believe we need failures in order to learn, grow and gain self-confidence. If we don't try, none of this will happen.

Generally now I feel that if I take risks, like in trying a new project, I have nothing to lose even if I fail. I only have something to gain in trying something new. Yesterday, for example, I was washing the floors, which always gives me sore knees, as does bending on my knees to work under machinery. I said to Bobby, "You know, I'm going to invent something to make work like this easier, maybe a pair of pants with foam in the knees, something loose and comfortable to slip on over cloths." Bob said, "Why don't you go for it, do it!" It's just a silly thing, but maybe if I made a couple of pair and see if somebody would want them – who knows?

Also, I now realize now that time goes so quickly. Here I am, at midlife. I'd like to stop rushing around quite so much and enjoy some of the things that there are to enjoy.

AM: Has your relationship with your husband changed now that the children are leaving and you have more time for each other?

HB: Bob and I have always been good friends. He greatly encourages and supports me in anything I want to do. We've made a point of having coffee together every morning. It's an important time for us, and that's when we usually make our major decisions. We just know we have to depend on each other a lot. It's kind of comfortable.

For our thirtieth anniversary last year, our kids had a surprise party. "Mom and Dad, you are going to go on a holiday to Mexico," they said. Well, we didn't know how to tell them. Bob thinks water is okay to drink and to bath in, but not to go and sit beside. However, California has a big farm show that we always wanted to see and never had the opportunity. So we said, "Well, would you mind if we went to California instead?" "Oh no," they said. "As long as you go away from the farm." So we went, and it was very nice. Now our kids are starting to see what we need. In the past, we were always concerned about their needs.

As I get older, I've certainly had a number of physical changes that I always try to look at with a sense of humour. You know, the aches and pains: maybe your knees are hurting today, or your elbow or neck. Or maybe you have a bunion here or there. You think, "How do these young people view me? Do they look at me like I used to look at old people, and say, 'Ho, look at those bunions!'" So I try to keep a sense of humour. You can either be really down about the physical things that are happening to you or else just make the best of them.

I think about that saying: "Life is like a grindstone. It either wears you down or hones you up, depending on what you're made of." We can learn from our frailties too. When my mother started wearing glasses, I remember thinking that would never happen to me because my sight was so perfect. Of course, it did happen, and that's okay.

AM: How do you manage with all the demands of physical work on a farm?

HB: I try to do things in a different way, like lift things differently. On the farm now, we have big machines to do a lot of the work. There's much more climbing up and down, mind you. I really do try to exercise in the off times so that I keep my muscles in shape. And I find that I can work out stiffness, like cricks in my neck.

I do find that it's hard to lose the weight now. But I look at it this way: am I going to spend all the rest of my years worrying about my weight, or am I going to be happy in what I'm doing, and try to be as healthy as I can be. You can start to feel really self-conscious about yourself, which can hinder you from going on and doing some other things, like water-skiing or whatever.

Because of fibroid tumours that gave me pain all the time, I had a complete hysterectomy three years ago. It actually made me feel a little better. Then, because my ovaries were removed, I was supposed to take estrogen. I had a lot of problems with that, because you read so many different opinions about whether or not to take hormones; so, on my own, I decided to cut back to half of the dosage. Just recently, I read a list of all the benefits of hormones. One is that anybody with heart disease definitely benefits from taking estrogen. Many people in my family have died young because of heart disease – my father, aunts and uncles, grandparents. So, I take half.

AM: What plans do you have for the future – for the farm or other activities?

HB: If William is going to farm, I would like to be a support to him in a non-interfering way. If he's not going to farm, I would like to see if we could gracefully retire, which I know will be difficult for me because I am so tied to this farm. Bob and the kids have always laughed at me because I often rub my hands on my knees and say, "Well, it's time to get going," and want to be on top of everything.

AM: With nineteen hundred acres, I imagine you have to keep on the move.

HB: It's going to be hard to scale back and leave it for another generation. But then, on the other hand, there's part of me that says, "Oh, I can't wait." Bob and I have talked about going to a developing country to give expertise and support. He has already travelled internationally with an agriculture group. We're on the verge of a complete change in Canadian agriculture, in terms of our markets, our inputs, the way we do things. At fifty, it's scary, but it can be a very exciting time too ...

AM: I think I hear you saying that you're not at the point of seriously thinking of giving up the farm?

HB: Yes, that's right, because physically we're still very able and don't feel ready. For financial reasons, I don't think we should quit either because, in the farming sector these days, nearly every farmer owes a lot of money. I feel we should be able to retire properly.

As for other activities, I don't think I'll ever quit doing community work until I'm in a wheelchair. Even then I think I'll keep it up. I've worked with young people for years; our community has a wealth of children. We have sixty-three in our Sunday school, where I've been teaching since our children were small. I love and care about each one of those kids. No matter what happens to them in their lives, even if they go to Timbuktu, I'll still care about them. We have a little skating rink, which we couldn't have if we didn't put money into it and if we didn't have people who voluntarily work for it. We try to be supportive of all our community events. People usually ask me to donate my time and cooking. And I really like doing that. We put on a lot of fundraisers.

We have so much in our lives. In addition to our children, Bob's family and my family, we know that our community – the people from the Brunkild and Rosenort areas – really care about us. They've shown us that time and time and time again; sometimes it overwhelms me.

AM: How have they shown that they care?

HB: Like, when Jamie passed away, all our family took it so hard, but the work still had to be done. It was fall, a critical time for getting some fertilizer banding done. We were planning to start the day he died. A neighbour came to work in the fields all day, and another neighbour came to work that night. Then more neighbours came to do the chores, and they kept coming. They were just doing things for us all the time, supporting us mentally, physically and spiritually. They really were there for us, upholding our whole family with such love and devotion that we could not do anything else but start to heal.

When we have fun times, the community is there for us too. The support that we got when we put on the concert for Rwanda was wonderful. And I like to know that we show how much we care about them in certain ways.

Recently, when my aunt had a kind of stroke and was put in a home, I began to think that I would like to do some work with the elderly in the community. When I go to visit her, I see all these people just sitting there. None of them has a smile, and I wonder what is in their hearts to make them look so sad. So many times, people get put into these places, and they don't have the extended family to help them. Even if the elderly have the best of physical care, they need a person to visit every so often to talk, or write letters, or just be there. Then they would have something to look forward to for the week.

There's got to be something we can do to help.

T O B I K L E I N

Committed to her work as a therapist for almost three decades, **Tobi Klein** has now begun to explore new worlds in her leisure and work activities.

Tobi has overcome illness to work at the "cutting edge" in several fields of therapy: psychodrama and sex therapy as well as divorce mediation. Whether she is assisting a divorcing couple to separate more amicably or advising a single woman on sexual matters, Tobi says that her greatest satisfaction is in helping people. She is a popular commentator in the Montreal media.

TOBI KLEIN: The head counsellor at summer camp was my idol; she was in social work and went into group work. Until then, I had never met a therapist in my entire life, didn't know what they did. I loved that camp, where I was in my element, and waited for it ten months of the year. I was like the Pied Piper, the camp spirit, playing the piano, the accordion, getting everyone to sing on rainy days.

So eventually, I went to McGill's School of Social Work and pretty well talked my way into it because, having studied maths and sciences, I didn't have one required course. I was their first student to have a combined group-work major and casework program. I really think that my forte is working in groups. My thesis was on group work with adolescents in hospitals.

When I graduated, I worked at the Montreal Children's Hospital, where I did a lot of work with groups and a lot of role playing. The hospital was a great place to work. There was so much to learn and I was having a super time. Then, after I'd been there for about five years, the Jewish General Hospital wooed me away. I went there and started up a group therapy department.

ANDREA MUDRY: If you enjoyed hospital work so much, why did you go into private practice?

TK: I was sick with a severe circulatory problem. My hands would ulcerate when I went out to work in the winters. I used to have my coat torn so that I could wear burn bandages that were like boxing gloves. For two or three years, I spent weekends in the hospital getting treatment, then going to work on crutches, with my hands in bandages. It was very, very difficult. Because of my illness, I was told I shouldn't work, that it was too hard on me. So I decided to go into private practice as a way of working and being sick.

I want to say that battling illness has made me tremendously appreciate the hospital system, which has been very helpful to me. It's also made me realize just how resilient people are. You can go through hell on fire and come out standing on your feet. It's amazing. My family has always helped a lot too. I have a wonderful sister and three brothers.

The change to private practice came at a good time. I had a great reputation in the hospitals and was fairly well known. I just walked out and set up in private practice. I'm probably one of the only people to be in private practice for such a long time. It's not an easy arrangement because you're isolated, and you have to do a lot to get a check on yourself. So, in order to have my work judged by people other than my patients, I was always giving talks in public or presenting at conferences.

You also have to ensure that you get out, which I couldn't for many, many years. Really, I was pretty home-bound because of my illness, which is a peripheral vascular disease, probably one of the worst cases. Now I'm on medication that works very well.

Some people used to call me the capitalistic social worker because I did my work but I also charged for it. These days it's a lot more normal to be in private practice and to charge people.

AM: Are there connections among the various therapies that you practice – the psychodrama, sexual therapy, divorce mediation and individual therapy?

TK: Nope. I've been practising for a long time, and I tend to become very focused on one area, such as psychodrama, and become certified in it. Then I practise for a while and develop an interest in something else. Some of my changes have come about by accident.

AM: The psychodrama was one of your first therapy specializations. How does it work?

TK: The aim of psychodrama is the same as any other kind of therapy. It's a group therapy that uses dramatic methods in order to portray a person's problem. You use members of the group to play the important characters in a person's life. All the members can learn something from each psychodrama by identifying with the problem. We're all more alike than different.

Sessions usually take about three hours, including a warm-up, which is an exercise where you try to find the person who's going to be the protagonist. In the warm-up, I'll say something like: "Think of a time in your life where you were very angry with someone and couldn't express yourself." So that's your opening scene. Then you trace the problem and try to sort it out.

Psychodrama can be used in numerous ways. If you have unfinished business with a person who's dead and you haven't told them that you love them, you can do all that. In psychodrama, dead people can come alive. It's a healing process. And in anticipating major changes, like divorce, people can go through what they would do, who would have to know, and also reverse roles. Then, if they decide to proceed with the divorce in real life, they may have learned how to better proceed, or they may decide it's too hard, and forget about it.

AM: So you can use it to deal with the past, the present or the future.

TK: Yes. Some of my groups are specialized: abused groups or groups of people with physical handicaps, such as cancer and other chronic illnesses. Because of Medicare arrangements, many hospitals are not going to hire a psychodramatist, even though it's probably a much more efficient method of treating people than others that are used. When I was at the hospital, I used it, and I swear by it.

AM: You indicated that it can be a problem to manage as a consultant. Was there a degree of pragmatism in some of the therapy specialties you chose to practise?

TK: I think I was following my interests and following things that I felt I could do well. Like several of my colleagues, I just as easily could have become a psychoanalyst, but I couldn't see myself doing that. I'm active and like getting results fast. Also, I tried to find things that I believe in, such as divorce mediation; I've seen people just taken down the tubes by lawyers. I got into mediation by accident because my clients didn't want to go to lawyers, so I started helping them with their divorces. Now it's not allowed to be both a therapist and mediator for the same people.

The most rewarding work I've ever done in my life was with an AIDS person in the early 1980s. He was someone who had worked in very well known films and other media, was bright and dynamic, but very depressed. Partly because of my encouragement, he wrote his memoirs and became a spokesman on the subject of AIDS. And I became involved in various ways. I did psychodramas at the AIDS conferences and learned much about the problems: Should we tell the family? How do we deal with the lover? The gay community in Montreal was just amazing, organizing volunteers to look after him twenty-four hours a day. He had organized his funeral and memorial service, and it was all perfectly executed.

AM: How did you begin to work in sex therapy?

TK: I began that by accident, too. At the Children's Hospital, my first specialty was in epilepsy. After I left, they sent me a couple with a child who was epileptic and had a behaviour problem. Over time, the child was getting better, but the parents were getting worse. So I had the parents come in alone, and they told me that things weren't good, that the husband was impotent. This was in the seventies, when Masters and Johnson were becoming well known. I said to them, "I don't know how to treat you, but I'll find somebody to refer you to." However, it had already taken them two years to tell anybody about this problem. They said, "We're not telling anybody else. You find this person, you go learn about it and then treat us. We'll pay you for your time." I did, and I helped them.

The interesting thing about this couple was that he became impotent because his wife was pressuring him to have a vasectomy, which he did not want. So he became impotent and then didn't need a vasectomy.

After helping them with their problem, I became interested in sex therapy. I always go to the source, so I went to Masters and Johnson to study and became a certified sex therapist.

AM: You mentioned impotence as a sexual problem. What are the most common sexual problems?

TK: The most common problem I treat today is what we call inhibited sexual desire or sexual anorexia, which is difficult to treat because it is mainly psychological. One person in the couple loses the desire for sex; they never think of it, never want it, never miss it. The causes vary and can include depression, stress, fear of intimacy or the death of someone close.

Another problem is that some people – especially two-pay-cheque couples – just can't fit sex into their lives. They're too busy with the children, the family, jobs. At the end of the day, they pick the kids up from day care and give them supper, a bath, get the dishes done, and then they're ready to flop. On the weekend they're shopping and trying to get organized for the next week. It's hard.

Impotence and premature ejaculation are common problems I get. I also treat a fair number of people in their thirties and forties who haven't had any sexual experience and are intimidated because they feel so out of step with others. I think that the older you get and the less experience you have, the harder it is. It's not easy for some people. And there's a lot of pressure on kids. I worry about them, and have been involved in advising parents on how to talk to their children about sex.

For women, not having orgasms is probably the most common complaint, and it is one of the easier problems to treat. I tell them how to masturbate so they can have orgasms by themselves; then it's easier for them to teach their partner what they need. "Let your fingers do the walking," I say. I'm like a Fuller Brush salesman for masturbation; I really am.

Many people believe the myth that they may have to practise in front of the sex therapist, which is untrue. Everything that's done sexually is done at home.

AM: Have you dealt with many female problems that come with middle age?

TK: Yes. During menopause women develop dryness in the vagina because of hormonal changes. Penetration hurts and many, not realizing it's because of menopause, stop having sex. There's a simple answer: they could use an over-the-counter lubricating hormone cream or KY jelly to solve the problem.

Another problem in middle age is not having a partner. There's a double standard. Men who are fat and bald, if they're in any way successful and have some money, can twirl beautiful young things around their fingers. Whereas women who are very attractive, bright and accomplished intimidate men or have a hard time finding a decent match. I don't think it's worthwhile going out with jerks to have a sexual relationship. It's a pretty depressing thing for women to try to find male companionship, let alone a sexual partner. I mean male companionship that's fulfilling, that isn't abusive, that isn't intrusive, that allows you to be yourself. It's difficult in midlife to find someone who will allow you to be yourself. If you're accomplished, it's difficult to find someone who can accept the fact that you're accomplished and who doesn't want you to give up your accomplishments to be available for his every whim.

It's a problem. I don't know how we're going to solve it; I don't think we can. Also, women live longer than men, so there's a whole range of years where women's sexuality is going to be kind of dead unless women feel comfortable to let their fingers do the walking. The more women can enjoy themselves on their own, the better.

AM: What about lesbianism?

TK: For many women it's not an option. Emotionally, it's not a lifestyle that's going to appeal. On the other hand, I think that there's much to be said about it in terms of having somebody that you can love and have a relationship with.

AM: Now there seems to be a wider acceptance of the fact that people are potentially more bisexual than has formerly been acknowledged.

TK: I think it would be a good option if it were more acceptable. I certainly would encourage it. Women travel well together, do many things together and have companionship. And women do value their friendships. Being a therapist, I sit in a very jaded seat because most of the people that I see – whatever their sexual arrangements – are coming in with problems. But when you see happy gay couples, they're even happier than straight couples. Of course, many of them don't have the responsibilities of a straight couple, such as children. They live better, with panache and flair, and know how to have a good time.

But as far as I'm concerned, for middle-aged women who do not have a sexual relationship and are not looking after themselves, it can be a problem. Of all of the organs in your body, the sexual organs get better with use, and they don't wear out, whereas everything else wears out. Basically, if you're in good health, you could have sex for quite a long time. However, sex has to be enjoyable, and it is enjoyable if people have good communication. Otherwise, poor sex is nothing to write home about.

Women are not usually into casual sex. I always describe it as "kleenex sex": you use it, you throw it out. It's not very satisfying. But men don't feel the same. It's an interesting difference, but I don't think men need sex any more than women do.

AM: In the 1970s, Erica Jong was one of the first to open the door and encourage women to express themselves as sexual beings.

TK: One of the things I still find is that women are reluctant to ask for what they want sexually, despite everything that's been written. They're still not very good at it.

I also find that the double standard still kicks in if a woman of forty-five gets involved with a twenty-five-year-old guy. For older men, it's much more acceptable, which is unfair. As women become more economically independent, you'll see more of this. But for the woman of forty-five who has children in their mid-twenties and goes out with a man who is close to the age of her children, it creates a problem for the children. That's where it gets all mixed up. With men, somehow they do it – they don't care what anybody thinks, and society accepts it to a certain extent. But with women, people say, "How could you do this to your children? What kind of example are you setting?"

So, as women become more independent, there may be some change, but I hope they will use good judgment. Parents do have to take their children's feelings into account because they are affected by what parents do. Men and women often don't realize that their behaviour affects their adult children. It's not true that the children are not affected if you get divorced when they are older and out of the house. They are affected, even though they may be married with their own families.

And for women who are married, maintaining a happy mature marriage is important. Good communication is central. One big problem is that people often don't express their feelings, especially positive feelings, like saying, "I really appreciate what you did." "You're great." "I'm glad I spent my life with you."

I think of my parents when I say this. My parents were in the bakery business together. They had five kids at home, and they spent twenty-three hours a day, seven days a week together.

AM: I have to ask about the other hour!

TK: My mother slept an extra hour and my father sent a driver for her.

When they stopped working, they spent twenty-four hours a day together. If my mother went to the hairdresser, my father would go too.

The hairdresser was on one side, and my father was on the other. It was a phenomenon to watch them together. Then my father was sick for a long time and needed my mother around always. And my mother cared for him with a generous heart. I remember after his funeral, when we were driving out of the cemetery, she said, "It's wonderful not to feel guilty." I think that's the honest truth. She had done and said everything; there was nothing more she could have said to him. Also, my father was able to tell us all that he loved us, and we could tell him we loved him.

So if I have something nice to say, I say it. And if I have something not so nice, I try to work it out. Respect and honesty are so important, and so is expressing appreciation. You can't assume that the other person is going to know your feelings. And even if he or she does know, it's still nicer to hear it.

Couples certainly don't have to do everything together, but it's good to do at least one activity together.

AM: Has being a sex therapist affected your own personal sex life?

TK: I have to say that if you haven't experienced sex, I don't think you could be a sex therapist, but you could still be a therapist and help people. Sex is something you have to experience yourself.

I mentioned that I was really quite sick for many years and often in great pain. I've wondered why I got into sex therapy, and think that sex was the only thing from my body that didn't hurt, that felt good. That's probably what made the difference. It was something that was pleasurable.

Also, during my younger years I tried to have children with my former husband, and we had a policy that we weren't just going to have sex to try to make a baby, that it had to be enjoyable. In fact, I was not able to have children. I never thought I would have to live my life without kids. It took me a long time to get over it and to feel that my life was going to be worthwhile.

I find that when people know that you're a sex therapist, they're always assuming things about your sex life – that you have a wild sex life. But the other thing is that I don't look like a very sexy person and consequently people are always surprised.

AM: But you're attractive.

TK: You know what I mean.

AM: You don't look like a kitten.

TK: And I never did. One of the most striking features when I went to the Masters and Johnson clinic was that most of the people teaching there looked like they belonged in a church pulpit rather than a sex therapy course. The famous Dr. Ruth is the epitome of that. And regarding appearances being deceiving, I've treated a lot of very attractive people who were having sex problems. So I don't think you can judge people who are having sex problems.

Also, being a sex therapist has been helpful in terms of learning things and really coming to live by what I preach: having good communication, having a nice relationship, and respecting each other's wishes to ensure that you're both having a good time.

AM: Has middle age affected you at all sexually?

TK: Well, now that I'm on hormones I don't have problems, but before I had a hysterectomy I had seven months' worth of terrible migraine headaches daily, and nobody could help me. I was taking migraine medication but just felt life was getting unbearable. That's why I went to the menopause clinic at the Jewish General Hospital to see whether there was something that I could do, and they discovered that I had a benign tumour. My gynaecologist had missed it, this obstruction which caused no symptoms other than these horrible headaches. After the hysterectomy, I felt physically a thousand and one times better. I also discovered that I could never have become pregnant because my fallopian tubes were mangled. That was a relief because I had tried so hard to get pregnant, and even after my divorce I wondered if it was a mistake, that I could have tried harder.

AM: How do you find your patients react to hysterectomies?

TK: For some women that I've seen in my practice, just the idea of having a hysterectomy is terrible. And there have been women who've had hysterectomies but received no hormone supplements; hormone imbalance can cause real problems, such as horrible depressions. Sex is even not an issue. Some women are concerned with the idea that they want to be "whole," and that has to be dealt with. There are many myths, such as the idea that you can't have sex after a hysterectomy. I've dealt with people who've gone through that. But I think, by and large, women feel better after hysterectomies. Certainly for me, it was like a miracle – just not having headaches. They just went away as soon as I started hormones.

AM: Regarding hysterectomies, it seems best if women became informed of their options. What other notable changes are happening in your life at this time?

TK: At least for this part of my career, I feel that it's a winding-down time. I would like to write a book, or take some courses, or do some other activity, although I still want to work. I'm a big traveller. Stanley and I have been together for a long time, and we travel a lot. Stanley is also interested and active in politics, and I'm getting more involved too.

If I write a book, it will either be something on sex or divorce, two areas I know a great deal about, or it will be about my own life. When I look at my life, I'm amazed that I was able to carry on working as I did, given some of the difficult periods due to illness. Maybe it was fear that if I stopped I would never be able to get going again. But I also loved my work and was always happy when working. I chose very well, even though it was by accident – I think I was suited for it. It's been good to me; I've been good to it.

Stanley and I have been travelling together for a number of years. Sometimes we go on cruises. Last Christmas we went to the Persian Gulf. We go to exotic, interesting places. It's something we enjoy a great deal together. Stanley has travelled to 149 countries, and I've been to around 80.

I'm very interested in the different cultures. We went to the Persian Gulf for three weeks, and I was often the only woman around. When I came back, I started reading voraciously about Muslim women, trying to understand their way of life. On another trip we went to a part of Indonesia where they have Stone Age people. Last Christmas we went to Malaysia, Singapore and Thailand. I like the different cultures, to see how people live. It's what the whole world's about.

AM: It must help in your practice by enriching your knowledge and giving you a more objective view of our culture.

TK: No. It's purely for pleasure. I'll tell you how it has enriched me. It's made me realize that balance is necessary and that it's nice to do something totally removed from your work. At one time, for me, taking a holiday was ridiculous because I loved my work. Now I don't feel that I have to slog forever in order to feel fulfilled. It's important to work and also do other things to have a better balance in your life.

There are things that I could do in future. For example, if I went to the Eastern bloc countries, there are probably a lot of therapists who would be interested in being trained in psychodrama. Or I could go to live in a different part of the world and do some work as a sex therapist. I might not get paid but would get room and board. Money is still a consideration for me because I'm still fairly young and know that we live for such a long time and may need it. But I probably worry about money less than I did.

And I always tell my friends I'm going to start The Wilted Pussy Willow Manor, a home for all my friends. We're all going to live together and have music, sing-alongs and games. It's going to be like camp. I've maintained friendships with people I went to public school with and I always picture this. I say to them, "Wouldn't it be nice if all of us built this home ..."

RITA SHELTON DEVERELL

Best known as "the face of VISION TV," **Rita Deverell** is committed to shattering stereotypes and challenging people on the way they see the world. "If Canadians are serious about having a multicultural society, we've got to understand each other and be able to coexist," she says.

Rita's career at Toronto-based VISION TV represents the culmination of years of study and experience that included acting, hosting and producing several CBC-TV programs, and teaching at the University of Regina's School of Journalism.

RITA SHELTON DEVERELL: I hadn't thought very much about the demographic issue of a longer life span until a couple of seasons ago when I did a VISION TV show on the breakup of long-term relationships called "The 25-Year Itch." Then I began to notice that around me there were a number of long-term relationships that were breaking up. It seemed to be a bit of an epidemic from where I was sitting. One of the things that I think I found out from talking to a number of people is that the world has changed in at least the following way: when people get to about forty-five or fifty and have been married or together twenty or twenty-five years, they are no longer old because they have a longer life span. At the same age in the past, people may have been equally unhappy with each other or unhappy with their lives, but they were too old to contemplate a change. Now, they can actually say, "What am I going to do with this next twenty or twenty-five years and, for that matter, who, if anyone, do I want to spend it with?"

Later, when I was preparing a speech for people who work in stewardship for Protestant denominations, I began thinking that now men and women in the Western world really do have another twenty or twenty-five years of productive life, unlike people in the Second or Third World. In a classical faith sense, stewardship means more than money: it means how you deal with all of the resources that you have. One of the things I found myself talking to these people about was the stewardship of time, and the fact that many people have gained these extra years. Faced with this incredible opportunity, they can extend their lives by twenty-five years of more productivity or creativity or giving, or they can just throw it away.

So I am saying that, in the Western world anyway, this longer life span is a new development. It actually presents a kind of moral question. Now, maybe I am only thinking that because I think about morals all the time.
ANDREA MUDRY: Well, it's a fascinating perspective.
RSD: And, indeed, there are some differences between men and women in this regard, although I think they both are faced with this challenge. Men more traditionally have been able to follow a life pattern that allows them to experience the kinds of successes or fulfilments in many careers that they wanted to have. So it could be that men are more prone to what I'll call "throwing this time away." Whereas women, who have probably spent a fair amount of that time having children and so on, tend to be better stewards.

AM: This situation may well be changing with the current generation of young women who usually have careers.

RSD: I know a couple of people who, once their children were self-supporting, literally said, "I do not need to earn all this money." They didn't, however, go off swimming in the Bahamas for the rest of their lives.

AM: As in "Freedom 55."

RSD: Yes. One of them, a woman, had been a social worker for the Metro School Board for a very long time. She has a Japanese background and had always done a lot of volunteer social work for her community. When she retired, she set up a volunteer social service agency for the Japanese community and is devoting her time to it. The other person is Roy Megarry, a former publisher for the *Globe and Mail*, whom I interviewed. He retired and now devotes his time to matching industrial and technical needs in the developing world with people here who can provide assistance. The point he made is that he could have kept on in publishing, but he had basically fulfilled his work in this field and no longer needed to earn the money.

AM: If you tend to think in terms of the morality of the situation, how do you view people who choose to just throw this time away?

RSD: I don't feel comfortable judging other people. I'll speak mainly for myself. I think there are some different factors that come with being black as far as this subject is concerned. I never expected to be able to do the work that I do, because I'm black and because I'm a woman – both – although being black is the major factor here. That is, I work at things that in my own lifetime it has been very, very difficult for people of colour to think about doing. So these opportunities have come or have been created relatively recently. Therefore, it is very difficult for me to think of not doing these things.

Now, this is even more true for men of colour. The statistics show us that since employment equity legislation was introduced in both the States and Canada, women of colour have done relatively well. However, men of colour still have considerable difficulty making great strides in the work force. Aboriginal people and disabled people have done the worst. I haven't done any kind of study of this, but for men of colour who have managed to work their way into what they want to be doing, I don't imagine there is a "Freedom 55."

AM: What kind of difficulties have you had in your career?

RSD: I can only think of one occasion, or maybe two, when I've been paralysed by my problems, so to speak. I suspect that people looking from outside on those occasions wouldn't have thought that I was paralysed. But, in my own terms, I was paralysed, although I functioned during that period. All of the problems that I had – and some of them have been serious – came to me at an age when I was able to deal with them. You know, if you're paralysed at the age of two or four or six, you're likely to stay paralysed.

The one that is the most interesting in some ways happened when I was twenty-nine, because this was the first time I had a major discrimination battle at work.

In the mid-seventies, Adrienne Clarkson, the principal host of the CBC show "Take 30," was moving to a prime-time show. They needed a host, and there were a number of people who thought that since I had been hosting once a week, I would make a good candidate. I had a private meeting with a senior manager of the show who said, "I know a number of people think that you would do a good job of this, but I want you to know that you're not even going to be considered because you're black." I was completely dumbfounded. I was astonished. I couldn't believe it. But I didn't even complain. You see, it was like being raped. I said, "What did I do to bring this on?" For about a year, there were days that I couldn't get out of bed. I literally thought I had brought the discrimination on myself.

Then one day I was at a meeting of broadcasters and a journalist said, "You used to be on 'Take 30.' I thought you were doing a very good job. Why aren't you there anymore?" And it just popped out of my mouth, "Because I'm black." And he said, "What?" Of course, he smelled a story. And I said, "I don't want you to pursue this because I haven't pursued it." That incident prompted me to go back and see if I could deal with this matter before it became a scandal.

The person who dealt with it, once I actually complained, was Peter Herrndorf, who was head of news and current affairs at the CBC and became the chairman and CEO for TVOntario. Peter investigated, and one of the first things that came back to me was that the person who got the job was more qualified than me: that person was bilingual and more experienced. For a few minutes after I heard it, that information threw me. But by then, I was able to say, "That may be true, but the fact of the matter is I was told I wasn't even going to be considered for the position."

This tells us something about all of the equity disturbances that happen. You may find one person who's vastly more qualified, but the fact still remains that people who have the minimum level of qualifications should be considered as well.

I give Peter much credit for dealing with that issue fairly and equitably even a year later. The final result was that my request was met: CBC's current affairs producers were told about this incident and were also told that this was intolerable and not the policy of the CBC.

AM: I imagine that now the media are actively searching for people to represent the varied ethnic makeup of the country.

RSD: Yes, but there are traps in that, mainly two. One has to do with experience. This work does take a tremendous amount of background and a tremendous amount of practice for a person to have the necessary confidence. Some inexperienced people get put into positions that they are going to fall from. There is a lot of that going on.

The other trap concerns conformity. Will ethnic people be allowed to be genuinely diverse or will only those people who become clones be chosen – in the same way that women have become accepted in certain kinds of jobs if they act like men. The same thing can happen with ethnicity. So those are the traps. But, certainly, the world has changed, without a doubt. There was a time when nobody was looking for me and, in fact, they were very unhappy to see me. Now people like me are being sought out.

AM: You're turning fifty soon. Has that had any effect on you?

RSD: I don't know, I haven't done it yet. Turning thirty became a crisis for me. I had planned to have a party and invited a number of people. Then this incident at the CBC happened a week before my thirtieth birthday; I didn't feel like having a party and cancelled. It's probably no coincidence that only a few months earlier I'd had a child – so I might have been having post-partum depression – and I'd had this major serious career setback.

Before this incident at the CBC, I remember driving home and thinking – and I guess this is classic thirties crisis thinking – "I have it all. I have this beautiful baby, I have a fine husband, I'm living in a pleasant condominium, and I have all these years left to live. What am I going to do? How am I going to fill in all of this time?" Then I thought, "There's nothing left to do but get a divorce." I realized that was crazy and didn't make any sense.

I understand that at thirty many people have spent so much time trying to get somewhere that when they arrive, they don't know what to do next. So that's a similar situation to becoming fifty, only now there's the extra active years that you didn't think you would have. So now …

AM: Now, you're faced with the same problem. "Oh, not again!"

RSD: At this moment, I don't think there's any problem with being fifty at all. I'm aware that I have a limited number of years where I can physically work very hard. On the other hand, I know a lot more now and can get results with less effort. So that feels good. My ability to conceptualize large amounts of material is greater, as is my intellectual stamina. On the whole, my physical stamina is almost the same. I can still stay up all night for things that please me enormously, like rearranging the furniture or making toss cushions. One of the things that comes of always working long hours is that most of those pleasurable kinds of things are only possible in the middle of the night, and I can still quite manage that.

Last year, our son went to university and we moved. The real-estate agents call this "changing your lifestyle." We sold our house, a very modest semi in east Toronto, then bought a rural retreat and are renting an apartment very close to downtown Toronto – nine minutes from here. So that cuts down on travel time in the city, allowing me to work longer hours and to spend weekends in the rural retreat. Not having a child at home, of course, adds time to my life.

AM: How do you spend that time?

RSD: I work very long hours, especially during the season from September to March. The one day a week that I don't work at all, I spend with my family. My husband and I are quite capable of parallel silences; our biggest activity has always been reading. Although some would not consider two people sitting in the same room and reading books as being together, we do. That's what we've always done. Also, however long the working day may be, it always ends nicely with dinner, candles and wine. That generally happens late, between ten and midnight, but it still happens. And every day I start by cleaning the house, which provides a kind of physical warm-up and gets the task accomplished,

But still, when I turn fifty, it could represent a crisis. I could wake up and read in the *Globe and Mail* that I've just been fired by VISION TV; my husband could run off with a bimbo; or I could decide that choirboys are my thing, and off I go. I could decide that it's all been meaningless, and therefore I will hook rugs. I don't know. It could be that I discover a lump in my breast, as my mother has before me and all of her sisters. This is a kind of a one-day-at-a-time business.

AM: Did they survive the cancer?

RSD: My mother did, but all her sisters haven't.

So, there are all of these possible crises. The other thing that I would have to say about my own life, which harks back to the security question, is that some unfortunate things have happened to me. But none of those things happened when I was too young to deal with them. They happened after I had rock-bottom security. Also, here I am, almost fifty, and nothing bad has ever happened to me yet that cuts to the core of who I am. That's astonishing. I've not had major illnesses or the death of people I love. I have been little betrayed by people very close to me. My one child has never inflicted massive disappointment on me. There have been the usual slings and arrows of a parent and a child growing up, but on the whole he's a person I am proud to know. And I recognize that this is amazing. I can't take any credit for it. It's just the luck of the draw.

Generally, I think that around the age of fifty we should all do at least part of whatever it is we've always wanted to do. If we haven't done it before, then now is probably the time. If we find it's still impossible for this reason and that reason, some of these reasons may be artificial. But I want to add a caution. There's a kind of middle-class, middle-age mythology that suddenly, at this moment, everyone is going to turn into a princess, because I suspect, like all the other eras where one is trying to turn into a princess, that (a) it's not true for everybody and (b) being a princess is an awful lot of hard work.

AM: What are your thoughts on menopause?

RSD: I think it is good that women are talking about menopause in the same way that it's good that women are talking about the whole menstrual cycle and reproduction as something that is normal, natural, ours, and not in any way shameful. It's also important, I think, to realize some of the seasons of our lives. I could be wrong, but I think that the beauty myths are changing a bit and that now it's not only young women who are considered beautiful. That seems to be one of the things to come out of women talking about menopause. So, I think that focus on the postmenopausal years as potentially energetic, potentially attractive, potentially opening up other opportunities, is a really good thing.

Now, the danger with all of this is in universalizing experience: everybody's experience is not positive. I know a relatively young woman who had a baby last year. She's a very productive, organized, intelligent, career woman, and she had a difficult pregnancy. She didn't feel well, she wasn't able to do everything, and she felt very upset about this because she's almost been programmed to believe that this is supposed to go very well. It doesn't go very well with everybody. It just doesn't. Menopause is the same thing.

AM: All part of the superwoman myth.

RSD: Yes. I have one child, who was conceived exactly when I wanted him to be. I was twenty-nine; we decided this was when we were going to have a child. I'd been on the pill for years, went off the pill, we conceived and had this child. At the time, I actually attributed this to my own intelligence and brilliant organization. I have since come to learn that many women with the same profile as mine are infertile. Many in my generation of women who were on the pill and taking high dosages for a long time, and who decided when they were a bit older to produce children, have had terrible times. I only realized this fact when an intern, who was working with me, produced a show on this subject. That's the last time I attributed the functioning of my body to my own brilliance.

I also had a relatively easy menopause. But that's not my cleverness, it's just what happened. I feel that gives me a moral responsibility to make good use of my time and energy.

There is one negative about aging that I should mention. Sometimes I find myself being jealous of the young. This generally happens when I see people starting things: starting families, being in love, having breakthroughs in terms of their work for the first time. Then I want to do that again too. I think that's probably where the people who start all over again in midlife get stuck. You want to have all that fun all over again.

AM: Especially with knowing what you know.

RSD: I have to stop every time I have this feeling, and give myself a good talk about how foolish it is, because what I have to do at this point is be my age. If I'm going to make a contribution, I have to be my age with my experience, and I have to go on after that.

Similarly in teaching, if you put a lot into your work – or even if you don't – you will, of course, have students who exceed you. That's the way it's supposed to be. And the first time it happened, I was really annoyed at that person. On some level I'm still annoyed when that happens. But I'm not so annoyed because I can identify that this is going on. I'm not so annoyed that I only want to work with people who are less talented than I am. What kind of sense does that make? I know that the only way we're going to be able to increasingly do well at what we do is to work with the best people. I suspect that this happens to other teachers, and that's one of the reasons some teachers always want their students to be doing little bits of their work as opposed to their own work.

AM: So much of your education and work have been values oriented. Do you find that your personal values have altered with age?

RSD: No. I still value and am still looking toward the same things as always. It's true that my life has had a tremendous value orientation all along.

I guess the most basic value has to do with the stewardship of the resources that we're given – the profitable use of whatever we have. I have always worked very hard to be sure that, insofar as I have influence – and sometimes that's considerable – people have equal opportunity, equal access. It's also very important for me to create a sense of family in the workplace and in my own personal life – a supportive circle where people are valued. At work, since we're in broadcasting, this is important for the individuals involved, and it's also important because that's what people see on the screen. That's what they receive. And it's important to me personally. It's important that people create, find or build circles of supporting friends; everybody needs and deserves it. It may even be their right.

Something that I've said often is that I want my activity to be about what is ultimately important in terms of what ultimately concerns people. That's what I meant when I wanted to be an actor, and that's what I still think television is about, at least the television that we do at VISION. None of those values has ever changed; they have only grown.

Maybe I don't even have less time to do it. That's an interesting thought. The first time anybody ever did a substantial interview with me was when I was twenty-five and worked for a small experimental Toronto theatre that no longer exists. It was the Studio Lab Theatre and Ernie Schwarz was artistic director. We did a play that ran for more than a year; it was a kind of avant garde hit called *Dionysus in '69*. Nathan Cohen was the interviewer, and it was right before he died. In the interview, he asked me about my goals and I said that I wasn't in a hurry because, after all, I had twenty-five years to do whatever. Well, those years have now gone by.

AM: Yes, this is it.

RSD: And see, that's back to the demographics. When I was twenty-five, I thought there were only twenty-five more years. Whereas now, twenty-five years later, I suppose I can do portions of this work for another twenty-five years. After all, there is one person on my VISION team who is more than seventy.

AM: In future, do you see yourself moving forward with VISION or doing something else?

RSD: I see myself being here in the foreseeable future. There are too many things to do. We've been granted our second licence, and for the first time we have a little bit of money. Until last January, VISION existed on only the money that we earned. Now we have eight cents per subscriber per month, which effectively doubles our programming budget. So there are lots of things to do here.

VISION was licensed by the CRTC (Canadian Radio-television and Telecommunications Commission) to explore anything related to a human being's relationship to the spiritual and associated moral and ethical values. Since we've been on the air, we have increasingly grown into the role we promised to take as resources and skill become more and more available.

For me as a producer, the creation of shows, the creation of particular episodes of shows, and the development of human beings are all very satisfying. Some people adopt and advance our aims in ways that are breathtaking. And then, sometimes, there's a kind of audience response that is uniquely satisfying, either because exactly what you hoped would happen has happened or something even better.

I have a couple of letters here that I'm just working on. Okay, now here's the "bad news" letter. This person says:

> As a Canadian-born, I find many of your programs promoting paganism, homosexuality and liberal lifestyles are morally and culturally objectionable. In my opinion, many of your programs are toxic to the moral and spiritual Canadian environment. I grew up in a wonderful country with high moral and Christian standards. I loved Canada because it was a country filled with Christian love and true brotherhood and devotion. Canada is now spiritually and morally starved. This had led directly to our financial crisis. I would like to request that VISION TV promote Canadian culture and unity rather than diversity. We did have a culture before we became multicultural. Perhaps it's possible for something to be saved but I somehow doubt it. Perhaps through prayer we can find love again.

So, naturally, when somebody tells you that you've got a spiritually based television network and it's immoral and corrupt, that's a concern. On the other hand, that person is not confused; he is seeing what we do. But then you get somebody who writes the following:

> One thing I'm happy about – but I don't know how to say it without being politically incorrect – is that as a WASP type I'm glad to see so many excellent people of varied ethnic backgrounds taking positions of impor-

tance on your channel – many more than on other Canadian channels. Have I said this correctly? I certainly don't want to sound condescending. One doesn't know how such comments sound to others. Is it better to try and risk being misunderstood?

See. This person is right. What is happening here is unique in the world. There is nothing like VISION, certainly not in Canada, but there isn't anything like VISION any place.

AM: In what way?

RSD: First of all, it is an entire network devoted to the spiritual, to moral and ethical values; secondly, it is devoted to the idea that people can meet around some of the most conflicting areas in life, such as faith; and last, there is a kind of respect for diversity that you don't see anyplace else. And that diversity is not just ethnic, it's also cultural, it's also faith, it's also gender, it's also age, it's also sexual orientation, it's also class.

Now there are still two of us here who helped establish VISION more than seven years ago – Peter Flemington, who is in charge of programming and development, and me; I'm currently senior producer and anchor and responsible for all in-house productions. When we leave, that means leaving people and structures in place that will forever nurture the mandate and also evolve. One of the things I need to be doing now is arrange for that eventual departure.

I suspect, beyond that, I will do some teaching again. Given the opportunity, I would do some acting again. It is a very rich profession which I always enjoy. I hope to have the opportunity to be an old lady actor. There are not many in the upper ages, and the discrimination problems that have existed no longer exist, at least not quite so hideously. Only last night I was at the *King Lear* with Janet Wright as Lear, so there's gender gone as a barrier, and race is much less there as a barrier.

AM: Do you have a sense that VISION has contributed to this lessening of discrimination in our society?

RSD: Oh yes. And I think we have an increasing role. We're looking at a world right now that is full of civil war, full of ethnic warfare, ethnic cleansing. This can't continue to happen. There have got to be models for that *not* happening. Canada is a splendid country, and in our own bungling way from time to time we find ways to do things that are unique in the world.

LESIA GREGOROVITCH

"Unified," "integrated," "free" – these are some of the words Lesia Gregorovitch uses to describe herself at midlife after considerable changes in her attitude towards certain internal and external pressures. Lesia feels that she is finally arriving at the place she wants to be, despite pricey roof repairs, a slim budget and the occasional tremor of a tender psyche. And, by embarking on an academic program in theological studies and counselling, she hopes to harmonize a lifelong passion with her wish for a fulfilling life's work.

LESIA GREGOROVITCH: When I got married in the 1960s there didn't seem to be any choice. I didn't think, "Should I get married or not." I was not madly in love. All my friends were getting married. My moral upbringing dictated that I had to be married to have a sexual relationship. So, when you're in your early twenties, who knows whether it's love or raging hormones saying, "Look, let's get on with this. Let's get married! Let's have sex! Let's have a baby!"

I remember my wedding day very clearly. I was definitely not very excited. And that's sad, because I don't think it was fair to Richard. But then again, I didn't consciously know this. It was like a duty. I didn't look upon it as some romantic joining of soul mates. I had to pick someone appropriate for my family, so I chose a person of Ukrainian-Polish background, a member of the Orthodox Church. If I had had a different family structure, it's likely that I would never have married Richard.

My father, who probably understood me better than anyone in my family, said to my mother when I got engaged, "I really wish that instead of getting married she would go to university." Because he was so gentle and humble, he probably felt he had no right to suggest it. When my mother told me that many years later, it was very poignant for me.

ANDREA MUDRY: Yes. Had he said it to you, it could have changed your life.

LG: In any case, I realize now that a lot of women take a man and if he doesn't exactly fulfil their need for a romantic, idealized mate, they project onto him qualities that he doesn't even have. Maybe it's part of the chemistry of romance. I know that's what I did with Richard: I projected, then found out that he just wasn't the person I had made up. And Richard has many good qualities. He was a good provider – I hate that term. He is a good father. He is a good person in many ways.

When my divorce was in progress, I became romantically involved with Lloyd, a musician who had been my guitar teacher. We had a relationship for eleven years which almost ended in marriage three times, but never did. I think I was motivated a lot by the past. I had been with a husband who was so straight and so concerned about money and power. The part of me that just didn't have those values turned totally away. I found a gypsy rover and we had a wonderful time. Lloyd and I opened a music store together. I entered an artistic world which I should have inhabited all along. Again, maybe I hadn't lived that life partly because my family disapproved. I hadn't felt free to pursue the arts when I finished high school, so I became a public school teacher.

So, at that time, the passion inside of me motivated me more than anything. I've always taken great delight in the passionate side of my nature. I like and admire it. I have – maybe too often – given it free rein. I guess I equate passion with life. If I'm not passionate about things, then I don't feel about things, and if I don't feel about things, I can't be alive. Passion to me is the true celebration of my life force.

Some people really do lack passion. I don't know whether they weren't born with it, never developed it or are just afraid of it. I lived with a man for several years, and then he started going out with another woman. He came to me and said, "I'm now pursuing another woman. Our relationship has ended." I was supposed to then immediately cease all feelings, and he couldn't understand the fuss. He didn't have a lot of passion, let me tell you.

AM: You would really have to be dead not to respond to his announcement.

LG: A short time afterwards, on a snowy night, I had been drinking, he had been drinking, and we quarrelled. He said, "I want you out of this house right now." I said, "Alright," and ran down the street in my nightgown and bare feet, holding my wine glass. Then I went back because my feet got cold. He just could not understand why I had done such a stupid thing. It probably wasn't productive; I don't think it was to make him love me again. But, to me, it was a beautiful image – a way of confronting him. I guess I wanted him to see that you don't just say things. If you say things, people will react. He thought I was crazy. And I said, "Well, I like that image of passion – I ran out into the snow, with my hair trailing. It was very artistic."

AM: I certainly get the image clearly.

LG: As I grow older though, I have changed. This is partly from being at university with some incredibly fine professors. Also, I met Aristotle, Sophocles and Plato, and learned so much. As one professor said, "You know, the remarkable thing is that you're not just reading Aristotle, you're having a dialogue with him." I mean, two thousand years later, you're having a dialogue with this man! Those university experiences opened my eyes to the fact that, above all, we have to be balanced.

Now, I know that I'm a very passionate person, but I also know that I have a very practical side and an organized, analytical mind. Both of those are inside of me, and I have realized that passion running wild accomplishes nothing. It does nothing for you as a person, and it does nothing for the world. This doesn't mean that passion should be subdued, but it should be controlled. You can't allow passion to rule your being because it will be chaos, absolute chaos. What your rational mind does is decide when to allow your passion to express itself, so that it's not harmful. I think people who are passionate and don't do that harm themselves and harm others.

Until recently, I never liked this stodgy, rational, practical side because it didn't seem exciting, romantic or interesting. But in the end it *is* interesting. Now I see that part of my growth is in learning to use my passion and intellect together, so that I can become a whole person, unified. It's my feeling that you can't really separate your mind from your spirit, from your body. They're all integrated, part of you.

My view of the world is slowly becoming more integrated. Sometimes I feel as if I've walked to the top of a mountain and can look down and see all around. I can feel inside of me such a strong sense of growth and of being more comfortable with myself and with the world. And my love for the world keeps growing. I cannot understand people who do not enjoy growing older. They must not be growing inside, because if they were, they would have to enjoy it.

AM: You see things in a more complete way than you did before.

LG: Exactly. It amazes me that we live inside a body, yet don't totally know ourselves. Through our interactions, we learn about other people, but we also learn about ourselves. Now I know myself better, as well as others.

At this time in my life, I feel much freer than I ever have before. Maybe it's because I'm not married and my daughters are grown up. I'm certainly not affected by pressures from society or family or anywhere else, as I was years ago. I think that even if I was really being pressured to do something, I would just say, "Nah, I don't think so."

AM: Has your working life also profited from your time at university?

LG: At university I did a major in classics and a minor in sociology, and originally hoped to work in the social services field. Although I did well and got on the dean's list, this proved impossible because of the poor job market. In fact, my present part-time job as a salesperson in an appliances store was the first offered to me after I had sent out more than a hundred applications. I do not see the image of me as a salesperson.

Now I've returned to study part-time for a master's degree in theological studies with pastoral counselling at Waterloo Seminary. I'm currently taking two courses on the New Testament and psychotherapy. It's wonderful – learning, meeting different people and working on my own spirituality. Hopefully I'll get a degree from an American counselling association. This will enable me to do various types of work, in a psychiatric facility or privately with individuals and groups.

My undergraduate work in the classics was a very good background for the theological studies. It gave me a real sense of what the world was like when Christianity appeared, as well as a lot of respect for paganism and the pre-Christian period. As Christians, we usually think we developed such concepts as ethics and morality. They are, in fact, as old as the human race. I've never studied the Bible much, and it's very exciting.

So I see my life progressing as I try to accomplish a lot in my studies and do some other things that I really enjoy. I've become interested again in dance – Celtic dance – and took a weekend workshop with a friend. That was heavenly: dancing all day, learning, then dancing all night.

AM: It sounds as if you're finally where you want to be. How does it feel?

LG: It feels peaceful and right. In fact, a friend used to sing a hymn called "A Gift to Be Simple." The words are: "It's a gift to be simple, it's a gift to be free, it's a gift to come to where you want to be. When you find yourself in a place just right, you'll be in a valley of joy and delight." That's how I feel – which isn't to say I don't have problems!

AM: What problems are you thinking of?

LG: Dealing with my own psyche is one. I feel that I have a great deal of self-esteem but not much self-confidence. I know I like myself. My parents respected and loved me and raised me well to do the right thing. Yet, in class, for example, when I'm surrounded by a lot of people who are very knowledgeable, I become very quiet and introverted. I'm working on it!

The theology program I'm in will take another two or three years, and so I'll continue with my job. The funny thing is that I care so little about sales, yet I do extremely well. I've been selling appliances like crazy. That's amusing. I think it's simply because I like interacting with people. I don't like dishonesty, hard sales, or people pushing stuff on people.

You know, many artists and musicians have to teach because they can't survive by performing. So I'm not unhappy with my work. It's allowing me to survive financially, and if the truth be known, I enjoy the work atmosphere and the people, who are very relaxed and warm.

AM: A lot of people would be disappointed and angry to be selling appliances after sacrificing to attend university at midlife.

LG: I think we make the choice very early to be unhappy or happy. A cousin said to me, "Lesia, everything you do that seems like a disaster turns out well for you." Maybe it's just that when I can't get something, I set my sights lower, or I'm happy with what I have. Now I have a small, highly mortgaged fourplex in Guelph that pays for one of the apartments for me. I'm certainly not living high on the hog; in fact, I'm just getting by because the building has needed a lot of repair work, like a new roof. But I hope to survive financially.

I had a husband who tried to make me feel extremely guilty about not being money conscious. But I also had a father who was a true scholar and did things for the love of it, never because it would bring in money. And it sure didn't. We were poor, financially, but incredibly rich in other ways. I like having money, I like buying things with it, but I don't spend a lot of my time worrying about it and I always seem to manage. I doubt if there is any material thing that I would grieve for if it were lost – maybe something symbolic, like my mother's wedding band. If people saw the state of my finances, they would probably say, "What about a pension, what about when she's old?!"

There's no way except by the hand of divine assistance that I got to buy this building. An old friend brought me $20,000 in cash. It's amazing.

AM: A lot of people do worry about finances.

LG: I won't say I never worry, but I enjoy my life – my family and friends. I get a lot of affection and feel so loved, it astounds and overwhelms me.

I have a friend, a very dear friend, who is a concern because she says, "I really hate living and wish I could just disappear." She's a nurse, a wonderfully intelligent, giving person. I don't understand why she feels that way. What has happened? Is it the result of a difficult childhood, early experiences?

I was blessed with a close, loving family – my parents, a sister and three brothers. I probably bonded most with my father, who was on shift work and cared for me in the daytime while my mother worked. A very dedicated, intelligent, humble person, he spoke Latin, Greek, German and Polish, in addition to Ukrainian and English, and worked as a translator and teacher. He was also an amateur botanist; when we walked through a park, he would give the Latin name for every plant and tree. This incredible love and thirst he had for knowledge he passed on to us, to all the children. It was probably the greatest gift he gave. And I miss him, every day of my life.

AM: And you have two daughters.

LG: Yes. Rachel and Thaïs are two of the greatest blessings of my life and bring me much pleasure. Actually, I had a tubal pregnancy, so lost my first baby. That was on December 21; I'll never forget the winter solstice. Every year I remember that baby. The part that really saddens me is that the foetus was attached to the tube, so it couldn't grow. I just think of this poor thing, going towards death, hopeless.

The births of my two daughters were highlights in my life. I absolutely loved giving birth to my babies. I loved everything about the delivery room: the smell, the sounds, the sight.

It's such an incredible kind of love, that daughter-mother bond. And, at this time of our lives, I think we're especially close, perhaps because they didn't have a father in the house. We went through times, as any mother and daughters do, when there was antagonism, push and pull. But I admire and respect them very much as individuals. They're becoming productive human beings. I would hate to think that I raised two children who just took from the world and gave nothing back. They have different talents and personalities and have both graduated from university, one in history and one in fine arts. It's just so interesting to be with them. We're good friends, but I never lose sight of the fact that I'm their mother. You can have a lot of friends, but just one mother.

Concerning my relationships with men, the situation is less stable. I've always had a man in my life and wonder if it is a flaw in me: that I have to have one. I suspect it's because my father gave me lots of attention. I like men, and they respond with a lot of attention, not necessarily sexual. And I don't find that situation has changed as I get older.

AM: Would you consider marriage again?

LG: I like having a man in my life, I like having a companion. I don't like living alone. But I won't marry just to get married. I know two men right now to whom I could say, "Let's have a relationship," and they probably would. But I'm so focused on my studies that it's not even an issue.

The passion that is working very well for me now is the passion of my Christianity. I feel that it changes me, it allows me to love myself, to develop the way I am developing, spiritually and in other ways.

I was born into a Christian Orthodox home. Church attendance wasn't regular, but my mother was observant of all the religious holidays. And throughout my life Christianity has always been important. In my thirties I had an experience at my father's grave that was what I would call supernatural.

AM: What happened?

LG: About seven years after my father's death, I took Lloyd to my father's grave because I had an overwhelming urge to take a glass of red wine and pour a libation over it. Now this was before I had studied the Greeks and learned that this is actually what they did.

Lloyd and I were very close; we felt like soul mates. He had never met my dad but felt a strong kinship with him because of the things I told him, and there are many qualities they shared. So we went, and I poured the wine. Lloyd was standing on the side of the grave; I was kneeling. And I had this incredible sensation – I don't know how long it lasted – of being in a tableau frozen in time, as if we were in a cube of ice. It was like a flash, it was like thunder and lightning. I looked up at Lloyd, he looked down at me, and I knew something had happened to him too. He said to me that at that moment it was as if he saw me as a little girl through my father's eyes, as if he was my father. And he had the same sensation of being in a tableau frozen in time. Lloyd recently died, and I felt the loss keenly.

I think the Holy Spirit was present at my father's graveside that day. That was the first of two supernatural experiences I've had in my life.

This development with the Holy Spirit was really wonderful because I felt that my passion could express itself. Afterwards I started to study the gospel in a Bible study group. I also became very active in the Anglican Church. Then about six years ago, when I was confirmed in the church, I had a second supernatural experience.

At confirmation, traditionally, the Holy Spirit is supposed to enter into you when the bishop puts his hands on your head. Well, I didn't feel any magic at that point. But later, when I went up to the communion rail for the Eucharist, something happened that absolutely knocked me off my feet. People who don't believe say, "Oh, it was just your imagination." But I know it wasn't. I thought the Holy Spirit would come as a nice warm feeling, emanating inside of me. But when I was kneeling there, I felt a physical sensation of someone coming from the top through every single part of my body, right down to my toes, which just about knocked me out. It was amazing.

And so, since then I say that I have met Jesus Christ and truly became a Christian. Becoming a Christian for me was like falling in love with Jesus Christ. It's as simple as that. There's no other way to describe it. It has changed everything in my life, as being in love with someone usually does, but because I'm human, the intensity of this relationship varies.

AM: You've talked about positive aspects of Christianity. Have you experienced any negatives, concerning your passionate nature for example?

LG: There is not, by virtue of what it is, any negative experiences with the divine. It's impossible. Negative experiences come from the organized church. The people who organize the church are human beings, and human beings fail. However, each century there have been many enlightened church fathers who have struggled to understand the best way to present Christianity in the world. As St. Paul said, "We fall short of the mark, like an arrow." People confuse Christ and Christianity with church. Christ clearly tells us how to live in the New Testament, and you need nothing more than that.

I do have problems with organized churches, especially the hierarchical structure that places the clergy at the pinnacle. I say that I'm simply a Christian who happens to be worshipping at the Anglican church right now. I also worship at other churches.

Today Christians from various denominations are gathering together more. I think we all have to be really understanding and forgiving, because everybody is on a spiritual journey. I don't care if someone says, "Oh, I'm not a religious person." Part of everyone's earth walk is spiritual, whether they choose to pay a lot of attention to it or not.

AM: Where do you see this spiritual journey taking you?

LG: To be the best possible Christian I can, I suppose. I try more and more to walk in the steps of Christ. I'm so far behind. The older I get, the more I realize how very far behind I am. I keep making mistakes.

To be a truly loving human being has to mean to be as close to Christ as you possibly can. And that, for me, means thinking about it in everything I do. It's as simple as overcoming your annoyance with a person or refusing to cut someone off in traffic. Sometimes I think to myself, "How would He have done it?"

Christ's relationship with women was incredible. If you read carefully, you will see that all of the times he interacted with women, women recognized him. This is something we should be proud of. He never had to say to a woman, "Do you understand who I am?" He was constantly saying it to his disciples and other men. "Do you understand me? Do you understand?" They were always the ones who were sceptical. I could not be a Christian if I didn't know that Christ. Considering his times, the interaction he had with women was incredible, absolutely marvellous. He was probably the first feminist.

AM: Is feminism important to you?

LG: I have friends who are militant feminists and see men as the enemy. I can't see men as the enemy. But I do have strong views on what's fair and what's not fair. My idea of equality is that both sexes are of equal value as human beings, but I think that we have different functions because of the very nature of being male or female. It doesn't bother me to ask a man to lift something heavy. That, to me, is just common sense, because I'm not as physically strong. I believe in equal pay for equal work and women's right to gain positions of authority. These are very important issues.

We are affected by our social milieu. All three of my brothers went to university. My sister did not, and neither did I when I was young. This definitely was not due to our parents. It was other messages from society at large. But I still see many young women whose only goal in life is to get married.

AM: Where do you see these young women?

LG: I met them at university when I was doing my undergraduate degree. I see more independence in my own daughters. We like to think that the women's movement has helped, and perhaps these students are a little more independent than we were at their age, but not much.

AM: Perhaps we don't think that it's absolutely necessary to be married because we've been through divorces, and our daughters get that message from us. Most young women grow up in two-parent families, and if they see that model working well, then that's what they'll probably want for themselves.

LG: In one sociology course, where we had a group of young and older women, it was the older women who stressed the need for women to be able to take care of themselves. That was an eye-opener. It's said that once a woman has been divorced, she never loses that sense of independence. For that reason alone, I'm glad I've had the experience of divorce. And I'm certainly pleased that my daughters are more secure in their womanhood.

NANCY GREENE RAINE

Since childhood, when she first went down Red Mountain on her father's back, **Nancy Greene Raine** has belonged to the world of skiing. In the late sixties, her years of self-discipline and determination were rewarded by some glorious wins in competitive skiing – including gold and silver Olympic medals and two overall World Cups. Nancy retired from competition but stayed in the public eye, as she, along with husband Al Raine, was instrumental in the development of Whistler Resort in British Columbia. Now, at midlife, they have moved to Sun Peaks Resort in the B.C. interior, where Nancy is director of skiing and the couple are partners in Nancy Greene's Cahilty Lodge. Besides promoting the British Columbia ski industry, Nancy finds time to assist amateur ski-racing organizations, ranging from the local club to the National Ski Team.

ANDREA MUDRY: In working with your husband, Al, to develop British Columbia's ski resort industry you've certainly stayed in the ski world. How did that chapter of your life begin?

NANCY GREENE RAINE: I first met Al when we were both still racing. Then, after I retired and he took over as program director for the National Ski Team, our paths would cross regularly because quite a few of my promotional contracts involved spin-offs to the team. General Motors, for example, began to sponsor junior ski races, so Al and I would meet at press conferences. We fell in love and were married in the spring of 1969. Our twin sons – Charley and Willy – were born in January 1970. After living in Montreal for a year, we returned to B.C. We bought a little house next door to Al's parents in Burnaby, so I was able to keep up with a fairly busy promotional life for the next few years with the great help that I received from Al's mother, Fran.

Both of us come from B.C., which has such great mountains with lots of snow, and we had both spent much time in the Alps, which often has very poor snow. We felt that skiing in B.C. had real potential. In those days, however, not many people believed that ski resorts could be successful so far away from the major population areas. Al had always dreamed of building ski resorts in British Columbia. We had both worked at Whistler and felt that it had huge potential, not just for skiing, but also as a summer resort. In 1975, when Al left the national team, we began to make serious plans about ski resort development.

Over several years we negotiated with the B.C. government regarding the development of potential ski areas near the Whistler area, but without success. One day Al came back from a meeting with government people. "I've got good news and bad news," he said. "The good news is I've finally convinced them that skiing can have a major impact on the economy in B.C. The bad news is that they want me to go to work for them and draw up a policy for ski development."

AM: That wasn't what you had in mind.

NGR: No. Al and I always wanted to develop our own ski area, even back then, but it seems that we had to set the stage first. At the time we owned most of the private land at the base of Blackcomb Mountain, but without a pro-active government policy for development it would not have been possible to develop it. So we wound up selling our land to the government at our cost; then Al worked for them putting the policy in place and coordinating the development of Whistler and Blackcomb. He has received a lot of credit for Whistler's success, both from the community and from the ski industry.

AM: What were you doing during this period?

NGR: Well, I was sort of the "cheerleader" to Al's "coaching" role in the early years at Whistler. I played an important role in the promotion of the resort, and of course I was busy looking after the children and keeping the home organized.

It was wonderful seeing Whistler grow. When we built our first cabin at Whistler in 1970, there were less than fifty names in the phone book and just a handful of people lived there year-round. You could buy a piece of land for less than $5,000, and most cabins were simple A-frames. By the time we left in 1994, Whistler was a huge success, with a population of more than six thousand full-time residents. We were both delighted that it had fulfilled our highest expectations in terms of quality, not to mention the very positive impact on the provincial economy. It wasn't all smooth sailing though.

In the early eighties, when the recession hit hard at Whistler, it gave us a chance to take a break. Al had been working very hard, and we both wanted to take a sort of sabbatical to spend more time together as a family. We'd always hoped to be able to live in a place where our children could learn French, and I'd always wanted to spend more time in Europe. So we went to the French part of Switzerland, where Al and I were able to work as ski instructors. The boys went to local schools, did very well, and we all really enjoyed the experience.

We never intended to stay, and so after two years away we returned to our home in Whistler and built Nancy Greene's Olympic Lodge, the first Whistler hotel to be financed as a hotel. After working day and night for three years to build it into a very successful operation, we sold it in 1989 when we got an offer we couldn't refuse! We had worked very hard but not that hard.

AM: I heard that it cost you roughly $5.5 million to develop the lodge and that you sold it for about $9 million.

NGR: It was a private deal and we never released the figures, but let's just say that we did very well, as did our investors. When the new owners asked me to stay involved, I signed a promotional contract with them for the use of my name. Then, when the hotel was resold in 1994, it was a good time to change the name and for me to move on.

Al and I had been keeping our eye on Tod Mountain just north of Kamloops, one of the biggest ski mountains in B.C., but underfinanced for many years. The area had just been purchased by Nippon Cable

Company of Japan, which renamed it Sun Peaks Resort and began extensive planning and infrastructure development. We felt that Sun Peaks could become the next major year-round resort in B.C., so we began looking at developing a condominium hotel in their new village. When the Sun Peaks management realized we were serious about investing in the new area, they asked us to move to Sun Peaks and become part of their development team. So now Al is setting up the Resort Association marketing program and I am the director of skiing.

At Sun Peaks, Al and I have once again put together a limited partnership, this time to develop a major $12-million condominium hotel, Nancy Greene's Cahilty Lodge, named after a pioneer ranching family in the area. The first phase opened in time for the 1995-96 ski season, and the second phase the following October. Sales have gone well, and occupancies are ahead of projections. It's been a lot of work, with never a dull moment!

AM: At this time of your life, it looks as if you're "on a roll" and in a position to capitalize on the experience you gained in helping to develop Whistler into a successful resort.

NGR: Exactly. Whistler cannot continue to grow at the pace it's going now without losing quality, and many people there want to limit its growth as was always planned. We feel strongly that now is the opportune time to develop other destination resorts in B.C. Sun Peaks Resort will be the next major year-round resort; then the timing may be right for Cayoosh, a potential resort north of Whistler that Al has been studying since the late 1980s. It's amazing how long these projects take.

For Cayoosh, eight years have passed since we first discovered the area, and all kinds of planning and environmental studies have been done. It was only this year that we finally signed an agreement with the B.C. government giving our company development rights. Cayoosh has fabulous potential, but it's located in a remote valley with no road access, no power or services – nothing. It's a huge challenge that will take years to develop.

AM: This could take the rest of your life and more! What motivates you? It doesn't seem to be just to make money or to have an easy life.

NGR: Our motivation is to build and to create. Here at Sun Peaks we are developing our condominium project in a resort that has been planned by others. It's good experience, but eventually we would like to be in control of a resort's plan from the start. One of Al's great strengths is the ability to conceptualize, then to make the vision become a reality. He's very creative.

Our motivation is not just to make money, but of course we don't want to lose what we already have! Possessions and status and things like big houses, the latest this and the latest that, have never been important to me. Friends, family and relationships are what count. As I get older I appreciate this even more.

AM: What is your life like aside from your work? Have you been noticeably affected by changes at midlife?

NGR: If you mean menopause, for me, it's been pretty straightforward. I've certainly had hot flushes, but nothing that really made me uncomfortable. I remember talking a bit to my mom about what it was going to be like. She said, "Don't worry, it's nothing. I didn't have a problem, and you probably won't either." In terms of energy and emotions, I think it's an interesting period to go through because you're certainly aware that there is a transition and that you are moving on. A common experience for most women seems to be accepting yourself physically. You start saying, "I don't have to dress like a young kid any more." You can wear what you feel good in and be yourself, but I've always kind of done that anyway.

I still have the same short hairstyle I've always had. With a busy life and lots of sports it's great to have a simple hairstyle. After a shower I can just shake my head and don't have to fiddle. Every so often I think about dying my hair, which is starting to go gray. Then I think of the complication of looking after dyed hair and just keep putting it off.

I know that there are lots of cosmetics, plastic surgery and so on to keep you looking young, but if you're happy with yourself, why not let your age show? I'm not interested in taking hormones to feel better because I feel fine already. So, I'm just kind of sailing along through menopause, like most everything else I've done in life, and it's no big bother.

AM: What do you do to keep in shape now? You seemed to be very aware of fitness in the sixties, when a lot of your competitors weren't.

NGR: When I was training hard and competing, I knew that if I wanted to get to the top I would have to do more than everybody else – more physical conditioning, more skiing and just more thinking about what I was doing. When you have the drive, you do what you have to do, and I enjoyed the physical training. After I stopped competing, I still led a very active lifestyle that included jogging and running. I always was more involved in "doing" activities rather than going for a workout or going to the gym, where you're just training for the sake of training. It's the same now; I ski almost every day all winter, and in summer I keep busy with golf, tennis, cycling and hiking. I try to do things that I enjoy, so the physical activity part of my life is also part of my recreation.

AM: That's an important point: fitness can be fun and not just work or a workout.

NGR: Yes, but I respect people who do work out. Their recreation may be in other activities, yet they have the discipline to take the time, three or four times a week, to look after the physical side of themselves. My approach is less disciplined: "Hey, I have to get off my butt and do something!" Sometimes Al and I get really busy and then, because we don't have fitness as part of our routine, it slides. We're building a fitness room in the hotel so we won't have any excuses to get out of shape.

Remember physical education when we went to school? Very little attention was paid to lifelong sports. There was some conditioning, but by the time you got everybody assembled, the class wasn't really long enough to have an effective fitness workout. Those people who were already athletic enjoyed phys. ed. and were the first ones picked for teams. The others, who did not enjoy sports or were poorly coordinated, kind of lost out.

The school didn't recognize that it was important for every single person to come out with an appreciation of the physical side of their development. The situation seems to have improved now. There is a much greater awareness that vitality and youthfulness have to do with fitness and health. For example, thirty years ago, if you had said that intelligent, grown men and women would run through the streets in leotards of psychedelic colours, people would have said you were crazy. It was absolutely unthought of – the lycra phenomenon.

To me, the biggest challenge of getting older is keeping your mind young. I think that age is a state of mind. Someone who is narrow-minded at twenty-five is already old, while fit and vibrant seniors are definitely young at heart.

AM: Middle age is a transition, but you've had several dramatic transitions in your life. Shortly after you retired from competition, you got married and had twin sons. Was the transition from famous athlete to wife and mother a difficult time?

NGR: No, it didn't seem difficult. I was fortunate in meeting the right person, and we were both ready to start a family. It was quite hectic because I was juggling a promotional career and family, but I was lucky to have a lot of help from my mother-in-law. And Al was a big help too, being very supportive of my public role as well as my role as a wife and mother. On the whole, I've been very happy with my life. Sure, you always have some anxious moments about whether your children are going to be happy, but basically it's been good.

AM: How do you think competitive athletics today compare with the way they were in the sixties?

NGR: I think that most youngsters still play sports for the fun of playing. Though there seems to be a lot of opportunity for sports, if you don't have support from your family, it's unlikely that you will become a serious competitor. But that's okay. Many people get a tremendous pleasure out of sport for its own sake.

Sometimes I think it's sad that people spend so much time watching sports on television instead of getting out and doing them! And on television, it's a shame that so much emphasis is put on the lifestyle and the money that sports celebrities make. I've met many professional athletes and sport stars, and without exception, their first motivation is that they love to play their sport.

AM: What do you think about today's Olympics?

NGR: The thing that bothers me most about the Olympics today is that there is still a hypocrisy in some sports where people say that the athletes should be amateurs. Yet everything else around the Olympics depends on money.

When I watch the Olympics, I don't enjoy watching commercial after commercial. I would like to see more actual coverage of the sport. People are captivated by the beauty and the intensity of Olympic competition. I guess I'm being philosophical when I say that, on the good side, we have incredible technical coverage and that it comes as a result of the commercials. The commercial side of sport pays the bills and creates a lot of opportunities for star athletes. I guess that's just the way the world is today.

Time will tell, but sometimes I worry that when successful athletes retire today, they don't give back to their sport in the same way as they did in the past. They don't have the same attachment to their club or team because their careers have, to a certain extent, been taken over by an agent. When you have a chance to give something back to the community and country, I think you should.

I follow closely the very talented athletes – men and women – on our current National Ski Team. It reminds me of the situation that we had in 1965, when the team was based at a university in Nelson, B.C. We were breaking new ground, doing things differently. Today, because of cutbacks in government funding, the team must find new ways of doing things. The athletes realize that if they want to get to the top, they will have to do a lot of things for themselves. I know they'll manage because people in the sporting world are aggressive, dynamic, competitive. They'll get lean and mean and survive.

AM: With that description, I wouldn't want to get in their way!

NGR: Really. But you know, setting a goal to be the best in the world is not normal. You must not only set the goal, but you have to be tenacious enough to stick with it over the long haul. As the years go by, you become more intense and focused, and you willingly postpone having a normal life. As you move up the ranks, the number of people you're competing against gets smaller and smaller, but each and every one of those people is also very intense and very focused. When you are going for the gold, you put up with pain, you put up with deprivation, you put up with lousy travel schedules and all of the negative side of the competitive life. You don't even notice it. You are so tough physically and mentally that you're beyond it. And the interesting thing is, once you finish your sports career and get back into the real world, you still have that mental toughness and an ability to really focus.

AM: Yes. I was wondering how your experiences as a competitive skier have stood you throughout your life?

NGR: Well for sure I developed self-confidence and a positive self image. Some of what I learned came as a by-product, like public-speaking skills, which we used when thanking race organizers or making speeches at fundraising events. Today I have a nice income from public speaking because of this experience.

My own experience was somewhat unusual, since not everyone who competes winds up on the winner's podium. But when I look at my teammates, I realize that they also got a lot out of their competitive experience. They also developed a competitive character and tenacity. In some ways, a person who retires without winning, and then carries on, better demonstrates the real lessons and values of their sports training. It's amazing when you see how many international athletes have gone on to be successful in other fields.

AM: I'm not surprised by that at all. Who are the people you've admired both in and out of the skiing world?

NGR: Lucile Wheeler and Anne Heggtveit both were role models for me. I was fourteen when Lucile became the first Canadian to win a World Ski Championship, which definitely got me interested in ski racing. At sixteen, I made the team for the Squaw Valley Olympics, and had the good fortune to room with Anne Heggtveit when she won her gold medal. I realized that she was a normal person, just like me, and that she was the fastest down the course because she had trained harder and had honed her skiing skills and mental toughness. I knew those were all things I could learn, so it was easy for me to set a goal to win the Olympics. I was right there when she won, and I saw all the telegrams, excitement and her happiness.

When I think of other people who have influenced me, I always think first of my mother and then of Al's mother. They were both down to earth and natural, devoted to their families but also secure in their own values. My mother was a "can do" type of person. In spite of a partially paralyzed arm, she was active in sports, an excellent skier and always game to try something new. She never backed away from a challenge. Both my mother and my mother-in-law were steady and unflappable, with really solid values. Even today, many years after they have passed away, I still try to measure up to their standards. Both of them were true "helpmates" to their husbands, but they also had their own personalities. One of the negative things that I see in the women's movement is a denigration or putting down of the role of homemaker and supporter – helpmates in the true sense of the word. Through my life, I've been a helpmate to my husband.

AM: Has he been a helpmate to you as well? Do you help each other?

NGR: Of course. He's my best friend, and we do all kinds of things together besides work! I know my husband respects me intellectually, physically and for the supportive role I play, and I respect and appreciate him in return.

Everybody's situation is different. If the husband is immersed in business while the wife is busy raising the family and they don't share common interests, there might be a void in the woman's life when the children leave home. At that point I think it would be very important for her to develop new interests, whether it's business, politics, community work or whatever.

I certainly can see how this time of life would be a wonderful time for many women to go out and "do their own thing." The children are grown up, so you don't have to look after them any more, and often you don't yet have grandchildren to baby-sit. Even if you haven't worked outside the home or had your own career, you would have a lot of time-management and organizational experience just from running a household.

For some women, this is a period of freedom. However, others must look after their older parents at this time of life. In today's reality, with Canada's debt situation leading to cuts in social spending, we will not be able to count on support from the government for all our social programs.

AM: It sounds as if you're concerned about our economy. Have you ever considered politics as a career?

NGR: Politics definitely interests me, but not being a politician. When our children were in school I served on the local school board, and my husband served on the municipal council. I've always felt reluctant to lend my "name and fame" to other people's political causes. I think that Al and I are making a good contribution to Canada in working to expand the ski industry. I know the jobs we are creating are real jobs, not government jobs that must be paid for by taxes!

Over the years I've done a lot of reading on economics and politics. Last year, for a contest, I wrote a 5,000-word essay in response to the question "If you were the prime minister, what would you do to improve the standard of living for Canadians and unify the country?" I was thrilled to win the contest against essays submitted by professional writers, academics and economists, and to have the essay published in a Key Porter book.

Perhaps more important, writing that essay gave me the incentive to study our constitution and to think through my personal thoughts on many issues. I am definitely in favour of less government and of the free enterprise system. Like many Canadians, I am very frustrated with the inability of successive governments to solve our deficit and debt problems. Our generation is leaving a terrible debt burden for the coming generations. It is not too late to change, but we need strong leadership.

As our governments run out of money, it is essential that social funding be targeted to the truly needy and that average Canadians take responsibility for helping their own families and communities. In the final analysis real security comes more from strong families than from relying on government support programs.

NONITA YAP

Nonita Yap's childhood in the Philippines has affected her in many ways, especially her attitude towards age and poverty. After years of working as a political activist and then as an environmental planner for developing countries, she has recently undertaken the leadership of a large CIDA project in southern Africa. Nonita views this as an opportunity to implement her vision for development.

Despite growing responsibilities and the fact that she is a self-confessed workaholic, Nonita is learning to relax more and is claiming back part of her life for herself and her family.

NONITA YAP: I haven't had much time to think about age, but I do see the signs of it. I guess it came creeping in. When I first noticed that I had some grey hairs, I would ask my son to pull them out. And I used to blame everybody for these hairs: my son, all my collaborators and the problems of working overseas and whatever. Then I actually remember a moment when I saw that it's the natural process: I am getting old. It's interesting because I then saw it differently. Instead of saying, "Oh, I'm getting old, I'm going to die." I thought, "Gee, I look more dignified!" It wasn't just resignation, but actually wanting to take full advantage of it. You can actually earn some respect with grey hair. In the Philippines they say that Maria Clara is the symbol of the very feminine one – really graceful and almost coquettish, but very slow, gentle and almost fragile. Well, it just couldn't fit me because I'm loud and active.

Jose Rizal said, "Depending on what you do in life, your grey hair can be a crown of thorns or a crown of glory."

ANDREA MUDRY: That's lovely. Who is he?

NY: Rizal is our famous Filipino author. He wrote political books at the turn of the century. This is what he wrote in a dialogue between an old man and a political activist in a book called *Do Not Touch Me*.

I always thought that my grandmother, who brought me up, was very dignified and had the respect of everybody, even though she was probably among the poorest of the poor. When my grandmother passed by, all heads turned because she was known to be a wise woman and had the respect. Given that she was one of the poorest, it was amazing. I always thought of her and said that it would be nice to grow up and grow old like my grandmother. But we are so different. I can't imagine my grandmother running around the way I do.

AM: Why were you brought up by a grandparent?

NY: My mother died when I was two and my sister was five. Upon her deathbed, my mother asked for us to be given to an orphanage because she was so sure that my father would marry again and that all stepmothers are just evil. My grandmother promised. But then, when my mother died, my grandmother decided to keep us.

My grandmother had been widowed at twenty-five and was a very strong woman. She was deprived of all the land that her husband had brought to the marriage by her husband's family, and she would fight for others but never for herself. So, basically, our lives were hand-to-mouth. I don't mean to glamorize poverty, but at that time you could be poor yet still survive and be happy. We were in a place where, basically, you could live off the sea. I'd come home, and we'd go to the sea and we would crack open oysters and eat them raw with some leftover corn grits. It was fun. I'm sure it wasn't fun for my grandmother, but I don't remember really going hungry for a long time. However, today I don't like soup because I ate so much of it then. When there was nothing to eat, my grandmother would get roots in the backyard, boil them, and that was what we had. So I can't stand soup; I can't stand soup. I try.

My grandmother shaped me more than anyone. Recently, my son tells me I'm foolish because I'm travelling so much and not earning more money. I said, "I do it because I have a skill in raising money for my work, and I feel good that I am able to use it to help others." I was glad that I was forced to explain to him, and I think he will remember. I was brought up to think of others, to think of society, to think that there is a value and personal reward in serving others.

My grandmother didn't sit me down and say, "There is a value in serving others," but that is what she did. She would be going out, and I would say, "Nanay, where are you going?" She would say, "Oh, there is a family that is having trouble." And she would walk many kilometres just to be there, because her advice had been sought. So her priorities were very clear to us. She is always my term of reference. When I'm trying to decide something, I often wonder, "What would my grandmother have done in this case?"

From my father, I learned how to look beyond the boundaries of my culture and to appreciate the beautiful. He was Chinese and presented the wisdom of the Chinese sages to my sister and me. But he also appreciated the beauty of other people's cultures; my father spoke beautiful old "Cebuano," my mother's language, and knew traditional Filipino music.

AM: I understand that years ago in the Philippines, when you were probably just a teenager, you were president of the Legion of Mary and worked with the rural and urban poor.

NY: That's right.

AM: Then when you emigrated to Canada in 1970, you belonged to a number of activist groups.

NY: Oh, yes.

AM: Your commitment goes way back. How did it develop?

NY: I think many things made me what I am. There was a time when I did work with the Legion of Mary. I was a very devout Catholic, but even then I got into trouble because I would advocate family planning when the priest would say no. Although I was very devout, I never desisted from analysing and questioning. My grandmother was also critical. She was not mesmerized by the cloth or by position. And you pick that up. So, I was never intimidated or impressed by position.

I especially remember one time, when I was working in the slum in Cibu City as a university student, there was a squatters' area next to the university – just a few blocks away – and we worked there with the Legion of Mary. There was a family and – oh, there was so many kids in this one room. One time, after visiting this family many times, I noticed that there was what I thought was a piece of rug, but actually it was a child. She was severely malnourished and deformed. I think it was Kwashiorkor. Really, it was a child. My mission was to get the parents married in church because the couples living in sin must be married in church. But I saw this child is really in serious illness, so I decided to baptize the child – an emergency baptism. When I came back next time, the child had died. And that, to me, just leaves a vision: what I thought was a piece of rug that turned out to be a five-year-old child. I mean, that doesn't leave you.

There were times when I'd go back to report to the legion, and I was so mad. The impacts of poverty were just so severe. I remember being in tears, and the spiritual adviser said, "You lay off that job. Don't go to that slum for about two months. Go to teach children catechism."

I don't think I've become more hardened to poverty now. I think I have become a little bit more realistic and look for a way of maybe making a little contribution.

AM: You seem to have contributed in many ways over the years. Could you talk a bit about some of these involvements.

NY: I became very involved in anti-apartheid and in a Philippines support group when I emigrated to Canada to do a Ph.D. in chemistry at the University of Alberta. In the early 1970s, anti-apartheid was not mainstream. You could end up being questioned by the RCMP; it was a serious business.

So I was working at all these things, but I was enjoying myself too – going out and travelling. I went to mainland China when it was hardly allowed. And I always had fun with the French Canadian students who also worked for my academic supervisor at the university. They have such a different sort of *joie de vivre*.

When I finished my studies and returned home in 1977, determined to serve, the Marcos regime was in power. Holy Moses, it was scary because my friends were afraid to talk, to express opinions. And then you start looking behind your back. I couldn't live like that. In Canada I had the freedom to discuss, debate and be challenged. There somebody would disappear, and I would ask questions: "Why? What happened?" Silence. Nobody would talk. After three months my brother-in-law actually told me to get out because I was definitely going to get into trouble. So I returned to Alberta because I was already an immigrant.

I was really lost back in Canada. What sustained me at that time was my politics. I became involved in Latin American politics: Nicaragua, Guatemala and so on. But I had lost my bearings; it was not my plan to return. "What am I going to do now with my life in North America?" I wondered.

AM: That would be difficult, to have to leave your homeland.

NY: Yes. Over the next few years, I had many changes. Because I could not settle down in Canada, I applied to CUSO and worked in Mozambique for two years, teaching science to teachers. While there, I married John Devlin, who I knew from Alberta, where he had been an adviser to the Federation of Alberta Students. When we returned to North America, I became pregnant with my son and left chemistry because I was worried about the effects of toxic materials on my child.

Soon I became one of those really radical environmentalists, and my husband couldn't put up with me. He told me to go through another academic program. So, when John got a job at Dalhousie, I backtracked from a Ph.D. and did a master's degree there in environmental studies. When I finished, I encouraged John to do a Ph.D., and I worked as a consultant for different organizations, then eventually came to the University of Guelph's University School of Rural Planning and Development.

I feel that it would be a waste if I didn't use my science background, if I didn't actually deliberately make it contribute more explicitly and strongly to my work. That's what I've been trying to do, especially in a two-year project in India, by emphasizing the role of science and technology in development. I've done work in low-waste technology and policy, which was my focus in my master's program. So both – the policy and the technology – complement each other.

AM: The change in your professional life is dramatic. Have there been other changes in your personal life?

NY: Physically, not much, other than the grey hair. I am more sensitive in the skin, and it's probably hormonal change. A while ago, I had a severe case of eczema, which has never happened before.

We're faced with so many problems, why worry about menopause? I'm concerned about this push for hormone replacement therapy, which treats menopause as a disease. It's not a disease, it's part of the normal cycle. But if we're told a thousand times that we must have a full bosom and to continue to menstruate in order to attract our partner, then we begin to believe it. I have a friend here, a beautiful woman with a wonderful figure, who had surgery on her breasts because she thought they weren't nicely shaped!

In the Philippines, power comes with age, so you almost welcome it because you're not as repressed as when you were young. Once the daughter-in-law reaches a certain age, she gains stature.

AM: How are the young women repressed there?

NY: They have to do all kinds of tasks, such as cooking for the in-laws. Meanwhile, the mother-in-law can decide the names of the children, the schools they should attend, and she can even decide if the young woman can visit her own family.

AM: So your grandmother was respected for her age as well as her wisdom?

NY: Yes. And Filipino culture is matriarchal too. My grandmother brought us to live with my father for just one year, because he wanted to see his children more. She didn't believe in cutting our hair, but my father wanted to because it always had to be washed and braided. One day my father told the maid, "Take the children to the hairdresser." Grandmother just sat there and said, "Go ahead, take them." The maid froze; she never took us. Although my father paid the maid's salary, my grandmother's position as an older woman and the head of the house meant more. That's power. Grandmother didn't have to scream; she knew she had the power.

AM: How does our attitude towards age in Canada compare?

NY: There is no comparison at all. When I first came in Alberta, I actually did some volunteer work for an old people's home. It used to just grab me because you would see these old people so alone. Sometimes I would spend two hours feeding them. I remember there was this one man, and one day his face was just lit up because his family had visited. I inquired where the family lived, and it was just like ten blocks away. That just really answered the whole thing. I mean, they have a car and hardly ever came to visit. I see that there is no respect for old people here.

You know what I love? One of my favourite programs on CBC is "Fresh Air" on the weekends. Old people come and talk about their experiences, and they say happy birthday to eighty-five-year-olds. I think we are missing something. And it's too bad. As they say in the Philippines, "If you didn't know where you come from, you won't know where you are going."

AM: Are attitudes changing in the Philippines now?

NY: There are some changes. In the past, if a young woman eloped, it was like committing suicide. But I know of a recent case of an elopement, and the parents were not upset.

AM: It seems that your perception of age is certainly affected by the culture of your youth.

NY: Yes. I would also like to say that I really appreciated having a child. This was a big change. I never dreamed of having a child. I dreamed of having a house when I was little but I never dreamed of having children. My son, Seán, is a teenager now, and is my greatest source of pride and my husband's accomplishment. I've been living in and out of suitcases, and John has nurtured Seán. A child is a source of frustration and challenge, but also of pride. The child can really teach you a lot about yourself.

When Seán was not even three, I was ready to leave for a conference in Ottawa and I'd had a big fight with my husband. It was seven in the morning, and my son was trying to talk to us. "Excuse me. Excuse me," he kept saying. And we were ignoring him and ignoring him. Finally we said, "What do you want?" He said, "The thing is to compromise."

AM: This is a three-year-old?

NY: I tell you my husband and I stared at each other. And, you know, we stared at each other and we stopped. We actually stopped. But I'd like to add that my son pointed his finger at my husband, not me!

So there are all kinds of things. He really does come up with the most important reminders of priorities in life. I think he has helped me set my priorities straight.

For a time, I travelled a lot as a consultant. Then I realized that my son will be gone in a few years. That's why I decided to take a regular job and came to the university, where I don't travel as much. My husband wanted to come to Guelph because he says this is the place to raise a family. He is very determined in this. Our son is going to have Canadian roots.

Over the years, I've changed in other ways. I used to be a workaholic, and I have deliberately stopped. I'm not going to always work on the weekends. And in the morning I used to wake up at three and start working. Now I can wake up at three, four, five, and for a while just have my coffee and stare out the window.

Many times I've said, "I am very lucky. I love my job, I am making good money, I have a reasonably healthy family, and I am doing what has been fun and I'm having fun." And I think it's important. My husband says, "You must realize that you are one of the very few who have that opportunity to absolutely be doing what they enjoy doing. The majority just slug at a job." And he had to really come down hard on that because I take so many things for granted, and now I really appreciate it. What more do I want? I've got everything going, and it's just at the right time.

AM: It's true. Many times we don't appreciate our luck.

NY: And when I go on my missions in different countries, I live and stay in a hotel or wherever, but I usually work twelve to fourteen hours a day. I never went out for a night because I felt I'm there to work. Now I'm trying to learn to relax. It's been just in the last year that I've learned to actually go out. I went to a jazz concert the last time I was in Capetown, and we had fun. And I didn't feel guilty about it because I'm supposed to be working or because of my family. It's ridiculous. I've been all over the world, but I haven't seen anything of the so-called tourist attractions. I can't remember anything at all. I mean, ask me about Brazil; I can't tell you what night life is in Brazil. So I have learned to be kinder to myself.

AM: But you still must work very hard. I understand that your environmental planning project in ten countries in southern Africa is an ambitious undertaking.

NY: It took a few proposals and a needs assessment, but CIDA accepted my proposal with no changes. I feel like they said to me, "You claim you have a vision for development. Here's $5 million. Use it." This is so unusual, and I feel that I have to appreciate it. That's what is exciting: this is my idea. I don't think such a thing will ever happen again.

And I think I have learned over the years. My development philosophy is totally embedded and intertwined in this project. I try not to use the word "development"; I talk about capacity enhancement because I believe that there is capacity in the region. We need to enhance it, okay? What we are trying to do is strengthen local institutions by strengthening the people in them through training, research, internships and networking.

People who benefit from the project are going to be ones already working, not fresh graduates, not freelance people. The other thing is that we are trying to influence policy. So we are working with people two or three levels down from the assistant deputy minister level in government. And we are also dealing with the private sector and non-government organizations. The project is addressing environmental issues such as sustainable agriculture, as well as planning and management for watersheds, wetlands and ecotourism.

And for resource persons, on subjects such as conflict resolution, we will use people from the regions even though our university has expertise in all these areas. What I am saying is that we are trying to provide an opportunity for Africans to learn from each other. All the consultants that are engaged in the project will be from the region, none from Canada.

It's tricky because we want to show we've made an impact, and this is not so much money for ten countries, but things are going well.

I'm always learning. When I was working on a project in India, I would say, "I'm not Hindu but I swear to you I'm going to be a Brahmin in my next life because of all the sufferings I've gone through. Spare me the lessons, please!"

AM: Does the Africa project have any special focus on women in these countries?

NY: Three out of four of the project's senior staff happen to be women, as are 25 percent of the people in the training program. We're doing a session on gender and land use because it's a major issue. For example, in some areas crops are split by gender: cash crops to men and food crops to women.

I was just talking to some sociologists at our university, saying it's a problem that women in developing countries are portrayed as victims of culture and biology. We have to be careful about generalizing. I think women assert themselves in many ways in different cultures.

A book that I reviewed on development literature showed – sometimes in amusing ways – how women take control of their lives. For example, it told of a Peruvian man coming home to his wife after being with his mistress for a few days, and asking his wife for breakfast. Afterwards, the wife goes to a shop, asks for chocolate and gets contraceptive pills. It's understood that's what chocolate is. So she is taking control of her body. She doesn't have to confront her husband. As outsiders, we only see our struggle here over male domination and how we'll gain a greater role in the professions and government. In different cultures, the struggle takes on different forms. We have to acknowledge what women lose by taking on a struggle. They make the risk assessment themselves. We should try to understand the strategies of the women and facilitate, rather than trying to define what the struggle should be.

AM: I know your hands are full at the moment with this project. Do you have plans for the future?

NY: I think I have been very lucky, so one hopes it doesn't run out. But, you know, because we were so poor when I was a child, I never knew if there would be food when I went home. Yet I never starved; I just went hungry occasionally. And you realize that there's really no point in worrying. I mean, in some ways, things do take care of themselves.

PATTI JOHNSEN

If you're unhappy with your life, there is time enough to make changes, insists **Patti Johnsen**, who urges women to take the risk and "go for it." She reasons that it is okay to have the fear, which gives momentum. In fact, she is only concerned when people aren't afraid or don't recognize their fear.

Patti is no stranger to fear or failure. When she was learning disabled, teaching authorities failed to recognize her liability. When she was an abused woman, society barely recognized her condition. Yet she has embarked on a new career and is helping other women in Alberta.

PATTI JOHNSEN: Some women don't have the advantage of a healthy family in childhood that I had. Because of that background and a lot of hard work, I've managed to accomplish a few things. I've also had a lot of help from other people, especially women. There were times, many times, when I said I couldn't do something: "There's no way I can leave my husband." "I can't raise my children alone." "I can't fight the academic establishment." It was the people who knew me through my marriage, raising the children, trying this and that, who constantly said, "You can do it."

ANDREA MUDRY: So if a person hasn't been born with a solid family background, he or she can go out and find support?

PJ: Yes, that's right. I'm here in Alberta by myself with no family geographically close by, but I've developed a whole family, a surrogate family, of friends, both married and single. Some of them are here without family too, so we celebrate the traditional holidays together and stuff like that. It's possible to make your life, to recreate it to fit you.

The ability to take risks is so important, and I hope more women will risk leaving a job or a relationship or taking on a challenge. A classmate asked me why I exposed myself so, and I said, "Maybe I'll get some answers in life and some healing."

AM: As a social worker now, you often deal with abused women. How important is your own experience of abuse in this work?

PJ: I don't work with abused women because of my own past experiences. I set out to be a social worker, then fell into this work, and here I am. In fact, it frightened me in the beginning, when I was at a college placement, because nobody there knew that I had been an abused woman. When I asked one of the profs at the college what to do, she said, "It's not a problem; just tell the director." And I found it wasn't. In my profession, we talk about self-disclosure, and I kept thinking, "Well, maybe I should tell some of the abused women that I've experienced this." So, when I was working at the shelter as a student, I told a few women. They didn't seem to care. Of course, they were experiencing their own crises. Now I share some of my story only if somebody asks me.

What I do find is that I can meet these women wherever they're at in the process. I guess, because of my own experience and this whole body of knowledge that I've acquired about the feminist model of working with women, I just know how to manage. If, for example, the phone rings on the crisis line, it may be a woman struggling to just get the words out about what's happening. Wherever they're at, I know and I'm able to meet them. It's so important not to try to "rescue" women.

When I'm working at the shelter and a woman has decided to go back home, I find that I'm able to offer her some support. She may be packing her bags and not wanting to look me in the eye. I can say, "It's okay. You've got our number. Don't forget to develop a safety plan, and don't feel embarrassed if it doesn't work out. Check in with us." Then I just have to let her go, let her experience what she has learned, let her be. She will do what she has to do. Women are the best experts of their own situations, and we must never forget that in working with abused women.

However, in order to help pull a woman out of denial, I do use some challenging methods. I'll say, "You just said that he smashed your head up against a brick wall, and now you're saying you can take care of yourself? But you've told me about all these violent incidents."

I can remember my own experience when I was married and first started with a self-help group. I knew that I was at risk if I violated any secrets outside the home. One woman in our group was challenging me to do something that would put me at risk. Now I listen to my gut, and when I'm working with women, I say, "You do what's best for you." Yes, I do find I have a real niche in this work.

AM: Do you mind talking about the kind of abuse you personally had to deal with in your marriage?

PJ: I've done my healing and don't mind talking about it. The abuse varied in degrees and took many forms: emotional, mental, psychological, sexual, financial. It became horrendous after my son was born in 1974. We had married in 1967 and adopted Shauna in 1973. Within two months, I was pregnant with Kevin. Sometimes I like to say I slept through these years, but in reality I was oppressed and didn't realize my basic human rights.

After the children arrived, I was allowed out to get groceries and go to church. We'd go and present this happy little family on Sunday morning. Because we lived out on an acreage and had one car, which I wasn't allowed to use, I was really isolated.

He wanted to control everything. Friends – he really didn't want me to have friends and would make my life miserable so I wouldn't see people. I needed his permission to spend money that I earned at home using my hairdressing skills for the neighbours.

One of the things I did to keep myself busy when the children were little was sewing. I learned to make tailored suits and was really good at it. He did nothing but constantly criticize me about this and everything else: "You're not good enough, just not good enough." "You don't have rights." "It's my way or the highway." "I'll control you and tell you how to spend your money."

Sexually, he had no respect for my wishes. If I didn't want to have sex, that was just too bad. Physically, there was a lot of pushing and shoving, slamming my head around, grabbing me by the throat, threatening me. He always blamed me for his violent behaviour.

AM: In retrospect, do you now understand the basic dynamics of what was happening – why he was acting the way he was acting, why you were acting the way you were acting?

PJ: I think one of the things that kept me in the marriage was that I couldn't figure out why he was acting the way he was acting. We both came from loving families. It was partially a drinking problem. I knew that, and he did get himself involved in AA. When the kids were toddlers, I did take a stand and said, "You do this or else." He did, he cared enough that he did. For a couple of years afterwards, it wasn't too bad, then the mental and the psychological abuse really escalated. By then he knew he couldn't drink and he couldn't physically abuse me. But I wasn't aware of emotional and psychological abuse. I just knew that he had been physically abusive to me and that I had put a stop to it.

Now I see his view of women's place in society. It is to be kept down, oppressed, controlled; he has the right to do what he has to do, and women don't count.

I know now that if a woman stays after the first assault, she is caught in that cycle, unless she gets other information to break it.

AM: Why did you stay?

PJ: Well, we moved to Alberta after our marriage because he couldn't find work as a welder in British Columbia, and we didn't know anybody here. I had experienced so many failures in my life around school. I dropped out of high school when I was in grade ten because I was failing for the third time, but had started to be successful in my work as a hairdresser. I felt that my work was a big achievement, that I was going to marry, and it was going to be good, not a failure.

My one sister was here at the time. She was appalled at what was going on but didn't know what to do. We know now that I wouldn't have listened. I just got caught, you know, I became more isolated and disempowered, and was really caught in it. And of course at that time, I don't even think we knew the label "domestic violence."

I really believe in divine intervention because I decided I had to get outside help when my son was about six months old, and I finally found someone – a priest – to talk to. This was 1974. I expected to go to this priest, tell him everything, and he was going to say, "You'll make it. You'll do okay," and support me in staying in my marriage. I'm so grateful to him because instead he mirrored what was happening to me. "You don't have to put up with this," he said. I needed to hear that, and I needed to hear it from an outside source. From that day, that's when I got into a self-help group, started taking a stand and began to really make some changes, although I didn't actually leave until 1981.

AM: Were you trying to change the marriage during all those years?

PJ: Yes, and also working on myself. Looking back now, with what I know, I realize that the self-help group gave me some mixed messages. But at the same time I knew our marriage wasn't right. My spirit was dying; I could feel it happening. That was a strong incentive to leave.

Just before I left the marriage, I managed to get myself a job in an auxiliary hospital working as a nursing assistant, and I stayed for ten years. It was meaningful work, the pay was reasonable, and it got me out of hairdressing, which I had begun to view as the female ghetto.

Then, in 1986, realizing that I would be working for many years, I began to look around for alternatives. Finally, the only out I could see was to go back to school, despite my terrible school record and learning disabilities. So I went back and did four years of upgrading to get myself to college level.

AM: When did you discover that you were learning disabled, and what does it entail?

PJ: In the early 1970s, my sister, who is a social worker, happened to say to me in a factual, non-judgmental way, "You know, I think what happened to you, Patti, was that you were learning disabled." I never forgot that. Also around 1989, I was in a parent/teacher interview with Kevin and his teacher. The teacher was telling me about Kevin's learning problems, and it dawned on me: "He's talking about me too!"

My disability is pockets of different things, and when you feed in anxiety, the going gets tough. I have a mild attention deficit. I have a deficit in spelling, and I process slowly, as in reading comprehension. I also believe I have a bit of dyslexia. Basically, I compensate by working hard and really paying attention to what helps me to learn. I realized right away that I have to have a quiet place to study, so I would get up at the crack of dawn every morning to study before I had to be on duty at 7:00 a.m.

At every step of the way I thought, "I can't do this." I kept thinking somebody is going to come up behind me, tap me on the shoulder and say, "You're out. You're too dumb, you're too stupid to do it." But, in fact, one little bit of success built on another.

But when I finished college and went on to do social work at university, I knew that I had met a brick wall and needed some kind of help or intervention. Then one of my profs, who started the Learning Disabilities Association in Alberta twenty-five years ago, said in class, "Any of you sitting here who think that you are learning disabled, come and see me afterwards."

So we met and discussed my past record and situation. She told me to get myself assessed on paper so that I could have special consideration, such as a closed room for exams. That was a help, but it was like coming out of a closet at the age of forty-six, and saying, "I'm disabled." I don't like the term anyway; I prefer to say I learn in a different way.

However, the administration later tried to boot me out because I was 0.11 away from a 2.5 grade average after my third year. In order to stay in the program, I had to go and sit in front of university administrators through an appeal process. Another student went through it at the same time. My profs were behind me 100 percent of the way. An instructor from my college, who had become a friend, came and supported me through the appeal process. Finally, the administration backed off. The fact that I was learning disabled enabled them to save face.

AM: This is like one of your worst nightmares coming true. You talk about your disability as "coming out of a closet," then end up having to go and plead your case in front of a group of academics.

PJ: It was awful, absolutely awful. But I thought, "Damn, you guys, you're not going to do this to me." And I had a lot of support on the campus.

So I graduated with my bachelor of social work, and right now I have a contract position with the City of Edmonton's Community and Family Services, which I like very much because their philosophy is preventative rather than reactive social work. It's a generalist position; I work in three areas: with groups, one on one, and in the community. Currently I'm working with a group of abused women, and about 80 percent of the work with individuals is with abused women. The community work entails working on various projects, such as helping mothers establish funding for a preschool.

We're all worried about the effects of government cutbacks. The shelter that I work for may not get any funding in the next few years. Some five hundred families come through there a year. It's scary. What will these people do?

Also, working in a community public service that gives women support when they go back into the community, I see how badly needed it is. I've seen women coming in, getting information and networking with other women, sharing their stories. And when they were struggling – slipping back into denial, saying "yes but, yes but, yes but" – it wasn't the professionals who were helping them, it was the other women. People like me facilitate, provide the forum to bring women together.

I really believe that as more women are brought together, brought out of their isolation, they can learn from each other. If that avenue is cut off, I don't know what will happen.

Then there's the children. There's not enough services or enough resources put into the children that are in these abusive situations. If we really want to stop the cycle, we need to look at the kids. Psychological abuse and emotional abuse are forms of child abuse. So all kids coming out of abusive homes are abused. But unless there's blood on the floor, society isn't going to respond to that. Unless a child has got physical bruises or can say he or she has been sexually abused by a family member, society is not going to respond. So we've got the children in training: the girls in training to fall right into being married to abusers, and the boys in training to abuse women.

AM: Certainly sounds like a serious situation.

PJ: In any case, there's no question that this is the right kind of work for me. I would like to stay working for the city, but I'll bloom wherever I get planted. In my wilder daydreams, I think about renting out my condo and going up north for a year. The other day at work, we were talking about doing social work in Saskatchewan. But then networks dry up when you're away. The people who you know, being in the right place at the right time – it's all so important. It's possible though; I'm in transition. My kids are grown now. Shauna has graduated from university and Kevin is an apprentice welder, and maybe he'll go back to school some day. But they're launched. I believe you can make your life, recreate it to fit you.

I guess that also means that I'm getting older, but that seems to be okay. If I hadn't gone back to school, it may not have been okay because school was unfinished business from the past. Even if I'd failed, at least I tried. Having made it, I can really look into the future and turning middle-aged and say, "Hey, it's not so bad."

The only thing that I don't like is my grey hair. I actually detest it.

The three of us sisters always had this gorgeous natural curly red hair; it was always noted by people. It's a loss to see my hair turn white, but I'm not comfortable with altering it. Some people say, "You look like a platinum blonde now. Did you colour it?" So I'm getting feedback that it looks okay.

AM: But it's not what it was.

PJ: That's right. I certainly feel healthier than I did twenty years ago. I've joined a women's health centre and am so much more aware of good eating habits. I've learned a lot, have a real sense of who I am, and I won't sell myself out for anybody.

When one of my aunts was here last spring, I asked her about menopause. I wanted to clarify matters because I'd heard so many negative comments about it: women saying to me, "Just you wait until you start." I always assumed that my mother, who died in 1972, sailed through it. My aunt agreed with that assumption. "You just tell your friends you're too busy to have it; you're just going to go through it, and you're not going to react to all this kind of stuff," she told me. I'm fortunate enough that I'm not really going through heavy-duty symptoms, but I also think that my positive attitude is important. Sometimes I find myself turning the heat way down, and people don't like it. Other than that, I say, "Okay, let's just get going here, and roll with whatever comes."

My mother really did a lot. I didn't know how much I had lost until I started healing and going through university. Then I began wondering where I got all this strength and these ideas from.

AM: What are you thinking of?

PJ: Well, when I went to school in 1952, she went to work. We often laughed at the story in my family, but it wasn't laughable at the time. When my parents got married in the early 1940s, my mother was working as a telephone operator, and my father said, "No wife of mine is going to work." So she had to quit work; she didn't speak to him for three weeks. But there she was ten years later, putting me in school one day and going to work the next.

"Good for my mom," I say when I look at that. She knew she needed something beyond the home, and she went out and got it. Good for my dad too; he was able to go along with her by that time.

My mother was also very much involved in the community, working at bazaars and so on. And she knew how to put herself together on a shoestring to present herself to society. She came from a family that liked fine things, such as good china, quality suits. She would have one good suit instead of six cheap ones. Knowing how to carry myself into the world, I believe I got that from my mother.

Her passing really took the fear of death out of me. She had a brain tumour and was gone within a few months. My father only died a few years ago. He had Alzheimer's. He wouldn't want us to wail and whine and cry and stamp our feet and say, "How come this world is so unjust." Neither would my mother. We have an optimistic outlook on life and a real faith that there is something beyond this human world of ours.

AM: What relationships have you had with men since you've been on your own?

PJ: When I first left my husband, I went out with someone for a few months. But early on I made a decision to stay celibate. It's not that I'm a prude or don't enjoy sex. Certainly, I was scared of walking back into another abusive relationship. However, remaining celibate gives me the freedom to really get to know the other person and assess the relationship without the distraction of sex.

AM: It's interesting that you made a conscious decision to remain celibate. Men and sex then became a non-issue and you could get on with other things.

PJ: Yes. It was a healthy decision at the time. Not that anybody came my way because I was really busy raising the children, working and going to school. Now I could be involved with somebody because I have the time. If someone comes along, fine. I will still live by the standards I've set. In working with women, I've become convinced that their relationships often get distorted because they become caught up in sex with men too early. Instead of first getting to know each other, becoming friends and companions, they're so often in the sack the first night or within a couple of weeks. They don't get to know each other as whole people. That's the goal: to stay as two separate people. I have a clear vision of what I need and won't sell out for less. So if that person happens to come along, fine. I'll consider. If it doesn't happen, I'm not going to sit back and whine and pine away. Now I honour who I am and what I'm about.

AM: You work with women and see so much. What do you think is one of the most important issues older women have to face today?

PJ: Pensions is one, certainly for me personally. Right now, I'm on contract, and there are no benefits whatsoever. I'm trying to rebuild my RRSPs. What I had was spent on going to university, and now I have a student loan. Within the next few years, I'm hoping that I'll be able to throw extra cash against my student loan to reduce it quickly. It may not be possible for me to get a pension through a permanent job, although I hope it will be. I'm very resourceful, and although money may become more scarce as the years go by, I'll manage and cope with less.

Finances are important for women generally. I also see women in my community here – never mind the women I work with – whose marriages are breaking up, and they have no pensions, no nothing. It's really scary. Yet at the same time, I'm seeing women who are also extremely resourceful, creating and carving a living for themselves, and doing what they want to do. Still, finances are a major concern.

AM: Your life has been very focused on particular objectives until now. What would you like to do?

PJ: Travel is one of my main goals. I want to do what I missed out on in the sixties: staying at hostels, bed and breakfasts, meeting people. There won't be much money, but there are all sorts of different ways to go. I have an aunt in Washington who travels very frugally. We laugh about it. This frugality must be in our genes, but we are creatively frugal, and we have fun seeing how far we can go with it.

This aunt has just returned from Costa Rica. She's seventy-eight, divorced with no children, and has been everywhere – China, Russia. She was always the fun aunt in our family. She told me about a pair of plain black pants that she'd worn as she travelled through numerous countries. Finally they began to wear out. "Well," she said, "what did I do? I just turned them around and wore them backward. Who gives a damn? Who cares when you're going through foreign countries?" To carry and protect her money, she bought men's pants at Goodwill, cut the deep pockets out of them and pinned these pockets inside her own pants. She used to go up into Alaska to pack fish for a couple of months in summertime, to make big dollars to travel.

When she's at home, she lives a lovely life in her community, even though money is scarce. Every Sunday afternoon, a group of women come over and they play Mah-jongg. One evening is set aside for bridge. My aunt believes that if you have a goal and you set your mind to it, you can achieve it. I've decided to take a page out of her book.

WILMA STEWART

Wilma Stewart's candid comments about women's lives in the present and past reveal a perceptiveness that has been sharpened by experience and study. The creator of a day-care operation in Dartmouth, Nova Scotia, she became a business woman who encouraged other business women and advised the provincial government on day-care matters. More recently, her thoughts have turned to history, to the founders of Nova Scotia, and especially to the settlers of Lunenburg County.

"I've jumped so many fences, been the token woman on X, Y and Z," she says. "Now I want to do things that I feel comfortable doing."

WILMA STEWART: When I first started to go through menopause, I was still sitting on a lot of boards that were primarily controlled by men. So you do your very best to be there in your little white blouse and navy blue suit. And about halfway through the meeting, your body temperature begins to climb and climb.

On one board, I had a really sweet man who sat next to me. He could tell by my colour and would just slide that nice beaded pitcher of cold water down to me. One day, when I thanked him, he said, "My wife is going through the same thing, and I really understand."

I found it very harrowing – I mean, it is one thing if it happens in your home, where you can just throw off a sheet or open a window. But if you're in a situation where men may not understand, you don't want to be seen as somebody who has a weakness and you don't want it to affect you.

ANDREA MUDRY: So you try to control it.

WS: That's right, but you cannot be in control, even on medication. You have to accept it. You have to think, "I can ride up and over this and it will finish." I am still waiting for that day!

AM: Do you have any other symptoms to deal with?

WS: Sometimes I get cycles of depression, but I can't tell if it's menopause or just overwork. You get to the point where you can't tie down a cause: maybe you have done too much work, or maybe you have had too much interaction with people, or maybe you headed too many committees. After a while, you can't tell what you need a rest from.

I remember saying to my doctor, a man I've been going to for a long time, "I would like to talk to a woman specialist." He said to me, "What do you mean a woman specialist? That is very sexist." I said "Listen John, you are never going to go through this; I want to talk to a woman who is."

So I went to a physician at the Halifax women's clinic who was remarkable. She said to me, "This is just something we can all get through, and I am going to talk to you in a matter-of-fact way. You can go on your way, not take medication and suffer twice as long. That is entirely your choice. I am not going to say that you must do this or you must do that. I'm going to give you choices, and you decide." There was none of this, "Well, my dear, this is just a fact of life." She was very informative and I appreciated that.

AM: When you talk about medication, are you talking about hormone replacement mainly?

WS: Yes, and I strongly recommend the entire world to have it because you don't even know you're taking anything.

Of course, there are other aspects. You really have to face the fact that you're getting older when you look in the mirror. Last year a woman I know said, "I am going through this, I am getting old." I said, "Oh, that's baloney, we are all getting old. I think you must understand that you are at a different phase of life. You were a young girl, you were a teenager, you were a young mother, you were a mother of teenagers, you were at this point in your career or that point. It's foolish to think that everything is just going over the falls now."

AM: There are usually some notable changes.

WS: Yes. You are not going to be a mother again. You have to face that. However, my mother and my husband's mother had menopausal babies. Those are little surprises in life that you may not need. But generally, you are not likely to be creating a life again, and even though your brain tells you that is logical, your body may grieve. It really may. Sometimes, if you're living with a really obstreperous teenager or whatever, you may think a little baby would be so painless. And you grieve the ability to begin again, to have a fresh life, to have the thrill of this tiny little person that is yours. I have already had four thrills. Who needs any more? But it is not logical, it is an emotion.

Also, so much of life is about your appeal to the opposite sex. Even if you are married, you think, "How does this person see me? Does he see me this way because he loves me, or is it that he doesn't want to say anything to hurt my feelings?" Going through menopause, it seems that all I have done is gain weight, gain fluid and get grey hair, and I just don't have the energy I used to have. I am told that this will pass and I will have twice as much energy if I live through it in a positive way. I am waiting for that to happen because I generally have a lot of energy and certainly a lot of creative ideas. I'm not worried about that. But you do examine your relationship with the person that you live with, or the person that you spend the most time with.

The other person that you examine is that person in the mirror. At so many times I still see myself as someone who is young. I think my life changed when I was about thirty-five, and I still can't decide about that middle-aged, grey-haired lady in the mirror and wonder who in the hell she is, because it can't be me! So as long as I feel young, I guess it is okay.

I had a partial hysterectomy some years ago because I had a lot of physical problems and just couldn't cope. My periods were horrendous and had been since I was young. After I had given birth they were not so bad for a while, but then it reached the point where I couldn't operate, couldn't do anything for four or five days a month. Meanwhile, I had a business, four children of varying ages and a husband who was redirecting his career. Also, I was brought up by my Scottish parents to believe that sickness does not excuse you from doing what is expected of you. After I had the hysterectomy, I didn't have those draggy days where I couldn't do anything.

However, there are a number of positive aspects to this time of life. My children suddenly think I know a lot because now they have children. When they were growing up it was "Oh, Mother!" At age seven your children think that you have "lost it." This goes on until they are twenty-six and have a child and all of a sudden you are brilliant again. I like that, I like being brilliant, and I like my children thinking that I am just wonderful. Now they say, "How in the name of God did you stand having four children? How did you do it? You are wonderful."

AM: What about your relationship with your husband?

WS: I hate to say this out loud because maybe something negative will happen. I feel I am at a wonderful point in my life because I have been married to the same man for thirty-three years and we still are each other's best friend. That is very important and was not the case when we got married. But we have established this "best friend" thing: a lot of exchange, a lot of interaction, a lot of planning together, which our parents did not do. Rick has always been very supportive. When I started to emerge at thirty-five and talked about things I wanted to do, he never said, "Don't be silly. You can't do that." He may sometimes question my rationale, and sometimes I get defensive, but he is a smart man and knows me well. When you have the security of that kind of relationship, then I think you are more bold to try other things.

Yesterday, I said to him, "Well, I think we have about fifteen years of optimum time ahead of us." We may not. How do you know? But now it is just like cresting the wave. What are we going to do? Rick is going to retire in a few years; I'm not because I think we need to have space between us. But we will plan to do things in the winter together, to go away. I have that option because my partner can look after our day-care operation.

Now I think I'm finally growing into myself. I've learned that there are a lot of things that I don't need to do for somebody else's sake. It takes a long time, first to learn that, and secondly, not to do those things. I am getting to that point.

AM: Yes. I've found that it can take a long time to appreciate the distinction between realizing and acting accordingly.

WS: My children are very happy that I got off a lot of boards. My two older sons particularly have lobbied to make me stop things. "Mother, you started this; Mother, you're involved in that. Get off it." You see, you get on this power roll and think you have to be involved, but you don't. There are lots of keen young women coming up behind you to do these things. If you stay in something too long, you think you are the only person who knows how to do it. And you're blocking other people behind you who can do it differently – not necessarily better – but differently.

I take great pride in the Association of Atlantic Women Business Owners, which I helped to found. Now all I do is attend meetings, but I enjoy seeing how other people are carrying it on. The real trick is knowing when to let go and still be able to sit back and enjoy, keeping your mouth shut. I haven't learned to keep my mouth shut yet, but I'm working on it.

I'm really enjoying watching my children as young adults bring up their families. It shows that I did something well. When the children were young, my husband, who was a career naval officer, was at sea a great deal. So I was alone, but I did a lot of activities with my children. Now, I am just thrilled to see my sons doing the same little games and reading the same stories we used to read. Well, my goodness, all of those things stayed in their minds, and that is wonderful. I never knew being a grandmother was so enriching.

Both of my daughters-in-law, of whom I am very proud, are career women who combine working and child-rearing, and they both do an excellent job. My daughter, who is adopted, met her birth mother a couple of years ago after a long search. Now she is very clear about what she wants to do. So I have lots to look forward to just in watching the careers of all the fine young women in my family.

My sons, much to my pride, do everything with their children. They did not learn that with their father, who was never around, and certainly not from either of our parents. It shows you that people have come a long way.

AM: Is middle age a subject that you discuss with your friends?

WS: Everybody is trying to be positive and ride over it. I think that everybody's mother was the same as my mother. I really think that it was a generational thing. It was just difficult for women in those days. I'm sure my mother never even mentioned it to Dad. Now you can read about it, you can write about it, you can take pills, you can talk to your friends, to your husband, who can help you get through it. My biggest fear was that I would be like my mother, who had a very hard time. Talking to friends of my age, I discovered they are afraid of the same thing. For my mother, menopause was horrendous, physically and emotionally.

AM: Did she talk to you about it?

WS: Oh, no. She never talked about physical symptoms or being a woman or any of those things, never discussed it. But I know she hemorrhaged and was very emotional. I was quite ill in high school. After two visits with me, a psychiatrist said to my father, "This young lady doesn't need to see me, but I think her mother should." My parents took me away from that psychiatrist and would not allow me to go back. So my mother tipped the balances at that point. The rest of her life, my father made excuses for her and levelled the ground around her. So I don't know what she was like as a woman, but I do know that the change of life did radically change her life.

AM: Do you think she was better before?

WS: She must have been because she was terrifying afterwards. My mother had an incredible imagination, yet because of her emotional instability, you never knew from one day to the next what form it was going to take.

She was an impossible mother but a wonderful grandmother. When I had our first son, she was ecstatic. She sent parcels from Quebec. The little drawings, the stories, the letters were wonderful; those were little things I remember. That is how I knew the kind of person my mother was inside, even though I hadn't seen that for a long time. I also saw it through the way she interacted with my children. Then, as she got older, she got worse again. I really don't know what her physical symptoms were. For me, that is very difficult because now I'm going through the change of life and specialists have asked me about my mother's symptoms. My sisters and I are going to get together and talk this year. Perhaps I'll learn some more about my mother and her symptoms, and that in turn will help me, I hope.

AM: This is an important point – that you need to know for practical reasons.

WS: I think so. Back then nice ladies didn't talk about periods or being pregnant or anything related. There was a great deal of ignorance and covering up.

When my mother came to visit me about two weeks before I had my first child, she never looked at me below a certain level. She did not discuss pregnancy or childbirth. When she came to visit after the baby was born, she was just royally disgusted by this nursing baby. My mother grew up in a family of thirteen children; only three of them lived. Her parents were incredibly poor, and as the oldest, she was the resident sitter. Her mother was constantly pregnant, miscarrying, aborting or nursing. So you can see why my mother just froze around this whole subject. She, of course, made up her mind that she wasn't going to have any of that stuff done to her. She had all of her babies in a nursing home in Britain, although home births were the norm then. In fact, I was born during an air raid. A bomb hit, blasting off the roof of the delivery room when I was born, which probably accounted for why I was a nervous child!

AM: It certainly didn't slow you down. Tell me about your professional life and your day-care operation, Children's Corner.

WS: Our total registration is about two hundred children at four sites. We have the main site, another site that is preschool and after school, and two sites that are just for lunch and after-school children.

AM: How did this all come about?

WS: I taught elementary grades for many years and really prefer little children because they are very open to things. After living in British Columbia, where I was a good naval wife, we returned to the East Coast, and I worked with small children as a substitute teacher and then in a preschool program before I decided to open my own preschool. That was in the late 1970s, and it really springboarded a change in my life.

I opened a preschool for eight children in my home, and within three years it had a long waiting list. So we built a bigger house up the street. During the day the two lower levels were used for the preschool. I had thirty children every morning and every afternoon, but even then I soon had another waiting list.

One day the person who used to do the licensing in day-care services came to me and said, "You should open a day care." My husband, Rick, drew up a business plan, and we arranged to build a day care in the area where we lived. It took two years of planning and construction. When it was completed, my husband worked with me for a while, but later I took a partner, and then we doubled the size of the day care. It took three or four years before we were actually making any money.

AM: Why do you think it was so popular? What needs were you meeting?

WS: We were in a young and growing yuppie community in Dartmouth, where women understood the need to go back to work. I had an interest and experience in the preschool program and wanted to use it in the day-care program. And I was hiring young women who had their degrees. Also, when we doubled the size of the centre, we added infant care, which can be particularly demanding. We even conduct grandmother tours so they can understand that it is a healthy environment.

We expanded to after-school care as well and now have about seventy schoolchildren. This means we can have a child from the time he is four months right up until he is twelve years old. During that time we are part of the child's family. Our children's parents will ask us when we'll have an opening in the program because they would like to have a second child. They will ask us where they should buy a house because they want to be part of our route for after-school care. Sometimes it is unnerving.

AM: What are the parents of your children like?

WS: Many are very stressed for a number of reasons. Imagine a mother who is a lawyer and returns to work after having a baby. At work, everything is fine for her. She has a schedule and knows what she is doing from eight-thirty in the morning to six at night. But the baby does not understand the schedule and can be up at night or teething or coming down with something.

The worst thing is the grandmother or mother-in-law who is giving parents guilt trips for putting the child in day care. And there is information everywhere: there are parents magazines, there is stuff on television, in newspapers. It is very difficult to know where you are as a parent.

I tell parents to relax, to enjoy the child. They say, "It has to be good quality time." I say I don't want to know about this "quality time" stuff. Why not just turn off the television and have supper together? Many of these parents are so programmed, they say, "He should be having lessons. He is four, he should be ..." Who said "should"? Why "should"? So he learns to swim at seven instead of four and a half.

AM: How did you manage through the growing demands of the business?

WS: You do what has to be done, and then you begin to learn that there are areas where you could expand, skills that you need. When I got involved with other business women, it was just like somebody put a light on; I couldn't believe it. Here I was doing my stuff, and here are all these other women out in isolation doing theirs. It was wonderful.

I was the president of the Association of Atlantic Women Business Owners from 1986 to 1990. But even before it was formed, what worked for most of us was just getting together and sharing.

At one point I was the only woman sitting on the big Nova Scotia loan board. I did all those things, and I can understand why people think women need to be visible. But we would do better to mind our own businesses as good managers and good employers. I don't think enough women are paying attention to that. When I sit down and listen to women talk about the businesses they're in, they are still apologetic, still saying words like "just." For years, I said of my employees that they work "with" me. The day that I grew up was when I said these people work "for" me. I pay their salaries, I sign the cheques. So now, with my partner, we realize that we are responsible for these thirty women.

Staying power is very important in having a business. You may work so long without making money that you think you'll never make money. Some people think I should feel guilty and will say, "You don't make money at this do you?" I say, "I have a family to feed too."

AM: Are more women starting businesses now?

WS: Yes. And many do well. But a lot of women still think of going into business for themselves as something that they "just ought to try just once." I say, "Like, why? It is not easy, honey. Why do you want to do this?" You have to have a real dedication and a will to succeed because you have a lot of things to transcend, and they are not just thrown at you because you are a woman. It is just life. I don't think that men have it any easier.

Nobody tells you how long it takes or what it does to your digestion system. That's what I remember – the ulcers. They don't tell you what it does to your family life. There are certain times when your business becomes the only thing in your life because it has to survive. So you always have to struggle for balance. It's very hard.

AM: Do you find at the association that more women are starting their own businesses at midlife?

WS: More often they do it by default, if their marriage has broken down or they have lost a job. It can be a good option for women as they get older, but a lot has to do with the experience they have had in life. For example, I know a woman on the board of the South Shore branch who ran a restaurant with her husband. Now she's on her own, and I'm really impressed. This is a smart woman who will do well.

AM: You've been involved in organizations concerned specifically with day care.

WS: Yes. For a number of years I was on the provincial minister's Round Table for Daycare, which was formed during a day-care crisis about six or seven years ago. This is a voice that the day-care community can use to speak to the minister, and we looked at many aspects such as salaries and benefits, legislation and finance.

AM: You've also become involved in heritage work, which is certainly a departure from your day-care operation. What is the crux of your fascination with the past?

WS: Part of it is the mystery and part of it is a fascination with a segment of Nova Scotian history that seems to have been invisible up until recently. For example, our house, which was built around 1774, was just covered over with wallboard and linoleum. When they ripped it off, all the original house was there underneath. People covered them up in the 1950s and 1960s because the houses were considered tacky and embarrassing. How many places in Canada can you find thirty-five houses built in the late 1700s? Many are still owned by the original families. It's an important part of Canadian history and certainly of Nova Scotian history.

I don't have any roots. My family disappeared in Scotland, and I have no idea where we came from. But when we moved to Mahone Bay in Lunenburg County my mother-in-law just idly said, "Oh yes, we had some relatives who came from Lunenburg." We found out we could trace my husband's family back to one of the original Lunenburg settlers, and it was just an act of God that we had bought an early house in this area.

Now, I think, more and more people come to Nova Scotia with a very specific interest in learning about early architecture, because in this province we have many gems and a lot of them are right here under our noses. I'm curator of the Mahone Bay Settlers' Museum, and one of the fundraisers we do every year is a tour of six to eight heritage houses.

I've also been doing a lot of research about the town, which once had many shipyards. It was settled in 1754, mainly by two thousand Lutheran farmers from the fertile fields along the Rhine.

Being a woman settler must have been horrible because they were constantly having children. After getting a thirty-acre lot, the family had to work together to clear the land and build a house. They had to grow everything they wanted. Imagine what this house would have been like in the summer, when that fireplace was going twenty-four hours a day, throwing out heat to cook on.

Most of these women didn't even live until middle age, although some lived into their seventies and eighties. But when you look at the records, a man would generally have two wives. What does that tell you? A woman had nine or ten children, then died, often in her early thirties. The men would then marry a younger woman and have another family. So I think it was very rare if they got to middle age, and those that did must have been exhausted, just because everything was so physical and there were no creature comforts. Their only social occasions would be church, christenings – of which there were many – weddings and funerals. I think that would be it. I'm sure they had happy times, but physically their life was very hard. They didn't have to worry about menopause in those days because they didn't get that far.

AM: Your description underlines the fact that it's not just the extra years that women have now, but our whole lifestyle that enables us to have more choices.

WS: Yes, we have the luxury of choice, more than our mothers had. And our daughters will have even more choices.

AM: You think so?

WS: Yes. And hopefully they have us as mothers being good examples in middle age, rather than the examples that many of us had. You just have to look around at all the talk and writing about the subject. The more women understand that it's just a phase, another part of life, the better. It's not the end of life and it's not the beginning of the end of life. How do we know what else we're going to do, how do we know what other options we may have?

AM: Are you entertaining other options now?

WS: There are lots of options, but I don't have to set challenges for myself as much any more. I'll never be able to do all the gardening I want to do, to read all the books I want to read. I read a lot of biographies about women. We can learn a great deal from women like Sylvia Plath or the Brontës, who have tried things and been unique in their own ways. We are not really cutting new paths. Somebody has already done some of these things before. Perhaps not in the way we do now, but for centuries women have been in their own quiet way doing a lot of things.

I read a book called *The Mad Woman in the Attic*, about women who wrote, and they wrote because of confined situations in households, marriages and families. There have been so many women, such as Mary Wollstonecraft, who had brilliant ideas but were repressed or never published because they were not men. All those people preceded us and got us to this point. So we can really help the next generation to do it right.

I don't even know exactly what "right" means. I do know it doesn't mean being militant, or being like a man at the boardroom table, or being taken with your own power. I think we've gone beyond the need to be a man in a skirt. There are more women coming up who can act and interact in a male world. You don't have to be the helpless little flower, you can just be your own person.

DIANE GRIFFIN

Diane Griffin has an easy-going manner, but she is earnest about her conservation work. Recently, her long-term efforts on behalf of conservation – through writing, teaching and working in government and non-government agencies – resulted in her appointment as deputy minister of Prince Edward Island's Department of Environmental Resources.

Through the years, Diane has developed many strategies and attitudes that can be useful personally as well as professionally. However, time is taking a toll on one strategy: her determination to outlive opponents. She says it was a wonderful tactic in her youth, but now she's becoming "a little dubious about how much time I'll have to outlive everyone who blocks any progress I hope to make!"

ANDREA MUDRY: You have the reputation of someone who likes to "make things happen."

Diane Griffin: Unfortunately, we each only have one lifetime, and it goes quickly! If you want to make things happen, you can't put it off. You've got to be prepared to do things all along. And you don't stop at retirement either. If you believe in a cause or idea, you'll continue with it, even on a volunteer basis, as long as possible.

One great example is General Bert Hoffmeister, who became the president of British Columbia's Nature Trust and did a lot of fundraising across the province. This was after he retired from the presidency of MacMillan Bloedel and other business interests, including partnership in a Whistler resort, and he still had a big cattle ranch. Of course, he had also retired as a general from the Canadian army. That guy was making things happen to everything he touched. I didn't meet him until seven or eight years ago, and I found him to be a great model. Wow! That's the way I want to be when I retire.

AM: Not everyone is motivated by an urge to bring about change. In fact, many don't even realize they can.

DG: That's right. Feeling empowered is very important.

AM: When did you first feel empowered?

DG: I guess in my life there's been a series of small successes that grew into larger ones, although it's not clear when the turning point was. I just felt that there are ways to get things done: plugging away and finding allies who seek the same objectives. It's pretty hard to do things all by yourself. Allies are often necessary, but you have to cultivate them so that everybody works together as a team. Then great things can be done in a short time.

Feeling empowered certainly wasn't a sudden big leap for me because sudden leaps are pretty scary! It was mainly a case of hard work. In school, for example, other students may be brighter or getting higher marks, but I found that if you want to give the time and have the determination to do something, you can cover a lot of ground. Ninety-five percent averages don't mean everything.

Knowing what you don't want to do can also help guide you in knowing what you want to do. Realizing some directions that you don't want to take can point you in the general right direction; then specific choices must be made and they often depend on circumstances. I knew, after growing up on a farm on P.E.I., that I didn't want to marry a farmer.

...a a lot of allergies to cats, dogs, cows,
...eathers. I couldn't even raise chickens. So

...st in the environment develop from your childhood
...all?

...I I was young, I think my greatest connection to the environ-
n... was hauling turnips and harvesting potatoes. The environment
meant work out there because everyone in the family helped on the farm.
We also played baseball and whatnot outside, but it usually meant work.
The interest in conservation of the environment really came later.

Originally, I wanted to be a physical education teacher, just like
Anne Murray. We would have overlapped at the University of New
Brunswick, where she did her phys. ed. program! But seriously, my career
path became clearer after I started working as a summer student for the
Biology Department at St. Dunstan's with Dr. Ian MacQuarrie. I graduated with a degree in biology, became a high school biology teacher, then
did a master's in biology.

Botany was my main interest. Some people remember china patterns, but I can tell you when and where I saw a certain plant. When we
were driving along I'd yell, "Hey stop! I saw something yellow!" Some
blossom in the ditch would have caught my eye, perhaps because it was-
n't normally found in that place or blooming at that time of year. When
we were collecting plants for the university in the summers, we were
always on the lookout for new things, so it became a habit.

All my government careers have been in areas of nature protection
and ecological reserves. Now my interests have broadened because my
new employer, the Department of Environmental Resources, has responsibility for a wider range. That is perhaps the biggest change I've made
in quite a long time. The rest was just changing from one end of the
country to another, changing from government to non-government
employment, as when I left working with P.E.I.'s parks to become a natural areas coordinator for the Alberta government, then returned to
P.E.I. to be executive director of the Island Nature Trust.

AM: What have you learned over the years – both in your professional
and personal lives – that is particularly helpful in your present new position as deputy minister of the Department of Environmental Resources?
DG: Probably my greatest experiences derive from all the exposure I've
had to contacts and new ideas at the national and international levels
while serving on national boards and committees. Experience has taught
me that there are many different viewpoints and many different ways to

approach a problem. Sometimes it is necessary to work together in partnership to negotiate solutions. Very few issues are clearly black and white. If they were, they would be so much easier to deal with.

I've also discovered that you cannot let the perfect be the enemy of the good because, if you are inflexible, you can end up with nothing. In working on legislation and recommendations for legislation in Alberta and P.E.I., I've seen that you don't always get what you want. Unfortunately, you may not get the perfect endangered-species protection legislation the first time around, and sometimes, sometimes you take what you can get the first time around with a view to getting stronger amendments later. Not that you compromise principles, but sometimes you have to be tenacious to get what you want in the long term, making gains when you can.

AM: Good thing that we have longer lives now!

DG: True! And I'd like to add that, compared to the short life span women could have expected a century ago, today's longer life span means a great opportunity to raise a family and still go on with a career or other interests that wouldn't have been possible before. Not only our life span, but our social climate has changed. When my grandmother was born in 1900, women couldn't even vote. When we look back on that now, we say, "How could that situation have existed?" But there were people – women as well as men – blocking the idea that women should be able to vote.

I assume that there are going to be a lot of things that we will look back on and wonder, "How could it ever have been allowed?" Child labour is an example of a practice that we wouldn't tolerate now, yet once it was quite acceptable. Slave labour is the same. So twenty years hence, when we look back at how we've abused our resources, being very wasteful of our natural resources and careless in our disposal of by-products, toxic chemicals and whatnot, hopefully we will say, "How could we have been so short-sighted?"

AM: You compared yourself to your grandmother. How would you compare yourself to your mother at midlife?

DG: She still had a house full of children at home. There were eight of us; I was about eighteen years old and the eldest. It was a very different situation. Kevin and I are now on our own and, believe me, we don't have the empty nest syndrome! We quite love it, and we love it when our daughter visits us and we visit her. But we are all very comfortable with our own spaces.

AM: I'm thinking that the pattern of your birth family is representative of part of the change in women's lives. In addition to having longer lives, we are also younger when the children leave home. In the past, women were often busy with many children who were at home for a longer period, and then they would help with the grandchildren after that.

DG: That's true. My sister and my daughter are only a few years apart; they almost overlap.

My mother was also in the traditional situation, in that she had no participation in financial planning for the family and the farm. My father was always very good at it, and that was the usual arrangement in families. So she and my father didn't have the opportunity, as Kevin and I have had, to financially plan together. We both have the same kind of financial values. There are no surprises. One of us doesn't just go off and buy a $40,000 car. Not that we carefully watch each other's bank account, but we agree on our goals, so there's no problem.

The fact is that women now have been more involved in planning for their own retirement. What I hope for my generation is that retirement will be beneficial for us in a way that perhaps it wasn't for the generation ahead of us. But only time will tell. Long-term financial planning for retirement is certainly becoming more important because of longer life spans and the coming impact of the baby boomers on the Canada Pension Plan and other pension plans.

AM: Your life has been very different from your mother's. What is her perception of your life?

DG: She is very pleased about how my career has progressed and the fact that I still have some time to spend with the family. My mother and father are coming down for dinner tomorrow, for instance. Like most parents, she wants to see all her children be happy with secure jobs that they like. And if they can't be secure, at least they should like their work.

Another thing Kevin and I did as a couple, which doesn't often happen, is that we followed my career as opposed to following Kevin's career. Between teaching and being a realtor and an appraiser, Kevin is very adaptable in meeting changes required by my career. This has certainly opened up opportunities for me, and I could take these opportunities when they arose. A big problem generally is being in the right place at the right time and being able to move. Timing and the place where you work and live can be thorny issues for a couple, but I have been very fortunate. Kevin likes variety and doesn't feel threatened by having to make changes. It's been great!

Anyway, when I look back, I guess my mother's path was set pretty clearly once she got married and children started to arrive. Women then wouldn't even think of going on to another career and moving to another province. So it's very different between the two generations.

AM: What else is happening for you at midlife?

DG: Well, my daughter has grown up! She left home and has her own apartment. She works as a waitress. I had hoped she might have been interested in biology and would consider university, but I finally realized that the wrong person is trying to make the decision here. So, relax. She'll do her own thing in her own good time, and I had better back off. She says that a lot of people go to university, don't know what they want and don't know what to do when they get out – and they have a big student loan to pay back. I have to say that she's right there.

In terms of physical change, a couple of years ago I found out that my glasses needed changing. I got those little half-moon executive specs, lost them two weeks later and haven't found them since. So I guess I really didn't need them all that badly. Now, when I'm driving I wear my old glasses, which are fine for distance. Up close, I'm better off without anything, so I don't wear my contact lenses any more.

Another change I'm finding is that I can't party for all hours like I used to be able to. When I was in my twenties, we'd celebrate the end of exams, even though we were exhausted, but I can't do that kind of thing any more. I need my sleep.

And occasionally I find the temperature in a room suddenly feels really hot and sticky; I don't think it's the temperature that's changed, it's my body. So all of a sudden, I'm opening the doors and I'm opening the windows in the office, and my thirty-year-old secretary is freezing to death! That's when it really becomes clear that it's me, not the temperature. She's shivering, sneezing, and I'm opening the windows! These have been some of the biggest changes for me. They're slow and subtle.

In terms of attitude, I find that experience definitely helps me to sift out what is important versus what's not important. When I was a teenager, everything seemed so dreadfully important; now I don't waste time with minor issues but deal with those that really matter. And the things that matter to me haven't changed, although minor expressions of them might.

I still believe in family and am very close to my own family, my brothers and sisters, parents, and until recently, my grandparents who lived until aged ninety-three and ninety-seven. None of that has changed and shouldn't change in the future either. And my concern for conservation, fish, water life, natural landscape, that's not going to change. And my appreciation for my husband, I hope that will never change! We'll be celebrating our twenty-fifth wedding anniversary this summer.

AM: Congratulations.

DG: Thank you. We're really looking forward to many more happy years together. We built this house to suit us now and in retirement, and we want to be able to look over the river for many, many years. Considering the good longevity we have in my family, I think I may be lucky that way. So I tell Kevin to watch his diet, get lots of rest and stay healthy because I want him to be around for a long time.

When we started out, we were graduate students at Acadia University. We met as undergraduates here, got married and went to Acadia. We were so poor. We had an old beater car, a 1963 Valiant that had over 200,000 miles on it. It was a clunker. But to us it was great; it got us back and forth to class and home to P.E.I. for Christmas. One year the engine wore out on the way. None of that mattered because we had high hopes for the future. We were going to get through, get our degrees at Acadia, and go on to interesting work. In looking back, I have to say that we have been lucky in getting careers that we have enjoyed, with lots of variety. I notice that some of the people I graduated with in 1969, who are still in the same careers, are finding it tough. Some of my friends teach, and I really admire their strength. If I had stayed in teaching from 1970, by now I'd be getting pretty worn down. As it is, I feel as if I'm always ready to meet challenges.

AM: What are some of the challenges of your new position?

DG: A deputy minister, who is a civil servant, runs the department, and the minister is the political head of the department. So, with these two, the political reality meets the bureaucratic reality. The minister and the deputy are the two that, in tandem, determine where the department is going, set policy. Technically, it's the minister from the provincial cabinet who sets policy, and it's up to the deputy and the civil servants who work with the deputy to recommend policy.

The ministry has a number of issues. Waste disposal is a major issue. We're in a province that has a very small land base of only 1.4 million acres. Generating waste and disposing of it in a way that keeps the volume down and doesn't pollute ground water is extremely important because all of our water is drawn from the ground. It's not like a lot of major cities that take their water out of rivers or other above-ground sources.

Many of our issues are related, such as the quality of ground water and soil conservation. The soil is under constant threat, not only from water erosion but also from wind erosion.

Generally, there's much more that can and should be done at the provincial levels and the national level for conservation. Nationally, we are certainly falling short in terms of what we could be doing. For instance, we were the first country to sign the bio-diversity convention in Rio, but we certainly haven't been the leader that we should have been at this point. There is no national endangered-species legislation, and only four provinces have such legislation. Something as simple as that, yet we haven't caught up with the necessary paperwork. And of course, then it gets bogged down in federal/provincial wrangling.

Compared to disaster areas around the world, we can say we are doing well. But we should be setting our own standards and trying to make this the best country in the world by the quality of the air we breathe, the water we drink, the food we eat, even human safety.

Part of the problem is that it's far too easy to fall back into the jobs versus environment blackmail. It doesn't have to be jobs or the environment; that's not the choice at all. We really need to have a better way of making decisions in our country than constantly running into adversarial situations – through courts, through commissions – where there's a winner and there's a loser. There's consensus decision making or other alternative dispute-resolution mechanisms that would give us fewer losers and more winners.

I'm hoping that as more women enter senior levels of the civil service and industry and the environment – and almost every other area that you can name – the tendency they have towards settling disputes in a less black and white manner should start to be felt through the system. But it will be interesting to see how long it takes for that to play out. There still seems to be a glass ceiling that women have problems getting above.

AM: Why do you think women have this problem?

DG: When you look at senior levels in government and industry – especially those dealing with natural resources such as oil and forestry, where my experience has been – these fields were traditionally male dominated. It has taken a long time for women to work up to senior levels, partially because people are not used to them being there. In the past, it was possible to say that women didn't break through the glass ceiling in these areas because they hadn't taken the right route by studying subjects such as law, engineering and geology. Now they are studying such subjects in greater numbers, so it will be interesting to see how this plays out.

In senior levels of the P.E.I. government, there was only one woman deputy minister until the last few years when three more were brought in. At the next level down, there are only two women directors in the whole P.E.I. government.

Certainly women have to plan and work at career development; it doesn't just happen. You have to work at it by making contacts, networking, doing volunteer work and looking for advancement possibilities.

AM: In your career development, you must have had failures along the way. How do you react when you fail at something?

DG: Sometimes, losing the battle doesn't mean you have lost the war. It is really important to keep it all in perspective. Getting up and resigning is only appropriate in a very small number of cases because then you have fired your last cannon and you are powerless to do anything else about a situation. Staying to fight or taking different tactics is far more effective. If you have lost one battle, maybe you are owed a success in another. That's the way things work on the political front too: there's a give and take. It's the same with almost everything we do in life. We can't win all the time.

Some people hang in there, and you learn a lot from them. There are a lot of people, like Silken Laumann in sports, who are models just for their sheer determination. Look at Jean Chrétien. When he lost to John Turner, it seemed that his career was finished. You really have to admire such people. If they had walked away, no one would have blamed them.

AM: I understand that you ran for public office a few years ago.

DG: Yes. When I was a student in university, I was interested in politics. Then it all fell along the wayside until several years ago. I actually planned to run at the federal level but was recruited to the provincial level after Joe Ghiz retired. I had also seriously courted the idea of running for the Conservative party leadership, but right then I was busy with the national round table on the economy and the environment. Then I did run in a provincial election in 1993. That was a great experience, although I didn't win. We only got one seat, the party leader's. We'd had two before that.

The challenge in something like this is not to take it too personally, and I didn't. Needless to say, I was disappointed. My husband had a way of putting it into perspective as we came home the evening after the election. He said, "Well, it could have been worse. You could have been the one seat that was elected." And I said, "Yes, you're right!"

AM: What prompted you to try in the first place?

DG: The decision-making power is in the hands of the politicians. They pass the legislation, make decisions, set the budget. So if you really want to make a difference, it's good to be in the political ranks, then in the party in power, then ultimately in the cabinet. That's where decisions get made. However, there are other senior people in the government who make recommendations and advise the politicians, so that's also a good place to be.

AM: You have many other interests and "druthers." I believe you won an outdoor woman award.

DG: Actually, it was the Canadian Outdoor Man of the Year award, started by the Winchester Rifles Company. Their headquarters are in the United States and they have an office in Canada. The award could be for somebody who had been active in hunting and the traditional forms of conservation, like stream improvement or improving certain areas for bighorn sheep – something along these lines, towards the traditional outdoors and sportsman kind of life. So I was a bit different in that I went hunting and fishing, although women aren't generally thought to do that kind of activity.

My husband and I both go pheasant hunting each autumn and would like to do it more, but there aren't enough days in the month. "Perhaps this year ..." We say that every year! There's so much to do: golfing, bird watching, gardening. I would also like to get back into writing. A friend and I are working on a book at the moment. Wayne Barrett is a well-known photographer on P.E.I., and we're looking at doing a book on ecotourism. We had collaborated – Wayne and his wife and myself – on an earlier book called *Atlantic Wildflowers*. I'd like to really be able to do more of that. When I retire, I will get back into writing nature-related material. But between now and then I probably will not have the time.